Frommer's®

W9-AXK-718

Yellowstone & Grand Teton National Parks

6th Edition

by Eric Peterson

Here's what critics say about Frommer's:

"Amazingly easy to use. Very portable, very complete."

—*Booklist*

"Detailed, accurate, and easy-to-read information for all price ranges."

—*Glamour Magazine*

WILEY

Wiley Publishing, Inc.

Published by:

WILEY PUBLISHING, INC.

111 River St.
Hoboken, NJ 07030-5774

ISBN: 978-0-470-18194-2
Editor: Billy Fox
Production Editor: Suzanna R. Thompson
Cartographer: Andrew Murphy
Photo Editor: Richard Fox
Production by Wiley Indianapolis Composition Services

For information on our other products and services or to obtain technical
support, please contact our Customer Care Department within the U.S. at
800/762-2974, outside the U.S. at 317/572-3993 or fax 317/572-4002.

Wiley also publishes its books in a variety of electronic formats. Some content that appears in print may not be available in electronic formats.

Manufactured in the United States of America

5   4   3   2   1

Contents

List of Maps

ABOUT THE AUTHOR

A Denver-based freelance writer, **Eric Peterson** has contributed to numerous Frommer's guides covering the American West, and written *Frommer's Montana & Wyoming, Frommer's Utah,* and *Ramble: A Field Guide to the U.S.A.* (www.speckpress.com). Peterson also writes about travel and other topics for such publications as *ColoradoBiz, Delta Sky,* and the *New York Daily News.* In his free time, he's an avid camper and hiker, a lifelong Broncos fan, and part-time rock star (at least in the eyes of his niece Olivia and nephews Mitch and Sam).

AN INVITATION TO THE READER

In researching this book, we discovered many wonderful places—hotels, restaurants, shops, and more. We're sure you'll find others. Please tell us about them, so we can share the information with your fellow travelers in upcoming editions. If you were disappointed with a recommendation, we'd love to know that, too. Please write to:

> *Frommer's Yellowstone & Grand Teton National Parks,* 6th Edition
> Wiley Publishing, Inc. • 111 River St. • Hoboken, NJ 07030-5774

AN ADDITIONAL NOTE

Please be advised that travel information is subject to change at any time—and this is especially true of prices. We therefore suggest that you write or call ahead for confirmation when making your travel plans. The authors, editors, and publisher cannot be held responsible for the experiences of readers while traveling. Your safety is important to us, however, so we encourage you to stay alert and be aware of your surroundings. Keep a close eye on cameras, purses, and wallets, all favorite targets of thieves and pickpockets.

FROMMER'S STAR RATINGS, ICONS & ABBREVIATIONS

Every hotel, restaurant, and attraction listing in this guide has been ranked for quality, value, service, amenities, and special features using a **star-rating system.** In country, state, and regional guides, we also rate towns and regions to help you narrow down your choices and budget your time accordingly. Hotels and restaurants are rated on a scale of zero (recommended) to three stars (exceptional). Attractions, shopping, nightlife, towns, and regions are rated according to the following scale: zero stars (recommended), one star (highly recommended), two stars (very highly recommended), and three stars (must-see).

In addition to the star-rating system, we also use **seven feature icons** that point you to the great deals, in-the-know advice, and unique experiences that separate travelers from tourists. Throughout the book, look for:

Finds	Special finds—those places only insiders know about
Fun Fact	Fun facts—details that make travelers more informed and their trips more fun
Kids	Best bets for kids—advice for the whole family
Moments	Special moments—those experiences that memories are made of
Overrated	Places or experiences not worth your time or money
Tips	Insider tips—some great ways to save time and money
Value	Great values—where to get the best deals

The following **abbreviations** are used for credit cards:

AE	American Express	DISC	Discover	V	Visa
DC	Diners Club	MC	MasterCard		

FROMMERS.COM

Now that you have this guidebook to help you plan a great trip, visit our website at **www.frommers.com** for additional travel information on more than 3,600 destinations. We update features regularly to give you instant access to the most current trip-planning information available. At Frommers.com, you'll find scoops on the best airfares, lodging rates, and car rental bargains. You can even book your travel online through our reliable travel booking partners. Other popular features include:

- Online updates of our most popular guidebooks
- Vacation sweepstakes and contest giveaways
- Newsletters highlighting the hottest travel trends
- Online travel message boards with featured travel discussions

Introducing Yellowstone & Grand Teton National Parks

Long before you reach the entrance to Grand Teton National Park, your sights will be set on the towering spires of the Teton Range—those signature hornlike peaks made famous through countless photographs. From afar, Yellowstone is not as dramatic because much of the parkland comprises heavily forested mountains, burn areas, and arid, high-country plateaus. However, at closer glance, Yellowstone's natural marvels are startling: hundreds of geysers, scores of inspiring waterfalls, and a gorge—carved by time and water—that rivals the Grand Canyon. Both parks command the imagination and envelop the senses from the moment of arrival.

Creatures great and small thrive in Yellowstone and Grand Teton national parks. In the wilderness of Yellowstone's southern corners, grizzlies feed on cutthroat trout during their annual spawning run to the Yellowstone headwaters. In the soft blue depths of Octopus Pond, microbes of enormous scientific value are incubated and born; in the mountain ridges, wolves make their dens and mountain lions hunt bighorn sheep. Bald eagles and osprey soar above the banks of the Snake River in Grand Teton, moose munch their way through meadows of native foliage, and elk and buffalo lazily traverse the park on the same roads as visitors.

When John Colter, a scout for Lewis and Clark, first wandered this way in 1807, his descriptions of geysers and sulfurous hot pools and towering waterfalls drew jeers and suspicion. No one doubts him now, but these are still places you should see for yourself. The explorers of today come in minivans and on bicycles, aboard snowmobiles and telemark skis, and in such numbers that the parks sometimes groan under the strain.

In the early days of Yellowstone, first established as a national park in 1872, visitors were so sparse that the things they did—catching a string of 100 trout, washing their underwear in the hot pools—left few noticeable scars. Now, with millions of people visiting the parks annually, the strain on everything from sewer systems to fish populations is immense.

While there are problems, these parks still radiate with extraordinary beauty: the jagged Tetons, the glassy surface of Jenny Lake, the awe-inspiring Grand Canyon of the Yellowstone, the towering Obsidian Cliff, the steamy meandering of the Firehole River. Wildlife that most Americans see only in zoos wanders freely here, from the grizzly to the river otter, the trumpeter swan to the rufous hummingbird. Aspen groves, fields of lupine, the howls of coyotes and wolves—all these testify to the resilience and vitality of the Greater Yellowstone Ecosystem, which extends outside the borders of the park to include Grand Teton and beyond.

This is not just a paradise for sightseers—it's a scientific preserve as well. The hot pools support a population of unique microbes known as thermophiles and extremophiles; studies of the elk herds and grizzly have yielded crucial information on habitat needs and animal behavior; and the rocks of Yellowstone are like the earth turned inside out, a treasure-trove for geologists.

Most visitors will see or know little of this. They park in a pullout on U.S. Hwy. 191/89/26 to pose in front of Grand Teton, or they sit on the crowded benches to watch Old Faithful erupt. If you have more time, however, I suggest that you take little sections of these parks—just the Jenny Lake area in Grand Teton, say, or Yellowstone's northeast corner, the Lamar Valley—and savor them in all their fine detail rather than embark on a madcap race to see every highlight.

Definitely get out of your car and away from the road, into the wild heart of the backcountry. These parks embody our country's beginnings: a nation of wilderness, of challenging and rugged extremes, and a landscape of extraordinary bounty and beauty. Use this guide as a set of footprints to help you find your way there.

1 The Best of Yellowstone & Grand Teton National Parks

A "best of" list could never do justice to Yellowstone and Grand Teton. These are just starting points, the best of the excellent accommodations and food the parks offer, as well as the unique sightseeing and recreational opportunities. Some involve backcountry expeditions; others can be enjoyed from behind the steering wheel. In the wildly diverse environments of these two parks, you can be as adventurous as you want, climbing peaks and spending the night deep in

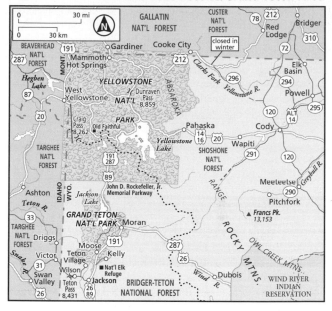

the wilderness, or simply enjoy the more civilized side of the park at grand lodges and enchanting roadside overlooks.

THE BEST VIEWS

You'll never get it all in a camera lens, but you'll undoubtedly try. Don't let that viewfinder get attached to your face; take a few shots, or run a little videotape, and then put it down so you can enjoy this place with all your senses.

- **Grand Canyon of the Yellowstone River** (Yellowstone): The waterfalls are spectacular, especially the 308-foot Lower Falls (twice the height of Niagara), and the steeply cut canyon walls are colorful and alive with life. Take the short, easy hikes to **Inspiration Point** or **Artist Point,** and you'll see the falls that stimulated Thomas Moran's creativity. If you're in reasonable shape, hike down the short but steep trail to the **Brink of the Upper Falls** or the 328-step steel staircase known as **Uncle Tom's Trail.** (Be careful of slick spots during the spring and following afternoon thundershowers.) See "Yellowstone: The Extended Tour," in chapter 3.

- **Lamar Valley** (Yellowstone): Bring your telephoto lens or binoculars to the northeast corner of the park, one of the best places to spot wildlife: **bison** and **elk** grazing along the Lamar River, **wolves** at Slough Creek and among the big ungulates, and the occasional **grizzly bear** on its never-ending quest for food. See "Yellowstone: The Extended Tour," in chapter 3.

- **Yellowstone Lake** (Yellowstone): Sunrise over Yellowstone Lake is stunningly beautiful, especially if there's fog on the lake, whether you watch it from the sunroom at the Lake Yellowstone Hotel or (better) from a campsite along the southern wilderness shore. For an equally spectacular sunset view, drive 10 miles east of the hotel to Lake Butte Overlook. See "Yellowstone: The Extended Tour," in chapter 3.

- **Cathedral Group** (Grand Teton): The three central mountains in the Teton Range rarely disappoint, except on the rare occasion when weather gets in the way—clouds tend to accent rather than obscure their majesty. You'll need a wide-angle lens to get it all in from the valley floor (there are pullouts along the highway between Moran Junction and Jackson), but if you want a panoramic shot, drive east on U.S. Hwy. 26/287 toward Togwotee Pass. See "The Highlights," in chapter 5.

- **Elk** (Grand Teton): While visiting the Jackson/Grand Teton area during the winter, take the opportunity to ride a horse-drawn sleigh out among thousands of elk on the **National Elk Refuge.** You'll get close-up shots of some of the biggest antler racks in the world, and you'll probably see coyotes and sometimes wolves. See "Jackson, Wyoming," in chapter 8.

THE BEST THERMAL DISPLAYS

Yellowstone has more thermal features—geysers, mud pots, and steam vents—than the rest of the world combined. When you're angling for a good shot of a colorful pool or a belching mud pot, obey the signs—otherwise, you could find yourself, literally, on shaky ground.

- **Old Faithful Geyser** (Yellowstone): While not quite as faithful as it used to be—the intervals average 74 minutes but sometimes stretch as long as 120 minutes—it's still the most predictable geyser on the planet, blasting water 130 feet into the air more than 20 times a day. How could you skip this one? See "Yellowstone: The Extended Tour," in chapter 3.

- **West Thumb** (Yellowstone): This lakeside thermal area is a must-stop for its collection of gemlike hot pools and steaming vents, as well as Fishing Cone, where early visitors poached their catch—until they realized the scalding water had natural traces of arsenic. See "If You Have Only 1 or 2 Days (the Short Tour)," in chapter 3.

- The **Riverside Geyser** (Yellowstone): This beauty sits on the bank of the Firehole River and sends 75-foot columns of water arching over the river. See "Yellowstone: The Extended Tour," in chapter 3.

THE BEST DAY HIKES

Just a few hundred yards off the road, things get a lot less crowded, and you'll have the views and the wildlife (almost) to yourself. The hikes described have an easy rating, but you'll find more challenging options later in the book.

- The **Mount Washburn Trail** (Yellowstone): Starting at Dunraven Pass, south of Tower Junction, this walk offers unsurpassed views of both parks plus the opportunity to see mountain wildlife such as bighorn sheep. See p. 86.
- The **Lonestar Geyser Trail** (Yellowstone): This gentle, 5-mile hike along the Firehole River presents several places to stop and take in the scenery, fish, and view this medium-size geyser. In the winter, this is a popular ski trail. See p. 89.
- **Cascade Canyon Trail** (Grand Teton): This hike can be short and sweet or long and rewarding. Make a day of it, or simply take a boat ride across the lake and hike to Hidden Falls, and you'll barely break a sweat. See p. 130.
- **Signal Mountain Summit Trail** (Grand Teton): The hike to the summit of Signal Mountain is rewarding for its solitude. While everyone else drives to the top, you'll have the same views and be closer to the greenery and wildlife. See p. 128.

THE BEST BACKCOUNTRY TRAILS

- **The Thorofare Trail** (Yellowstone): This hike will take you deeper into road-free wilderness than you can get anywhere else in the Lower 48 states. You'll spend a few nights on the trail, climbing up to the park's southern border and beyond to the Yellowstone River's headwaters, a high valley bursting with wildlife. Early in the summer, if the snow has melted, the cutthroat spawning run attracts grizzlies and fishers. It's not for the faint of heart. See "Exploring the Backcountry," in chapter 4.
- **Cascade Canyon Loop** (Grand Teton): Perhaps the most popular trail in Grand Teton, the Cascade Canyon Loop, which

starts on the west side of Jenny Lake, winds northwest 9.5 miles on the Cascade Canyon Trail to Lake Solitude and the Paintbrush Divide, and then returns past Holly Lake on the 10-mile Paintbrush Canyon Trail. The payoff comes at the highest point, Paintbrush Divide, with marvelous views of Jackson Hole Valley and Leigh Lake. See "Exploring the Backcountry," in chapter 6.

THE BEST CAMPGROUNDS

If you stay in developed campgrounds in the parks, the outdoor life is pretty civilized. You'll have running water and, in most cases, flush toilets, plus there are opportunities to meet fellow campers.

- **Jenny Lake Campground** (Grand Teton): Situated near the edge of the lake from which it takes its name, Jenny Lake Campground is nestled among spruce and fir trees just a short walk away from the South Jenny Lake area. It's the perfect place to spend the night if you plan to hike around the lake to Hidden Falls or up Cascade Canyon the next day. The only problem: There are no site reservations, and sites are usually taken early in the morning. See p. 161.

- **Norris Campground** (Yellowstone): Although it's away from the hotels and services, the Norris Campground has excellent sites with a little elbow room, as well as flush toilets and the Solfatara Trailhead. A small hillside amphitheater hosts campfire talks by rangers. The campground is across the street from the Norris Geyser Basin and within walking distance of the Museum of the National Park Ranger. See p. 150.

- **Slough Creek Campground** (Yellowstone): Another favorite is out in the Lamar Valley. The campground is smaller, but it's away from the crowds (and other services) yet close to fishing and wolf viewing. Because of the wildlife-watching and fishing opportunities here, it fills quite early. See p. 150.

THE BEST PLACES TO EAT IN THE PARKS

Don't expect five-star dining (with one exception) or a great variety, but the food is well prepared, the servers are cheerful, and the dining rooms are mostly big, convivial gathering places. All of these are detailed in chapter 7.

- The **Old Faithful Inn,** Yellowstone (© **307/344-7311**): Can't beat the ambience: a grand stone-and-timber lodge perched next to the most famous geyser in the world. The food's pretty good, too, but it can be inconsistent. See p. 147.

- The **Lake Yellowstone Hotel,** Yellowstone (© **307/344-7901**): Enjoy a bit of Victorian-era hospitality (without dressing up) and the finest food in the Wyoming wilderness. There are views of the lake from the dining room and the comfortable lounge area off the lobby. See p. 146.
- **Jenny Lake Lodge Dining Room,** Grand Teton (© **307/733-4647**): This place gets my five-star award: Dine where presidents have dined on five-course meals featuring such delicacies as smoked sturgeon ravioli. Breakfast and dinner are included in the price of a room; nonguests can call for reservations, but it's not cheap. See p. 166.
- **Signal Mountain Lodge,** Grand Teton (© **307/543-2831**): **Trapper Grill** and **Deadman's Bar** here make good casual meals (including mountainous plates of nachos in the latter), with a view of Jackson Lake and the Tetons or, in the lounge, a view of one of the few televisions in the park. **Peaks** offers finer dining, with a largely organic menu. See p. 165.

THE BEST PLACES TO SLEEP IN THE PARKS

My Yellowstone favorites are both grand hotels, but they're very different. In Grand Teton, I lean toward the rustic option. All of these are detailed in chapter 7.

- The **Lake Yellowstone Hotel,** Yellowstone (© **307/344-7311**): Try this recipe for a great vacation: a quiet drink in the sunroom overlooking the lake, a friendly meal in the big dining room, a walk by the lake, and then a comfortable bed in one of the big wings. See p. 146.
- The **Old Faithful Inn,** Yellowstone (© **307/344-7311**): As if the wonders outside aren't enough, this is an architectural gem, a cavernous lobby with an 85-foot-high ceiling and lodgepole balconies inside and out. Get a room in the old lodge, not the wings, even if the bathrooms are down the hall. See p. 147.
- **Jenny Lake Lodge,** Grand Teton (© **800/628-9988**): Solitude, great food, and beautifully appointed cabins with porches—there is just one downside: the high prices. See p. 159.
- **Colter Bay Village,** Grand Teton (© **800/628-9988** or 307/543-3100): Rough it in a roomy canvas tent with a stove and bunk beds and firewood delivered to your door (or flap).

The rates are relatively inexpensive, and the fresh air is free. For a step up, try the rustic cabins. See p. 158.

THE BEST PLACES TO EAT OUTSIDE THE PARKS

This is food so good that you won't mind spending $15 to $30 for entrees. These establishments are detailed in chapter 8.

- **In Jackson, Wyoming: Rendezvous Bistro** (✆ 307/739-1100) offers steaks, seafood, and game dishes with creative twists, not to mention the perfect balance of chic and casual. See p. 198. Mornings, though, you'll find me at **Nora's Fish Creek Inn** (✆ 307/733-8288), in nearby Wilson, with a bottomless cup of coffee and a huge plate of huevos rancheros. See p. 198.
- **In Cody, Wyoming: Cassie's Supper Club** (✆ 307/527-5500) is a brothel turned cowboy eatery, plating up some of the best steaks in the Rockies. After dinner, country bands hold court over the bustling dance floor. See p. 209.

THE BEST PLACES TO SLEEP OUTSIDE THE PARKS

All of the following are detailed in chapter 8.

- **In Jackson, Wyoming:** The **Wort Hotel** (✆ 307/733-2190) is a downtown Jackson landmark with comfortable "New West"–style rooms; it's also a good value for its downtown location. See p. 190.
- **In Gardiner, Montana:** The **Absaroka Lodge** (✆ 800/755-7414) has modern rooms and decks overlooking the Yellowstone River, near the center of town. See p. 174.
- **In West Yellowstone, Montana:** Sleek and opulent, but definitively Western, the newly renovated lodge rooms and cabins at the **Bar N Ranch** (✆ 406/646-0300) are the most distinctive lodgings in the chain-dominated town. See p. 170.
- **In Cody, Wyoming:** Centered on a serene and green courtyard, the new-and-improved **Chamberlin Inn** (✆ 888/587-0202) is now Cody's best lodging option, featuring charming historic rooms and apartment units. See p. 207.

THE BEST THINGS TO SEE & DO OUTSIDE THE PARKS

Don't assume a Yellowstone and Grand Teton vacation is limited to park boundaries. Here are a few attractions worth highlighting in the area. See chapter 8 for more information.

- **In Cody, Wyoming:** The **Buffalo Bill Historical Center** (✆ 307/587-4771) is the best museum in the region. See

p. 204. Another can't-miss is the **Cody Nite Rodeo** (📞 **800/207-0744**), the only rodeo held every night throughout the summer. See p. 205.

- **In Jackson, Wyoming:** Glimpse some of the finest artistic interpretations of the natural world at the fantastic **National Museum of Wildlife Art** (📞 **307/733-5771**), which houses 1,300 pieces within its red-sandstone walls. See p. 185.

- **In West Yellowstone, Montana:** For a look at Yellowstone's cultural history, pay a visit to the **Yellowstone Historic Center** (📞 **406/646-1100**) in the historic Union Pacific depot. See p. 168.

THE BEST SCENIC DRIVES

Roll down the windows, crank up your favorite music, and take time to relax as you travel these byways.

- Every stretch along the figure eight of roads at the center of Yellowstone has some scenic allure, but my favorite is the part along the western and northern shores of **Yellowstone Lake.** There's less traffic than around Old Faithful or the Grand Canyon of the Yellowstone, and you have a good chance of seeing wildlife east of **Fishing Bridge,** as well as steaming geothermal features near **West Thumb.** The drive is best in the morning, when the sun is rising over the steaming lake. See chapter 3.

- From the northeast entrance of Yellowstone, head across the Beartooth Highway (U.S. Hwy. 212) to Red Lodge, Montana; at Red Lodge, head southeast toward Cody (Mont. 308 to Wyo. 120), and then catch the **Chief Joseph Highway** (Wyo. 296) and return to the park. Imagine this: dramatic mountain peaks, river valleys, painted landscapes, and two Old West towns, all on this 155-mile drive. See chapter 3.

- A twisting, narrow road climbs **Signal Mountain** to a fine 360-degree view of the valley and the mountains. On the way up, you'll see wildflowers and birds, and from the top, you can study the moraines and potholes left by retreating glaciers. See chapter 5.

2 A Look at Yellowstone

Think about this: What other national park boasts an assortment of some 10,000 thermal features, including more than 300 geysers? Even when the rest of North America was largely a wilderness,

Yellowstone was unique. The geothermal area is greater than any other in the world, with mud pots, geysers, and hot springs of all colors, sizes, and performances. Plus, there's a waterfall that's twice as tall as Niagara Falls and a canyon deep and colorful enough to be called "grand." Sure, other parks have great hiking trails and beautiful geologic formations—Grand Teton is pretty spectacular in its own right, as is Yosemite—but a sizable percentage of the geology in Yellowstone is reachable by visitors in average shape.

Wildlife? Ever focus your telephoto lens on an untamed grizzly bear? Or a bald eagle? What about a wolf? Thousands of visitors have these experiences here every year. Protected by the national park and surrounding forests from development, Yellowstone is home to herds of bison, elk, grizzly bears, trumpeter swans, Yellowstone cutthroat trout, and more subtle beauties such as wildflowers and hummingbirds.

And the park doesn't appeal solely to the visual senses; you'll smell it, too. By one biologist's estimate, Yellowstone has more than 1,100 species of native plants. When wildflowers cover the meadows in spring, their fragrances are overpowering. The mud pots and fumaroles have their own set of odors, although many are less pleasing than a wild lily.

Your ears will be filled with the sounds of geysers noisily spewing forth thousands of gallons of boiling water into the blue Wyoming sky. After sunset, coyotes break the silence of the night with their high-pitched yips.

You can spend weeks hiking its backcountry or fishing its streams, but the park's road system makes it easy to tour in a day or two from behind the windshield. Yes, *really.* It's possible to see most of the highlights of Yellowstone without hitting the trail. Park roads lead past most of the key attractions and are filled with wildlife commuting from one grazing area to another. While there's no doubt that driving through the park yields vivid memories, those who don't leave their cars are shortchanging themselves.

Yellowstone is just as active after summer ends, when the park is open for snowmobiling and skiing for 3 months during the winter. (*Note:* For snowmobile policy updates, visit **www.nps.gov/yell**.)

3 A Look at the Grand Tetons & Jackson Hole

Because the Grand Tetons stand so tall, with the park curling snugly at their feet, visitors sometimes fail to appreciate this surrounding environment of rivers and high valley floor. The Tetons are a young range of old pre-Cambrian granite, abrupt and sharp-edged as they knife up from the Snake River valley, sliding upward along a 40-mile-long fault sculpted over the course of the last 13 million years, with help from geological upheaval, retreating glaciers, and erosion. The result is a masterpiece. Many visitors regard Grand Teton National Park as more dramatically and immediately scenic than its northern neighbor, with its shimmering lakes, thickly carpeted forests, and towering peaks blanketed with snow throughout most of the year.

It's also a very accessible park. You can appreciate its breathtaking beauty on a quick drive-by, or take to the trails and waterways in search of backcountry lakes and waterfalls. The Tetons themselves are especially popular with mountain climbers, who scale them year-round.

There's a dynamic relationship between the Tetons and the valley below. The elk and other wildlife migrate from the high country down to the open grasslands to forage during the winter, when the snowmelt curls across the valley floor and west through a gap in the mountains, and the moraines and alluvial soils that slough off the mountains provide rich soil for the pastures below.

Visitors can float and fish the lively Snake River, visit the National Elk Refuge in the winter, hike in nearby ranges such as the Wind River or the Gros Ventre, or play cowboy at one of the dude and guest ranches that dot the valley of Jackson Hole. Skiers and snow-boarders have a blast on the slopes here, as well as at Grand Targhee on the other side of Teton Pass. And the chic town of Jackson, with its antler-arched town square and its busy shops, offers everything from classy art galleries to noisy two-step cowboy bars.

4 Making the Most of Your Trip

Yellowstone and Grand Teton are more than photo ops and zoos where the animals roam free. They aren't museums, either, where magnificent scenery is merely on display. Both parks, unlike a picture hanging lifelessly on the wall of a museum, are works in progress; they are living, breathing wilderness areas. Plant your feet in a comfortable pair of walking or hiking shoes, find a trail head, and set off into the woods with a sack lunch and big bottle of water. Better yet, if you can afford the time, plan an excursion around Shoshone Lake or to the south end of Yellowstone Lake by boat to areas few visitors ever see. There are isolated areas in Grand Teton, too—even on the far shore of popular Jenny Lake—where, with a little hiking, you'll be rewarded by a pristine, forested glade with nothing to distract your attention but wild moose and an awe-inspiring mountaintop.

If you're more adventurous, take a white-water trip down Snake River Canyon, or let a guide take you up to Grand Teton's summit. In Yellowstone, sleep under the stars and listen to the wolves howl at Slough Creek Campground; or backpack for a week on the Thorofare Trail.

You'll never plumb the absolute depths of these parks—no one ever will. You could spend your whole life trying, though, and have a great and illuminating time doing it.

5 Some Historical Background

YELLOWSTONE NATIONAL PARK

Before the arrival of European settlers, the only residents on the plateau were small bands of Shoshone Indians known as "Sheepeaters," who lived on the southern fringe. Three other Indian tribes came and went: the Crows (Absaroka), who were friendly to the settlers; the Blackfeet, who lived in the Missouri Valley drainage and were hostile to both whites and other Indians; and the Bannocks, who largely kept to themselves. The nomadic Bannocks traveled an east-west route in their search for bison, from Idaho past Mammoth Hot Springs to Tower Fall, and then across the Lamar Valley to the Bighorn Valley, which is outside the park's current boundaries. Called the Bannock Trail, it was so deeply furrowed that evidence of it still exists today on the Blacktail Plateau near the Tower Junction. (You'll see remnants of the trail if you take Blacktail Plateau Drive, described in chapter 3.)

The first white explorer to lay eyes on Yellowstone's geothermal wonders was probably John Colter, who broke away from the Lewis and Clark expedition in 1806 and spent 3 years wandering a surreal landscape of mud pots and mountains and geysers. When he described his discovery on his return to St. Louis, no one believed him. Miners and fur trappers followed in his footsteps, reducing the plentiful beaver of the region to almost nothing, and occasionally making curious reports of a sulfurous world still sometimes called "Colter's Hell."

The first significant exploration of what would become the park took place in 1869, when a band of Montanans, led by David Folsom, completed a 36-day expedition. Folsom and his group traveled up the Missouri River and into the heart of the park, where they discovered the falls of Yellowstone, mud pots, Yellowstone Lake, and the Fountain Geyser. Two years later, an expedition led by U.S. Geological Survey Director Ferdinand Hayden brought back convincing evidence of Yellowstone's wonders, in the form of astonishing photographs by William Henry Jackson.

A debate began over the potential for commercial development and exploitation of the region, as crude health spas and thin-walled "hotels" went up near the hot springs. There are various claimants to the idea of a national park—members of the Folsom party later told an oft-disputed story about thinking it up around a campfire in the Upper Geyser Basin—but the idea gained steam as Yellowstone explorers hit the lecture circuit back East. In March 1872, President Ulysses S. Grant signed legislation declaring Yellowstone the nation's first national park.

The Department of the Interior got the job of managing the new park. There was no budget for it and no clear idea of how to take care of a wilderness preserve; many mistakes were made. Inept superintendents granted favorable leases to friends with commercial interests in the tourism industry. Poachers ran amok, and the wildlife population was decimated. A laundry business near Mammoth went so far as to clean linens in a hot pool.

By 1886, things were so bad that the U.S. Army took control of Yellowstone; iron-fisted management practices resulted in new order and protected the park from those intent upon exploiting it. (However, the military did participate in the eradication of the plateau's wolf population.) By 1916, efforts to make the park more visitor-friendly had begun to show results: Construction of the first roads had been completed, guest housing was available in the area, and order had been restored. Stewardship of the park was then transferred to the newly created National Park Service.

GRAND TETON NATIONAL PARK

Unlike Yellowstone, Grand Teton can't boast of being the nation's first park and a model for parks the world over. This smaller, southern neighbor was created as the result of a much more convoluted process that spanned 50 years.

The first sign of human habitation in the Grand Teton region points to people being here around 12,000 years ago. Among the tribes who hunted here in the warmer seasons were the Blackfeet, Crow, Gros Ventre, and Shoshone, who came over the mountains from the Great Basin to the west. Indians spent summers hunting and raising crops, before heading to warmer climes.

Trappers and explorers, who first arrived in the valley in the early 1800s, were equally distressed by the harsh winters and short growing season, which made Jackson Hole a marginal place for farming and ranching. Among these early visitors were artist Thomas Moran and photographer William Henry Jackson, whose images awoke the country to the Tetons' grandeur. Early homesteaders quickly realized that their best hope was to market the unspoiled beauty of the area, which they began doing in earnest as early as a century ago.

The danger of haphazard development soon became apparent. There was a dance hall at Jenny Lake, hot dog stands along the roads, and buildings going up on some prime habitat. In the 1920s, after some discussion about how the Grand Teton area might be protected, Yellowstone park officials and conservationists went to Congress. Led by local dude ranchers and Yellowstone superintendent Horace Albright, the group was able to protect only the mountains and foothills, leaving out Jackson Lake and the valley; Wyoming's congressional delegation—and many locals—were vehemently opposed to enclosing the valley in park boundaries.

Then, in 1927, something called the Snake River Land Company started buying up ranches and homesteads along the base of the Tetons. It was a front for John D. Rockefeller, Jr., one of the richest men in the world, working in cahoots with the conservationists. He planned to give the land to the federal government, while keeping a few choice parcels for himself. But Congress wouldn't have it, and Rockefeller made noises about selling the land, about 35,000 acres, to the highest bidder. In the 1940s, President Franklin D. Roosevelt created the Jackson Hole National Monument out of Forest Service lands east of the Snake River. That paved the way for Rockefeller's donation, and in 1950, Grand Teton National Park was expanded to its present form.

6 Issues Facing the Parks Today

In 2001, after 32 years with the National Park Service, Michael Finley left his post as superintendent of Yellowstone. His parting shot: "At some point, you just can't keep dumping people into the parks," he told the *Livingston Enterprise*. "The park's mission is not to sell more motel rooms in an adjacent community or more rubber tomahawks."

The struggle to balance recreation and preservation is as old as the park itself, and it's an issue that continually comes to a boil when long-standing park policies, such as the use of snowmobiles, are revisited with a critical eye. Superintendent Suzanne Lewis, Finley's successor, knows all too well that the mission of the Park Service is a tricky balancing act.

"How do you get your hands around 2.2 million acres?" said Lewis in an interview with Frommer's. "You just can't put it in perspective until you come here. And you have almost three million visitors a year who come for this once-in-a-lifetime experience. The magnitude of people's expectations is enormous, and it takes a lot of management."

BISON, BEARS & WOLVES

In the frontier West—where bison seemed to be everywhere, grizzly bears were fearsome, and wolves regularly raided livestock—wildlife was treated as more of a nuisance than a national treasure. Eventually, the bison and grizzly populations around Yellowstone and Grand Teton were whittled down to near extinction, and wolves were completely eradicated by the 1930s.

It took some intensive management to bring grizzlies and bison back to reasonably healthy numbers in the area, and now the wolves, which were reintroduced from Canada in 1995, are reaping the benefits of the huge ungulate herds that have enjoyed a nearly predator-free environment for quite some time. But these high-profile species—called "charismatic megafauna" by biologists—are not out of the woods yet. Given the pressures of development around the parks, they might never be secure again.

There are now more than 3,500 bison in Yellowstone and Grand Teton, and, naturally, they pay no mind to the park's invisible boundary. In the winter, when snows are deep, they leave the park to forage at lower elevations, sometimes in ranch pastures shared with domestic cattle. The ranchers fear that the bison will spread brucellosis, a virus that can be transmitted to cattle, causing infected cows to abort their unborn calves. There have been no documented cases of bison-cattle transmission, but because of the perceived threat to livestock, Montana officials allow them to be shot once they wander outside the park. Animal-rights activists are outraged, and park and state officials continue to search for some middle ground.

Wolves are another sore point with area ranchers. The reintroduction has been astonishingly successful. Rapidly reproducing, feeding on abundant elk in the park's Lamar Valley, wolves now number more than 300 in the Yellowstone area, and the packs have spread as far south as Grand Teton, where several have denned and produced pups. Although the Defenders of Wildlife have set up programs to compensate ranchers for livestock lost to wolves, the ranchers have gone to court seeking to have the wolves removed. The wolves have, indeed, been implicated in the deaths of sheep and cattle, and a federal judge in Wyoming ruled in 1998 that all reintroduced wolves should be removed. This decision was overturned in 2000, and the wolves are finally entrenched in Yellowstone for the long haul.

Grizzly bears once teetered on the brink of extinction in the parks, but they've made a slow comeback to a population estimated at about 500 animals in the Yellowstone area. (It seems the wolves have helped, because their hunting results in many more carcasses to scavenge.) Because of this success, in March 2007 the U.S. Fish and Wildlife Service removed grizzlies from the endangered list, a decision environmentalist groups subsequently attempted to reverse by filing a lawsuit. Nonetheless, the grizzly habitat in the Greater Yellowstone Ecosystem keeps shrinking, as more and more development takes place around the plateau.

A MULTIPLE-USE PARK

Grand Teton National Park is much more than just a preserve of mountains and lakes and wildlife. Its land is used for all sorts of things that most people don't expect of a national park. There's a big dam holding irrigation water for potato farmers in Idaho; a commercial climbing business that charges big bucks to take climbers up the peaks; and even a commercial airport and a country club.

Each year, one of these conflicting uses makes headlines. Lately, it's cattle, which graze in the fall only a short lope from a den of young wolves. What's the purpose of this park, critics ask—to feed a rancher's cattle or to protect wildlife?

As park spokesperson Jackie Skaggs points out, these are the sorts of public-lands conflicts that arise more often in modern times. With its pockets of private land, uses that predate the creation of the park, and heightened debate between park purists and multiple-use advocates, Grand Teton is a prime example of the difficulty of modern park management.

A BURNING ISSUE

Yellowstone's park managers faced the ultimate test of their noninterference philosophy of fire management in 1988, when nearly one-third of Yellowstone was burned by a series of uncontrollable wildfires. These violent conflagrations scorched more than 700,000 acres, leaving behind dead wildlife, damaged buildings, injured firefighters, and ghostly forests of stripped, blackened tree trunks.

The debate over park and public-land fire policies still rages, although things have quieted down some. After years of suppressing every fire in the park, Yellowstone, in 1988, was operating under a new "let it burn" policy, based on scientific evidence that fires were regular occurrences in nature, part of the natural cycle of a forest.

What you will see, as you travel Yellowstone today, is a park that could be healthier than it was before. Saplings have sprouted from the long-dormant seeds of the lodgepole pine (fires stimulate the pine cones to release their seeds), and the old, tinder-dry forest undergrowth is being replaced with new, green shrubs, sometimes as thick as one million saplings per acre. Visitors who want to better understand the effects of the fires of 1988 should check out the exhibits at the Grant Village Visitor Center; the coverage there is the best in the park.

SNOWMOBILES: TO BAN OR NOT TO BAN?

Winter in Yellowstone is a time of silent wonder, with fauna descending from the high country in search of warmth and food. The only dissonance to this winter wilderness tableau is the roar of snowmobiles, which inhabit the park's snow-packed roads in ever-growing numbers. The noisy, pollution-heavy engines are not exactly ecologically friendly, but the gateway towns are staunch snowmobile proponents because the activity boosts their economies in the moribund winter.

Before President Clinton left office in 2001, he "ended" the ongoing controversy by establishing a ban on snowmobiles in Yellowstone, effective beginning the winter of 2003–04. However, gateway communities and snowmobile manufacturers responded with lawsuits; and the Bush administration also voiced its opposition to a total ban, delighting the outfitters in West Yellowstone and Cody. In mid-2004, a judge overturned a ruling enforcing the ban.

Through the winter of 2007–08, snowmobiles continued to ramble through Yellowstone and Grand Teton; all trips were guided by licensed outfitters with a daily quota of 720 machines, and the technology met best-available standards. In late 2007, a new winter-use plan was issued that would institute a lower quota (540 a day), with over-snow travel on the Continental Divide Snowmobile Trail discontinued in Grand Teton National Park and the John D. Rockefeller Jr. Memorial Parkway. If you're planning a trip, you can get up-to-date information by visiting **www.nps.gov/yell**.

Planning Your Trip to Yellowstone & Grand Teton National Parks

2

It's no one's idea of a fun vacation to end up sucking exhaust behind a long line of cars waiting for a break in construction at Yellowstone's east entrance, or wearing a T-shirt in a Montana snowstorm. Few things can ruin a much-anticipated vacation more than poor planning. So look over some of the crucial information in this chapter before you hit the road—it might be the difference between a trip you'll never forget and one you'd rather not remember.

1 Getting Started: Information & Reservations

The primary entries to Yellowstone and Grand Teton are through Montana and Wyoming, so if you want information about the surrounding areas, contact these states' travel services: **Travel Montana,** 301 S. Park Ave. (P.O. Box 200533), Helena, MT 59601 (© **800/847-4868** or 406/841-2870; TDD 406/841-7202; www.visitmt.com); and the **Wyoming Business Council Tourism Division,** I-25 at College Drive, Cheyenne, WY 82002 (© **800/225-5996** or 307/777-7777; TDD 307/344-2386; www.wyomingtourism.org).

YELLOWSTONE NATIONAL PARK To receive maps and information before your arrival, contact Visitors Services, P.O. Box 168, Yellowstone National Park, WY 82190 (© **307/344-7381;** www.nps.gov/yell).

Information regarding lodging, tours, boating, and horseback riding is available from **Xanterra Parks & Resorts,** P.O. Box 165, Yellowstone National Park, WY 82190 (© **866/439-7375** or 307/344-7311; www.travelyellowstone.com). You'll find complete information about lodging, both inside the park and in the surrounding communities, in chapters 7 and 8.

For information about educational programs at the Yellowstone Institute, contact the **Yellowstone Association,** P.O. Box 117, Yellowstone National Park, WY 82190 (© **307/344-2293;** www.yellowstone association.org). The association also operates bookstores in park visitor centers, museums, and an educational facility open to the public; contact it for a course catalog or details about the books it offers.

GRAND TETON NATIONAL PARK   To receive park maps and information before your arrival, contact **Grand Teton National Park,** P.O. Drawer 170, Moose, WY 83012 (© **307/739-3300;** TDD 307/739-3400; www.nps.gov/grte).

Lodging information is available from park concessionaires: **Grand Teton Lodge Company,** P.O. Box 250, Moran, WY 83013 (© **800/628-9988** or 307/543-2811; www.gtlc.com), and **Signal Mountain Lodge Co.,** P.O. Box 50, Moran, WY 83013 (© **307/543-2831;** www.signalmountainlodge.com); just north of the park is **Flagg Ranch Village,** Box 187, Moran, WY 83013 (© **800/443-2311** or 307/543-2861; www.flaggranch.com). You'll find complete information about lodging, both inside the park and in the surrounding gateway communities, in chapters 7 and 8.

Educational and field trips are offered by the **Teton Science Schools,** 700 Coyote Canyon Rd., Jackson, WY 83001 (© **307/733-1313;** www.tetonscience.org). The school's **Wildlife Expeditions** (© **888/945-3567** or 307/773-2623; www.wildlifeexpeditions. org) offers tours that bring visitors closer to the park's wildlife.

The **Grand Teton Association** is a not-for-profit organization that provides information about the park through retail book sales at park visitor centers; you can also buy books about the park from the organization by mail. Contact the association at P.O. Box 170, Moose, WY 83012 (© **307/739-3403;** www.grandtetonpark.org).

National forests and other public lands surround the parks. For information about national forests and wilderness areas in Montana, as well as **Bridger-Teton National Forest** in Wyoming, contact the **U.S. Forest Service Intermountain Region Office,** 324 25th St., Ogden, UT 84401 (© **801/625-5306;** www.fs.fed.us/r4). The rest of Wyoming's forests, including the **Shoshone National Forest** east of the Tetons over Togwotee Pass, are covered by the **Rocky Mountain Region Office,** 740 Simms St., Golden, CO 80401 (© **303/275-5350;** TDD 303/275-5367; www.fs.fed.us/r2).

The federal **Bureau of Land Management** also manages millions of acres of recreational lands and can be reached at its Wyoming state office, 5353 Yellowstone Rd. (P.O. Box 1828), Cheyenne, WY 82009 (© **307/775-6256;** www.blm.gov/wy); or its Montana state

What Things Cost in Yellowstone & Grand Teton US $

Double motel room in or around the parks, peak season	$75–$200
Double motel room, winter season	$60–$160
Cabin with bed and bathroom	$66–$200
Dinner in a full-service hotel restaurant	$15–$40
Dinner in a coffee shop	$7–$20
Horseback riding for 1 hour	$35
Stagecoach ride	$7–$10
1-hour lake cruise	$7–$12
Bus sightseeing tour (Yellowstone)	$30–$90
1-day snowmobile rental	$175–$250
Round-trip snowcoach to Old Faithful	$99–$125

office, 5001 Southgate Dr., Billings, MT 59101 (© **406/896-5000;** www.blm.gov/mt).

GENERAL TOURIST INFORMATION   Other sources of information include **Yellowstone Country,** 1820 W. Lincoln St., Bozeman, MT 59715 (© 800/736-5276 or 406/556-8680; www. yellowstonecountry.net); **Gardiner Chamber of Commerce,** 222 Park St. (P.O. Box 81), Gardiner, MT 59030 (© 406/848-7971; www.gardinerchamber.com); **Cooke City/Colter Pass/Silver Gate Chamber of Commerce,** 205 Main St. (P.O. Box 1071), Cooke City, MT 59020 (© 406/838-2495; www.cookecitychamber.org); **West Yellowstone Chamber of Commerce,** 30 Yellowstone Ave. (P.O. Box 458), West Yellowstone, MT 59758 (© 406/646-7701; www.westyellowstonechamber.com); **Jackson Hole Chamber of Commerce,** 990 W. Broadway (P.O. Box 550), Jackson, WY 83001 (© 307/733-3316; www.jacksonholechamber.com); **Jackson Hole Central Reservations** (© 800/443-6931); **Cody Country Chamber of Commerce,** 836 Sheridan Ave., Cody, WY 82414 (© 307/ 587-2777; www.codychamber.org); and the **Buffalo Bill's Cody/ Yellowstone Country,** P.O. Box 2454, Cody, WY 82414 (© 800/ 393-2639 or 307/587-2297; www.pctc.org).

2 When to Go

Summer, autumn, and winter are the best times to visit the Northern Rockies. The days are sunny, the nights are clear, and the humidity is low. A popular song once romanticized "Springtime in the

> ### Tips Road Openings & Closings
>
> **In Yellowstone** Traveling Yellowstone's roads during spring months can be a roll of the dice because openings can be delayed for days (sometimes weeks) at a time, especially at higher altitudes. There is always some section of road in Yellowstone under reconstruction, with projects for Dunraven Pass and the stretch between Madison and Norris being the current hot spots; so call ahead, and get a road report (✆ 307/344-7381). It's irritating, but don't take it out on the road workers; they often labor through the night to cause as little inconvenience as possible.
>
> The only road open year-round in the area is the north entrance to **Mammoth Hot Springs.** From Mammoth, a winter access road to the northeast entrance and **Cooke City** is plowed throughout the winter. This service for Cooke City residents gives visitors a great opportunity to watch wildlife in winter in the Lamar Valley. Just be watchful of the weather; the road is often slick with ice.
>
> Snowplowing begins in early March. In Yellowstone, the first roads open to motor vehicles usually include **Mammoth-Norris, Norris-Canyon, Madison–Old Faithful,** and **West Yellowstone–Madison.** These roads might open by the

Rockies," but that season lasts about 2 days in early June. The rest of the season formally known as spring is likely to be chilly and spitting snow or rain. Trails are still clogged with snow and mud.

Typically, from mid-June on, you can hike, fish, camp, and watch wildlife, and if you come before July 4 or after Labor Day, you won't have to share the view all that much. Wildflowers bloom at these elevations in early summer—beginning in May in the lower valleys and plains, while in the higher elevations they open up in July.

Autumn is not just the time when the aspens turn gold, it's also the time when gateway motel and restaurant rates are lower and the roads are less crowded. That allows you to pay more attention to the wildlife, which is busy fattening up for the winter.

Winter is a glorious season here, although not for everyone. It can be very cold, but the air is crystalline, the snow is powdery, and the skiing is fantastic. If you drive in the parks' vicinity in the winter, *always* carry winter clothing, sleeping bags, extra food, flashlights, end of April. If the weather cooperates, the east and south entrances, as well as roads on the east and south sides of the park, will open early in May. Opening of the road from **Tower-Roosevelt** to **Canyon Junction,** however, might be delayed by late-season snowfall on Dunraven Pass.

The **Sunlight Basin Road** (which is also called the **Chief Joseph Highway**), connecting the entrance at Cooke City, Montana, with Cody, Wyoming, often opens by early May. The **Beartooth Highway,** between Cooke City and Red Lodge, Montana, is generally open by Memorial Day weekend.

Winter road closures typically begin in mid-October, when the Beartooth Highway closes. Depending upon weather, most other park roads remain open until the park season ends on the first Sunday in November.

In Grand Teton   Because Grand Teton has fewer roads and they're at lower elevations, openings and closings are more predictable. **Teton Park Road** opens to conventional vehicles and RVs around May 1. The **Moose-Wilson Road** opens to vehicles about the same time. Roads close to vehicles on November 1, although they never close for nonmotorized use.

and other safety gear. Every resident has a horror story about being caught unprepared in the weather.

THE CLIMATE   The region is characterized by long, cold winters and short, relatively mild summers. There is not a lot of moisture, winter or summer, and the air is dry, except for the brief wet season in March and April.

I've already warned you about the brief glimpse of spring in these parts. Cold and snow can linger into April and May—blizzards can even hit the area in mid-June—although temperatures are generally warming. The average daytime readings are in the 40s to 50s (5°–15°C), gradually increasing into the 60s or 70s (16°–26°C) by early June. So, during **spring,** a warm jacket, rain gear, and water-resistant walking shoes could be welcome traveling companions.

The area is rarely balmy, but temperatures during the middle of the **summer** are typically 75° to 85°F (24°–29°C) in the lower elevations

Montana's Average Monthly Temperatures (High/Low)

	Jan	Feb	Mar	Apr	May	June	July	Aug	Sept	Oct	Nov	Dec
Billings												
°F	32/14	38/19	45/25	57/34	67/44	77/52	86/58	85/57	72/47	61/37	45/26	36/18
°C	0/-10	3/-7	7/-4	14/1	19/7	25/11	30/14	29/14	22/8	16/3	7/-3	2/-8
Bozeman												
°F	28/2	34/9	39/15	54/28	65/37	72/44	83/48	82/47	71/39	59/30	43/19	34/10
°C	-2/-16	1/-13	4/-9	12/-2	18/3	22/7	28/9	28/8	22/3	15/-1	6/-7	1/-12
Butte												
°F	28/2	33/6	39/14	51/26	61/34	68/40	80/45	78/43	68/35	56/27	40/15	33/8
°C	-2/-16	1/-14	4/-10	11/-3	16/1	20/4	27/7	26/6	20/2	13/-3	4/-9	0/-13
Dillon												
°F	31/8	36/12	42/18	55/28	64/36	71/43	84/49	82/47	71/39	59/31	43/19	35/14
°C	-1/-13	2/-11	6/-8	13/-2	18/2	22/6	29/9	28/8	21/4	15/0	6/-7	2/-10
Glasgow												
°F	20/0	27/7	39/18	56/31	68/43	77/51	85/57	84/55	71/44	59/33	40/19	26/7
°C	-7/-18	-3/-14	4/-8	13/-1	20/6	25/11	29/14	29/13	22/7	15/1	4/-7	-3/-14
Great Falls												
°F	31/12	37/17	43/22	55/32	65/41	74/49	83/54	81/53	70/44	59/36	44/25	35/16
°C	-1/-11	3/-8	6/-6	13/0	18/5	23/9	28/12	27/12	21/7	15/2	7/-4	2/-9
Havre												
°F	24/3	32/10	43/20	57/31	68/41	77/49	84/54	84/52	71/42	60/31	41/18	29/7
°C	-4/-16	0/-12	6/-7	14/-1	20/5	25/9	29/12	28/11	22/6	16/0	5/-8	-2/-14

	Jan	Feb	Mar	Apr	May	June	July	Aug	Sept	Oct	Nov	Dec
Helena												
°F	29/9	36/15	44/22	56/31	65/40	74/47	83/52	82/51	70/41	58/31	42/21	32/12
°C	-2/-13	2/-9	7/-6	13/-1	18/4	23/8	28/11	28/11	21/5	14/0	6/-6	0/-11
Kalispell												
°F	28/13	35/18	43/23	55/31	65/39	72/45	81/48	80/47	69/39	55/30	39/24	31/17
°C	-2/-11	2/-8	6/-5	13/-1	18/4	22/7	27/9	27/8	21/3	12/-1	3/-4	0/-8
Lewistown												
°F	32/9	35/11	42/18	55/28	64/37	72/44	82/49	80/47	70/39	59/31	45/20	37/14
°C	0/-13	2/-12	6/-8	13/-2	18/3	22/7	28/9	27/8	21/4	15/-1	7/-7	2/-10
Libby												
°F	32/16	39/19	48/25	57/30	68/38	75/45	83/48	85/47	71/38	57/30	41/25	32/18
°C	0/-9	4/-7	9/-4	14/-1	20/3	24/7	28/9	29/8	22/3	14/-1	5/-4	0/-8
Miles City												
°F	25/5	33/11	43/21	58/33	69/44	79/53	89/60	87/58	73/46	61/35	43/21	31/11
°C	-4/-15	1/-12	6/-6	14/0	21/7	26/12	32/16	31/14	23/8	16/2	6/-6	-1/-11
Missoula												
°F	30/14	37/20	46/25	57/32	66/39	74/46	84/50	83/49	71/40	57/31	40/24	31/17
°C	-1/-10	3/-7	8/-4	14/0	19/4	23/7	29/10	28/9	22/4	14/-1	4/-4	0/-8
Sidney												
°F	20/-3	29/5	35/13	56/29	68/41	76/49	83/53	83/52	71/41	59/30	42/18	30/8
°C	-7/-19	-2/-15	2/-11	13/-1	20/5	24/9	28/12	28/11	22/5	15/-1	6/-8	-1/-13
W. Yellowstone												
°F	25/-1	31/2	39/7	49/19	59/27	68/33	79/38	77/35	67/28	53/21	37/9	27/1
°C	-4/-18	-1/-16	4/-14	9/-7	15/-3	20/1	26/3	25/2	19/-2	12/-6	3/-13	-2/-17

Wyoming's Average Monthly Temperatures (High/Low)

	Jan	Feb	Mar	Apr	May	June	July	Aug	Sept	Oct	Nov	Dec
Casper												
°F	33/12	38/16	45/22	56/30	67/39	78/48	87/54	86/53	74/43	61/33	44/22	35/15
°C	1/–11	3/–9	7/–6	13/–1	19/4	26/9	31/12	30/12	23/6	16/0	7/–6	2/–9
Cheyenne												
°F	38/15	41/18	44/21	55/30	64/40	75/48	83/54	81/53	72/44	60/34	47/23	40/17
°C	3/–9	5/–8	7/–6	13/–1	18/4	24/9	28/12	27/12	22/7	16/1	8/–5	4/–8
Cody												
°F	36/12	40/14	47/21	57/31	66/40	76/47	85/54	83/51	72/42	61/33	46/22	38/15
°C	2/–11	4/–10	8/–6	14/–1	19/4	24/8	29/12	28/11	22/6	16/1	8/–6	3/–9
Devils Tower												
°F	33/7	40/13	47/19	57/28	68/39	77/48	86/53	86/51	75/41	64/31	45/20	37/12
°C	1/–14	4/–11	8/–7	14/–2	20/4	25/9	30/12	29/11	24/5	18/–1	7/–7	3/–11
Dubois												
°F	33/10	37/12	41/16	50/24	60/31	70/38	79/42	78/41	67/34	56/26	42/18	35/12
°C	1/–12	3/–11	5/–9	10/–4	16/–1	21/3	26/6	26/5	19/1	13/–3	5/–8	2/–11
Gillette												
°F	32/11	36/14	43/20	55/30	66/40	76/48	87/56	85/54	75/45	61/34	44/23	36/15
°C	0/–12	2/–10	6/–7	13/–1	19/4	24/9	31/13	29/12	24/7	16/1	7/–5	2/–9
Jackson												
°F	27/5	32/8	41/15	52/24	63/31	72/37	82/40	80/38	71/31	58/23	39/16	28/6
°C	–3/–15	0/–13	5/–9	11/–4	17/–1	22/3	28/4	27/3	22/0	14/–5	4/–9	–2/–14

	Jan	Feb	Mar	Apr	May	June	July	Aug	Sept	Oct	Nov	Dec
Kemmerer												
°F	29/5	33/7	40/14	54/25	65/33	74/38	82/44	80/42	71/34	59/26	41/16	34/10
°C	-2/-15	1/-14	4/-10	12/-4	18/0	22/3	28/7	27/6	22/1	15/-3	5/-9	1/-12
Lander												
°F	32/8	37/14	45/21	56/31	66/40	77/49	86/55	84/54	73/44	60/33	43/19	33/11
°C	0/-13	3/-10	7/-6	13/-1	19/4	25/9	30/13	29/12	23/7	16/1	6/-7	0/-12
Rawlins												
°F	31/11	34/15	39/18	52/27	64/37	76/44	83/51	81/50	71/40	58/31	40/19	33/15
°C	-1/-12	1/-9	4/-8	11/-3	18/3	24/7	28/11	27/10	22/4	14/0	4/-7	1/-9
Riverton												
°F	35/7	41/12	48/20	58/29	67/38	77/46	85/51	84/49	74/41	63/31	45/18	37/9
°C	2/-14	5/-11	9/-7	14/-2	19/3	25/8	29/11	29/9	23/5	17/-1	7/-8	-3/-13
Rock Springs												
°F	28/10	33/13	39/19	53/29	63/38	73/46	83/54	81/52	72/43	58/33	40/20	32/14
°C	-2/-12	1/-11	4/-7	12/-2	17/3	23/8	28/12	27/11	22/6	14/0	4/-7	-0/-10
Sheridan												
°F	33/9	38/14	46/21	57/31	67/40	76/48	86/54	86/52	73/42	62/32	45/20	36/12
°C	1/-13	3/-10	8/-6	14/-1	19/4	24/9	30/12	30/11	23/6	17/0	7/-7	2/-11
Thermopolis												
°F	34/5	40/10	49/20	61/31	71/39	81/47	91/53	89/51	78/41	64/30	48/18	37/9
°C	1/-15	4/-12	9/-7	16/-1	22/4	27/8	33/12	32/11	26/5	18/-1	9/-8	3/-13
Yellowstone												
°F	22/-2	28/-1	34/3	43/15	52/25	61/32	71/38	71/37	61/29	49/22	34/11	25/3
°C	-6/-19	-2/-18	1/-16	6/-9	11/-4	16/0	22/3	21/3	16/-2	9/-6	1/-12	-4/-16

and are especially comfortable because of the lack of humidity. Remember, too, that the atmosphere is thin at this altitude, so sunscreen is a must. Nights, even during the warmest months, will be cool, with temperatures dropping into the 40s (4°–9°C), so you'll want to include a jacket in your wardrobe. Because summer thunderstorms are common, you'll probably be glad you've included a waterproof shell or umbrella.

As **fall** approaches, you'll want to have an additional layer of clothing because temperatures remain mild but begin to cool. The first heavy snows typically fall in the valley by November 1 (much earlier in the mountains) and continue through March or April. Aspen trees turn bright yellow; cottonwoods turn a deeper gold.

During **winter** months, you'll want long johns, heavy shirts, vests, coats, warm gloves, and thick socks. Temperatures hover in single digits (negative teens Celsius), and subzero overnight temperatures are common. Ultracold air can cause lots of health problems, so drink fluids, keep an extra layer of clothing handy, and don't overexert yourself.

AVOIDING THE CROWDS   Between the Fourth of July and Labor Day, the Northern Rockies come to life. Flowers bloom, fish jump, bison calves frolic—and tourists tour. The park roads are crowded with trailers, with the well-known spots jammed with a significant portion of the millions who make their treks to Montana and Wyoming every year. Your best bet: Travel before June 15, if possible, or after Labor Day. If you can't arrange that, then visit the major attractions at off-peak hours when others are eating or sleeping, and you'll have the park more to yourself. Or, as I suggest over and over, abandon the pavement for the hiking trails.

Whenever you come, give these parks as much time as you can; you'll experience more at an unhurried pace.

3 Special Permits

BACKCOUNTRY PERMITS   If you want to sleep in the Yellowstone or Grand Teton backcountry, you have to get a permit, follow limits for length of stay and campfires, and stay in a designated area. The permit is free if you pick it up at the park during the final 48 hours before you begin your trip or on the day of your trip. Or you can reserve a site by paying a $25 fee to Grand Teton or $20 to Yellowstone. If you wish to make a reservation, you must do so in writing, and you still need to pick up your permit in person upon your arrival in the park. Yellowstone reservations can be made starting on

April 1 of the current year and are generally not accepted after early November. In Grand Teton, you can reserve a permit from January 1 to May 15; thereafter all permits are first come, first served. If you're going during the parks' busy season, you'd be wise to make a reservation.

In Yellowstone, permits can be obtained at any ranger station (most of which are open 8am–7pm during the summer), no more than 2 days before embarking on a trip. To make a reservation by mail (for a $20 fee), write the **Backcountry Office,** P.O. Box 168, Yellowstone National Park, WY 82190. Phone reservations are not accepted, but if you want information about the system, call © **307/ 344-2160.**

In Grand Teton, permits are issued at the Moose and Colter Bay visitor centers and the Jenny Lake Ranger Station. For a $25 fee, you can make reservations from January to mid-May by writing the **Permits Office,** Grand Teton National Park, P.O. Box 170, Moose, WY 83012. Phone reservations are not accepted, but information is available by calling © **307/739-3602.** Reservations can also be made online at **www.nps.gov/grte** or by fax at 307/739-3438.

BOATING PERMITS   For motorized craft in Yellowstone, the cost is $20 for annual permits and $10 for 7-day permits. Fees for nonmotorized boats are $10 for annual permits and $5 for 7-day permits. Boating permits are required for all vessels. Motorized boating is restricted to designated areas. Boating is prohibited on all of Yellowstone's rivers and streams except for the Lewis River Channel, where hand-propelled vessels are permitted. In Grand Teton, the fees are $40 for annual permits and $20 for 7-day permits. Fees for nonmotorized boats are $10 for annual permits and $5 for 7-day permits. Powerboaters are permitted on Jenny, Jackson, and Phelps lakes; nonmotorized boats are allowed on most park lakes and the Snake River. Sailboats, windsurfers, and jet skis are allowed only on Jackson Lake. U.S. Coast Guard–approved personal flotation devices are required for each person boating.

FISHING PERMITS   In **Yellowstone,** park permits are required for anglers 16 and over; the permit costs $15 for 3 days, $20 for 7 days, and $35 for the season. Youths ages 12 to 15 also must have a permit, but it's free. Children younger than 12 may fish without a permit. Permits are available at any ranger station, any visitor center, Yellowstone Park General Store, and most fishing shops in the gateways. The season usually begins on the Saturday of Memorial Day weekend and continues through the first Sunday in November.

Exceptions to this rule are Yellowstone Lake, its tributaries, and sections of the Yellowstone River, which have shorter seasons.

In **Grand Teton,** State of Wyoming fishing licenses are required for anyone older than 13. An adult nonresident license costs $11 per day and $76 for the season. Youth fees (ages 14–18) are $3 per day and $15 for the season. An $11 Conservation Stamp is also required for all licenses except the 1-day variety. The river season generally opens April 1 and ends on October 31; Jackson Lake is closed all of October.

4 Getting There

If interstate highways and international airports are the measure of accessibility, then Yellowstone is as remote as Alaska's Denali National Park. But three million people make it here every year, on tour buses, in family vans, on bicycles, and astride snowmobiles—even from the other side of the world.

Grand Teton's gateways are from the north, south, and east. Drivers naturally enter from whichever side they approach the parks, but fliers have some choices to make.

THE NEAREST AIRPORTS

The closest airport to Yellowstone is the **West Yellowstone Regional Airport** (© 406/646-7631) in Montana, where the airport sits just 1 mile north of town (and the west entrance) on U.S. Hwy. 191. The airport has commercial air service seasonally, June through September only, on **Delta Connection/SkyWest** (© 800/453-9417; www. skywest.com).

Visitors can land right in Grand Teton National Park when they fly to **Jackson,** Wyoming, and will be only 56 miles of scenic driving from the southern entrance of Yellowstone. **American Airlines** (© 800/433-7300; www.aa.com), **Continental** (© 800/523-3273; www.continental.com), **Delta** (© 800/221-1212; www.delta.com), **Northwest** (© 800/225-2525; www.nwa.com), and **United** (© 800/241-6522; www.united.com) all have flights to and from **Jackson Hole Airport** (© 307/733-7682; www.jacksonholeairport.com).

To the north, **Bozeman,** Montana, is 87 miles from the West Yellowstone entrance on U.S. Hwy. 191. Or you can drive east from Bozeman to Livingston, a 20-mile journey on I-90, and then south 53 miles on U.S. Hwy. 89 to the northern entrance at Gardiner. Bozeman's airport, **Gallatin Field** (© 406/388-8321; www.gallatin field.com), provides daily service via **Delta, Northwest,** and **United** (see phone numbers and websites above), as well as **Horizon** (© 800/547-9308; www.horizonair.com) and **Big Sky** (see below).

Driving Distances to Yellowstone National Park *

Salt Lake City	390 miles
Denver	563 miles
Las Vegas	809 miles
Seattle	827 miles
Portland	869 miles
Omaha	946 miles
Washington, D.C.	2,081 miles

* The difference in distance to Grand Teton is about 70 miles, depending on your route.

Also to the north, **Billings,** Montana, is 129 miles from the Cooke City entrance. Billings is home to Montana's busiest airport, **Logan International** (✆ 406/247-8609; www.flybillings.com), which is 2 miles north of downtown. Daily intrastate service is provided by **Big Sky Airlines** (✆ 800/237-7788 or 406/245-2300; www.bigsky air.com), and regional daily service is provided by **Allegiant Air** (✆ 702/505-8888; www.allegiantair.com), **Delta, Frontier** (✆ 800/ 432-1359; www.frontierairlines.com), **Horizon, Northwest,** and **United** (see phone numbers above). From Billings, it's a 65-mile drive south on U.S. Hwy. 212 to Red Lodge, and then 30 miles on the Beartooth Highway to the northeast entrance to the park.

From **Cody,** Wyoming, it's a gorgeous 53-mile drive west along U.S. Hwy. 14/16/20 to the east entrance of the park. Cody's **Yellowstone Regional Airport** (✆ 307/587-5096; www.flyyra.com) serves the Bighorn Basin as well as the east and northeast entrances of Yellowstone National Park with year-round commercial flights via **Delta** and **United** (see phone numbers above).

Airfares to the small airports surrounding the parks can be pricey, so if you like to drive, consider flying in to **Salt Lake City,** Utah, and driving about 300 miles to Grand Teton National Park, a drive that has some nice scenic stretches. Even **Denver,** a drive of roughly 500 miles, is an alternative, although the route is not nearly as scenic.

RENTING A CAR   Most of the major auto-rental agencies have operations in the gateway cities. **Hertz** (✆ 800/654-3131; www.hertz. com) has operations in **Billings, Bozeman, Cody,** and **Jackson. Thrifty** (✆ 800/847-4389; www.thrifty.com) is in **Cody** and **Jackson. Alamo** (✆ 800/462-5266; www.alamo.com) and **National** (✆ 800/227-7368; www.nationalcar.com) have locations in **Bozeman,**

Billings, and **Jackson. Avis** (© 800/230-4898; www.avis.com) has locations in **Billings, Bozeman, West Yellowstone,** and **Jackson. Budget** (© 800/527-0700; www.budget.com) serves **Billings, Bozeman, Cody, West Yellowstone,** and **Jackson.**

5 Tips for RVers

You love 'em, or you hate 'em—the large, lumbering vehicles that serve some travelers as both transport and home. There are some retirees, self-named "full-timers," who sell their homes and their possessions and spend the rest of their lives chasing comfortable weather down the highway. Others might see it as a cost-saving way to vacation in the West—by renting a rolling room for the whole family at perhaps $1,000 per week plus gas. Is that a better deal than an economy car and less expensive motels? You do the math.

You don't have to carry your bags, or even unpack them, and you'll sleep in campgrounds instead of motels, hear the sounds of the night outside, and have great flexibility in planning your itinerary. The trade-off will be making your own beds, doing without cable television, and preparing your own breakfast most of the time.

A few years back, Yellowstone officials considered closing the RV campground at Fishing Bridge, on the north end of Yellowstone Lake. The outcry was enormous, testimony to the immense popularity of RV travel, so the Fishing Bridge facility remains open today. You can drive most of the major roads in both parks with an RV or a trailer; but there will be some areas where large vehicles are prohibited, and most of the camping areas don't provide hookups— Colter Bay, Flagg Ranch, and Fishing Bridge are the exceptions.

For details on rentals, contact **Cruise America,** a nationwide company that rents all sorts of RVs (© **800/671-8042;** www. cruiseamerica.com).

6 Learning Vacations & Special Programs

One of the best ways to turn a park vacation into an unforgettable experience is to join an educational program. There are no finals in these courses; they're just a relaxed, informative way to spend time outdoors.

The **Yellowstone Association Institute** ✦✦✦, P.O. Box 117, Yellowstone National Park, WY 82190 (© **307/344-2294;** www. yellowstoneassociation.org/institute), operates at the historic Lamar Buffalo Ranch in the northeast region of the park, and other locations in the vicinity. It offers more than 400 courses a year, covering everything from wildlife tracking in the snow, to wilderness medicine, to the history of fur trappers on the plateau. The courses, some of which are offered for college credit, run from 1 to 7 days, with forays into the field, and lectures and demonstrations at the Institute's cozy quarters. The classes are a study in camaraderie as well as natural history, with participants sharing meals and stories in the common kitchen. Prices are reasonable (starting around $80 a day for tuition), and some classes are specifically oriented to families and youngsters. To make the most of a class, you'll want to stay at the ranch itself, where simple, comfortable cabins are available for $25 a night per student. Customizable 1-day hiking and wildlife-watching expeditions with an experienced naturalist, dubbed **Yellowstone Ed-Ventures,** run about $500 per day for groups of up to five people— a rate that includes transportation and use of high-powered spotting scopes, but does not include lunch.

The Institute has teamed with Xanterra Parks & Resorts to offer the best of two worlds: days spent exploring little-seen trails with knowledgeable and witty guides, and nights at the comfortable lodgings throughout the park. These 3- to 5-night packages, called **Lodging and Learning,** are excellent options for those who want to delve into the park without too much of the traditional "roughing it." Rates (starting at about $600 per person) include box lunches, breakfast, and in-park transportation. Contact **Xanterra Parks and Resorts** (℡ **307/344-7901;** www.travelyellowstone.com), P.O. Box 165, Yellowstone National Park, WY 82190, for reservations.

The **Teton Science Schools** ✦✦, 700 Coyote Canyon Dr., Jackson, WY 83011 (℡ **307/733-1313;** www.tetonscience.org), is a 30-year-old institution, with a cabin campus in the park near the little town of Kelly, that offers summer and winter programs for students and adults. Classes cater to different ages, and the emphasis is on experiential, hands-on learning. College credit is available. Long and short classes review the ecology, geology, and wildlife of the park, with workshops in photography and tracking as well.

The school's **Wildlife Expeditions** (℡ **888/945-3567** or 307/773-2623; www.wildlifeexpeditions.org) offers and arranges trips on open-roof vans, rafts, and sleighs, and by foot. These tours bring visitors closer to wildlife than they're likely to get on their own. The institute offers trips from a half-day sunset safari ($115) to weeklong trips through the park, usually lodging in park hotels. Adult seminars usually run about $150 to $300 per day, but more inclusive ones cost upwards of $400 per day.

7 Clothing & Equipment

Nothing will ruin a trip to the parks faster than sore or wet feet. Take some time planning your travel wardrobe. Bring comfortable walking shoes, even if you plan to keep walking to a minimum. **Bring shoes that are broken in,** and if you plan to do some serious hiking, get sturdy boots that support your ankles and wick away water. Early in the season, trails might be wet or muddy; late in the fall, you can get snowed on. The more popular trails are sometimes also used by horses, which can make stream crossings a mucky mess.

Wear your clothing in layers, and bring a small backpack or fanny pack so that you can take those layers off and on as temperature, altitude, and your physical exertion change. Cotton is a no-no in the backcountry; synthetic fabrics are recommended because they dry much faster. Gloves or mittens are useful before the park heats up, or in the evening when it cools down again, *even in summer.*

The atmosphere is thin at higher altitudes, so protect your skin. Bring a strong sun block, a hat with a brim, and sunglasses. I also recommend bringing insect repellent, water bottles, and a first-aid kit (recommendations for its contents are discussed under "Protecting Your Health & Safety," below).

Take into account that elevations at the parks are between 5,000 and 11,000 feet; in campgrounds and on hiking trails, you'll want clothing appropriate to the temperatures—in summer, 40°F (4°C) in the evening, 75°F (24°C) during the day.

8 Tips for Travelers with Special Needs

FOR TRAVELERS WITH DISABILITIES

In recent years, both parks have become increasingly user-friendly for travelers with disabilities.

YELLOWSTONE   **Accessible accommodations** are located in the Dunraven and Cascade lodges and Western cabins at Canyon Village; in Grant Village; in the Old Faithful Inn and Snow Lodge and Cabins; and in the Lake Yellowstone Hotel. For a free *Visitors Guide to Accessible Features in Yellowstone National Park,* write to the **Park Accessibility Coordinator** (© **307/344-2017;** www.nps.gov/yell), P.O. Box 168, Yellowstone National Park, WY 82190, or pick up the guide at the gates or visitor centers. There are **accessible campsites** at Fishing Bridge, Bridge Bay, Madison, Canyon, and Grant campgrounds, which you can reserve by calling © **307/344-7311.**

Accessible restrooms with sinks and flush toilets are located at all developed areas except West Thumb and Norris. Accessible vault toilets are found at West Thumb and Norris, as well as in most scenic areas and picnic areas.

Many of Yellowstone's **roadside attractions,** including the south rim of the Grand Canyon of the Yellowstone, West Thumb Geyser Basin, much of the Norris and Upper Geyser basins, and parts of the Mud Volcano and Fountain Paint Pot areas, are negotiable by wheelchair.

Visitor centers at Old Faithful, Grant Village, and Canyon are wheelchair accessible, as are the Norris Museum and the Fishing Bridge Visitor Center. The Albright Visitor Center at Mammoth is also accessible via a rear entrance.

Accessible parking is available at Old Faithful, Fishing Bridge, Canyon, Norris, and Grant Village, although you'll have to look for it; at some locations, it is near a Yellowstone General Store.

GRAND TETON **Campsites** at Colter Bay, Jenny Lake, and Gros Ventre campgrounds are on relatively level terrain; Lizard Creek and Signal Mountain are hilly and less accessible.

Accessible dining facilities are located at Flagg Ranch, Leeks Marina, Jackson Lake Lodge, and Jenny Lake Lodge.

Visitor centers at Moose, Colter Bay, Jenny Lake, and Flagg Ranch provide interpretive programs, displays, and visitor information in several formats, including visual, audible, and tactile. Large-print scripts, Braille brochures, and narrative audiotapes are available at Moose and Colter Bay.

Accessible parking spaces are located close to all visitor center entrances; curb cuts are provided, as are **accessible restroom facilities.**

More information is available from **Grand Teton National Park,** P.O. Drawer 170, Moose, WY 83012 (© **307/739-3600;** www. nps.gov/grte).

FOR TRAVELERS WITH PETS

Domestic animals and wild animals don't mix well, and park regulations reflect that. So, as much as you might like traveling with Fido, don't bring him unless he likes the inside of a car and the end of a leash an awful lot. Pets must be leashed and are allowed only 25 feet away from roads and parking areas. They are prohibited on trails, in the backcountry, on boardwalks, and in thermal areas.

FOR TRAVELERS WITH CHILDREN

The best general advice I've discovered is in Lisa Gollin Evans's book *An Outdoor Family Guide to Yellowstone and Grand Teton National Parks* (The Mountaineers; www.mountaineersbooks.org). Another useful guide to consult is *Frommer's National Parks with Kids,* by Kurt Repanshek. Both guides are easy to find in bookstores.

Older children will be entertained and receive a nature lesson by enrolling in the **Yellowstone Junior Ranger Program** (no specific age restrictions) at any visitor center or ranger station. The $3 fee covers the cost of the activity paper for Junior Rangers, *Yellowstone's Nature,* which describes the requirements for attaining Junior Ranger status. Activities include attending a ranger-led program, hiking, and keeping a journal. When participants complete the program, it's announced to the public with great fanfare, and a patch is awarded.

The **Young Naturalist** program at **Grand Teton** provides children with a similar opportunity to explore the natural world of the park, following instructions from an activity brochure. It costs $1 to participate; when you complete the course, you're awarded a patch.

9 Protecting Your Health & Safety

Health hazards range from mild headaches to grizzly-bear attacks. Because most of us live at or near sea level, the most common health hazard is discomfort caused by **altitude sickness** as we adjust to the parks' high elevations, a process that can take a day or more. Symptoms include headache, fatigue, nausea, loss of appetite, muscle pain, and lightheadedness. Doctors recommend that, until acclimated, travelers should avoid heavy exertion, consume light meals, and drink lots of liquids, avoiding those with caffeine or alcohol.

Two waterborne hazards are *Giardia* and *Campylobacter,* with symptoms that wreak havoc on the human digestive system. If you pick up these pesky bugs, they might accompany you on your trip home. Untreated water from the parks' lakes and streams should be boiled for at least 5 minutes before consumption or pumped through a fine-mesh water filter specifically designed to remove bacteria.

To be on the safe side, you might want to keep a **first-aid kit** in your car or luggage, and have it handy when hiking. It should include, at the least, butterfly bandages, sterile gauze pads, adhesive tape, an antibiotic ointment, pain relievers for both children and adults, alcohol pads, a pocket knife with scissors, and tweezers.

10 Planning a Backcountry Trip

While I've given the particulars for both Yellowstone and Grand Teton national parks in their respective chapters (see chapters 3 and 5), the following are some general things for you to keep in mind when planning a backcountry trip.

REGULATIONS   The theme in the backcountry is "leave no trace," and that means packing out any garbage you take in, not taking pets, and avoiding leaving scars on the landscape by staying on designated trails and reusing existing, designated campsites. Fires are allowed only in established fire rings, and only dead and downed material may be used for firewood; fires are prohibited in some areas, but backpacking stoves are allowed throughout the parks. You must have a park permit for overnight stays in the backcountry. The complete list of do's and don'ts is available in the ***Backcountry Trip Planner,*** available at most visitor centers. For more information on "leave no trace" ethics, see **www.lnt.org**.

BACKPACKING FOR BEGINNERS   Be sure to wear comfortable, sturdy hiking shoes that will resist water if you're planning an early-season hike; cotton socks are not a good idea because the material holds moisture, whereas wool and synthetics, such as fleece, "wick" it away from your body. Your sleeping bag should be rated for the low temperatures found at high elevations; if you bring a down bag, keep it dry or suffer the consequences. Most campers are happy to have a sleeping pad. The argument rages about the merits of old-fashioned, external-frame packs and the newer, internal-frame models. Over the long run, the newer versions are more stable and comfortable, but a big frame pack can shoulder bigger loads. Good padding, a lumbar support pad, and a wide hip belt are pluses. Be sure that you've tried out the pack—wear it around the house!—before you take it on a long trip with heavy loads, so that your body and the pack frame have a chance to adjust to each other.

PERSONAL SAFETY ISSUES   It's best not to backpack alone, but if you must, be sure that you have told both park rangers and friends where you'll be and how long you'll be gone. Don't leave the parking lot without the following gear: a compass, topographical maps, a first-aid kit, bug repellent, toilet paper and a trowel of some sort, a flashlight, matches, a knife, a rope for hanging food supplies in a tree, and a bell or other noisemaker that hopefully will alert any bears in the neighborhood to your presence, as well as a tent, a stove, and a sleeping bag. At this altitude, sunscreen and sunglasses with UV protection are a wise addition. A recently developed bear repellent generically referred to as "pepper spray," available in most sporting goods stores, has proven successful in countering bear attacks. You'll also need iodine pills or a good water filter because that seemingly clear stream is filled with parasites that are likely to cause intestinal disorders. If you don't have iodine or a filter, boil water for at least 5 minutes before you drink it.

Tips **Bear Encounters**

Most people have a healthy respect for bears and are content to view them from a distance. But because a close encounter can happen unexpectedly, you need to know how to handle yourself. First, be aware that what matters most to a bear are food and cubs. If you get between a sow and her cubs, you could be in trouble. If a bear thinks that the food in your backpack is his, you have a problem.

Unless bears have already developed a taste for human food, though, they won't come looking for you. Make a lot of noise on the trail through bear habitat, and *Ursus horribilis* will give you a wide berth. Don't camp anywhere near the carcass of a dead animal; grizzlies sometimes partially bury carrion and return to it. Hang your food bag high in a tree, keep your cooking area distant from your campsite, and don't keep any food or utensils in your tent—or even clothes worn while cooking. Soaps and other perfumed items can also be attractants.

Avoid hiking at night or in the meadows of mountain areas if visibility is poor. Bears have an extremely good sense of smell but poor eyesight.

If you encounter a bear, here are some things you should and should not do:

11 Recommended Reading

The following books are interesting, informative, and easy to find: ***Yellowstone, A Visitor's Companion,*** by George Wuerthner, Stackpole Books, Harrisburg, Pennsylvania; ***The Yellowstone Story*** (two volumes), by Aubrey Haines, Colorado Associated University Press; ***Searching for Yellowstone,*** by Paul Schullery, Mariner Books, New York; ***Yellowstone Trails: A Hiking Guide,*** by Mark C. Marschall, Yellowstone Association, Yellowstone National Park; ***Top Trails Yellowstone & Grand Teton,*** by Andrew Dean Nystrom, Wilderness Press, Berkeley, California; ***Death in Yellowstone,*** by Lee Whittlesey, Roberts Rinehart Publishers, Boulder, Colorado; ***Grand Teton National Park,*** available from the Grand Teton Natural History

- **Do not run.** Anything that flees looks like prey to a bear, and it might attack. Bears can run at more than 30 mph. The bear might bluff charge, but you're best off holding your ground.
- Avoid direct eye contact.
- If the bear is unaware of you, **stay downwind** (so that it can't catch your scent) and **detour away from it slowly**.
- If the bear is aware of you but has not acted aggressively, **slowly back away**.
- **Do not climb a tree.** Although black bears have more suitable claws for climbing, grizzly bears can climb trees, too.
- Make noise and act intimidating if the bear does not retreat.
- If you're attacked, drop to the ground face down, clasp your hands over the back of your neck, tuck your knees to your chest, and **play dead.** Keep your backpack on—it can act as armor. Only as a last resort should you attempt to resist an attack and fight off a bear.
- If you carry **pepper spray,** be sure that it's handy when you're in potential bear habitat, not buried in your backpack. If you use it, aim for the bear's face and eyes. After you use it, leave the area: Bears have been seen returning to sniff about an area where spray has been used.

Association; *A Guide to Exploring Grand Teton National Park,* by Linda L. Olson and Tim Bywater, RNM Press, Salt Lake City, Utah; *Crucible for Conservation,* by Robert Righter, Grand Teton Natural History Association, Moose, Wyoming; and *Teton Trails: A Guide to the Trails of Grand Teton National Park,* by Katy Duffy and Darwin Wile, Grand Teton Natural History Association. Falcon Press (Helena, Montana) also publishes a long list of hiking, fishing, climbing, and other guides to the Yellowstone/Grand Teton region.

If you cannot find these publications in your local bookstore, many can be ordered from either the **Yellowstone Association** (© 307/344-2293; www.yellowstoneassociation.org) or the **Grand Teton Association** (© 307/739-3403; www.grandtetonpark.org).

3

Exploring Yellowstone National Park

You can scratch the surface in a day or two, or you can devote an entire summer to digging deeper. One trip, however long, never feels adequate; there's always a road not traveled. You can focus on the roadside highlights or venture deep into the backcountry. You can enjoy the old-style park hotels or pitch your own tent. You can learn about the geology and flora and fauna in visitor center exhibits or take an in-depth class with expert naturalists.

There are 310 miles of paved roadways in Yellowstone, with a figure-eight loop at the center that takes you to some key attractions: You can cover that ground in one long day. This is a common strategy, but it doesn't do Yellowstone justice. Ultimately, those who embark on it are selling the park short.

I recommend you give yourself at least 3 days. Despite the crowds, you should check the famous sites because they're deserving of all the attention: **Old Faithful,** the **Grand Canyon of the Yellowstone, Fishing Bridge,** and **Mount Washburn.** If you're seeking knowledge, take a class at the **Yellowstone Association Institute,** or follow one of the rangers on a nature hike. If you want solitude, go early in the morning up one of the less-traveled trails, such as **Bunsen Peak** or **Mystic Falls.**

You'll find more details in the chapters that follow on where to hike, fish, sleep, and enjoy yourself in the park.

1 Essentials

ACCESS/ENTRY POINTS   Yellowstone has five entrances. The **north entrance,** near Mammoth Hot Springs, is located just south of Gardiner, Montana, and U.S. Hwy. 89. In the winter, this is the only access to Yellowstone by car.

The **west entrance,** just outside the town of West Yellowstone, Montana, on U.S. Hwy. 20, is the closest entry to Old Faithful. Inside the park, you can turn south to Old Faithful or north to the

---

⌒Tips **Superintendent's Advice**

"People have trouble grasping the enormity of our park," says Yellowstone Superintendent Suzanne Lewis. So do your homework. "Really spend time on our website," Lewis suggests. "If you don't have Internet access, go to the public library. It's also important to tell folks, if you come between June and mid-September, you'll be sharing the park with a lot of people."

Norris Geyser Basin. This entrance is open to wheeled vehicles from April to November.

About 64 miles north of Jackson, Wyoming, the **south entrance,** on U.S. Hwy. 89/191/287, brings visitors into the park from Grand Teton National Park. On the way to Yellowstone, drivers get some panoramic views of the Teton Range. Once in the park, the road winds along the Lewis River to the south end of Yellowstone Lake, at West Thumb and Grant Village. It's open to cars from May to November and to snowmobiles and snowcoaches from December to March.

The **east entrance,** on U.S. Hwy. 14/16/20, is 53 miles west of Cody, Wyoming, and is open to cars from May to September and to snowmobiles and snowcoaches from December to March. The drive up the Wapiti Valley and over Sylvan Pass is especially beautiful, when not marred by road-repair delays.

The **northeast entrance,** at Cooke City, Montana, is closest to the Tower-Roosevelt area, 29 miles to the west. This entrance is open to cars year-round, but beginning October 15, when the Beartooth Highway closes, until around Memorial Day, the only route to Cooke City is through Mammoth Hot Springs. When it's open, the drive from Red Lodge to the park is a grand climb among the clouds.

Regardless of which entrance you choose, you'll be given a good map and up-to-date information on facilities, services, programs, fishing, camping, and more.

VISITOR CENTERS   There are five major visitor and information centers in the park, and each has something different to offer. Unless otherwise indicated, summer hours are daily from 8am to 7pm.

The **Albright Visitor Center** (© 307/344-2263), at Mammoth Hot Springs, is the largest and is open daily, year-round. It provides visitor information and publications about the park, has exhibits depicting park history from prehistory through the creation of the National Park Service, and also houses displays on wildlife.

Yellowstone National Park

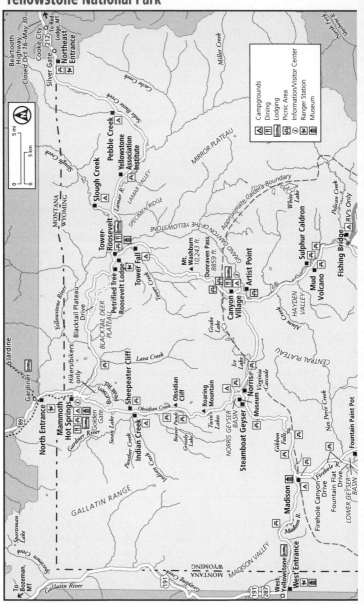

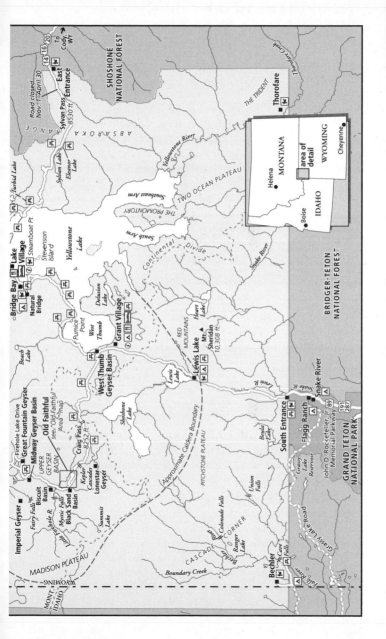

The **Canyon Visitor Center** (☏ 307/242-2550), in Canyon Village, completed in 2007, is the place to go for books and an informative display about the park's geology, with a focus on the underlying volcanism. It's staffed with friendly rangers used to dealing with crowds.

The **Old Faithful Visitor Center** (☏ 307/545-2750) is in a temporary facility until the Park Service opens a new, state-of-the-art building in 2009. A film on Yellowstone's thermal features is shown throughout the day in an indoor auditorium. Rangers dispense various park publications and post projected geyser-eruption times here.

The **Fishing Bridge Visitor Center** (☏ 307/242-2450), near Fishing Bridge on the north shore of Yellowstone Lake, has an excellent display that focuses on the park's bird life. You can get information and publications here as well.

The **Grant Visitor Center** (☏ 307/242-2650) has information, publications, a video program, and a fascinating exhibit that examines the role of fire in Yellowstone.

Park literature and helpful staff are also found at several small information stations: the **Madison Information Station** (☏ 307/ 344-2821); the **Museum of the National Park Ranger** (no phone; summer daily 9am–5pm) and the **Norris Geyser Basin Museum and Information Station** (☏ 307/344-2812; summer daily 10am– 5pm), both at Norris; the **West Thumb Information Station** (no phone; summer daily 9am–5pm); and the **Public Lands Desk** at the West Yellowstone Visitors Information Center, 100 Yellowstone Ave. (☏ 406/646-4403; summer daily 8am–8pm, limited hours the rest of the year). In Gardiner (but also within Yellowstone boundaries) is the **Yellowstone Heritage and Research Center** (☏ 307/344-2664), housing a library, archives, and other resources available to the public. It is open 9am to 4pm year-round, but is not equipped to handle standard visitor inquiries.

ENTRANCE FEES   A 7-day pass costs $25 per automobile and covers both Yellowstone and Grand Teton national parks. A snowmobile or motorcycle pass costs $20 for 7 days, and someone who comes in on bicycle, skis, or foot will pay $12.

If you expect to visit the parks more than once in a year, buy an annual pass for $50. And if you visit parks and national monuments around the country, purchase an **Interagency Annual Pass** for $80 (good for 365 days from the date of purchase at nearly all federal preserves). Anyone age 62 or older can get an **Interagency Senior Pass** for a one-time fee of $10, and people who are blind or who have permanent disabilities can obtain an **Interagency Access Pass,** which costs nothing. All passes are available at any entrance point to Yellowstone. While the Interagency Senior and Interagency Access passes must be purchased in person (to verify age or disability), Interagency Annual Passes are also available online at **www.store. usgs.gov/pass**.

CAMPING FEES   Fees for camping in Yellowstone range from $12 to $17 per night, depending on the number of amenities the campground offers. The RV Campground at Fishing Bridge charges $35 per night and has full hookups; while other campgrounds have sites suitable for RVs, this is the only one with hookups, and only RVs are allowed here. Flagg Ranch, just outside the south entrance, also has an RV camp with hookups.

For more information on camping, see the "Where to Camp in Yellowstone" section in chapter 7. It is possible to make advance reservations at some campgrounds in both parks.

SPECIAL REGULATIONS & WARNINGS   More detailed information about the following rules can be requested from the park rangers or at visitor centers throughout the park or at **www. nps.gov/yell**.

- **Bicycles:** Bicycles are not allowed on the park's trails or board-walks, but there are some designated off-pavement bicycling areas—contact the park for more information. Helmets and bright clothing are recommended because of the narrow, wind-ing nature of park roads and the large recreational vehicles with poor visibility.
- **Camping:** In any given year, a person may camp for no more than 30 days in the park, and only 14 days during the summer season (no limits at Fishing Bridge RV Park). Food, garbage, and food utensils must be stored in a vehicle or container made of solid material and must be suspended at least 10 feet above the ground when not in use.
- **Climbing:** Because of the loose, crumbly rock in Yellowstone, climbing is discouraged throughout the park and is prohibited in the Grand Canyon of the Yellowstone.
- **Defacing park features:** Picking wildflowers and collecting natural or archaeological objects is illegal. Only dead-and-down wood can be collected for backcountry campfires, and only when and where such fires are allowed.
- **Firearms:** Firearms are not allowed in either park. However, unloaded firearms may be transported in a vehicle when cased,

broken down, or rendered inoperable, and on certain trails for access to areas outside the park, with a special permit. Ammunition must be carried in a separate compartment of the vehicle.

- **Littering:** Littering in the national parks is strictly prohibited—remember, if you take it in, you have to take it out. Throwing coins or other objects into thermal features is illegal.

- **Motorcycles:** Motorcycles and motor scooters are allowed only on park roads. No off-road or trail riding is allowed. Operator licenses and license plates are required.

- **Pets:** Pets must always be leashed and are prohibited in the backcountry, on trails, on boardwalks, and in thermal areas. If you tie up a pet and leave it, you're breaking the law.

- **Smoking:** No smoking is allowed in thermal areas, visitor centers or rangers stations, or any other posted public areas.

- **Snowmobiling:** In late 2007, Yellowstone officials released a final winter use plan that will limit snowmobiles entering the park to 540 a day as of 2008–09.

- **Swimming:** Swimming or wading is prohibited in thermal features or in streams whose waters flow from thermal features in Yellowstone. (One exception is Boiling River near Mammoth, where visitors can take a warm soak between dawn and dusk except during spring runoff.) Swimming in Yellowstone Lake is discouraged due to the cold water and unpredictable weather.

- **Wildlife:** It is unlawful to approach within 100 yards of a bear or within 25 yards of other wildlife. Feeding any wildlife is illegal. Wildlife calls, such as elk bugles or other artificial attractants, are forbidden.

FAST FACTS: Yellowstone

ATMs There are numerous ATMs in the park: at Old Faithful Inn, Old Faithful Snow Lodge, Canyon Lodge, Lake Yellowstone Hotel, Mammoth Hot Springs Hotel, Grant Village, and Canyon Lodge, as well as Yellowstone General Stores throughout the park.

Car Trouble & Towing Services If you have car trouble, you'll find car-repair shops in Old Faithful, Canyon Village, Fishing Bridge, and Grant Village. Call the park's main information line (© **307/344-7381**) 24 hours a day if you need to be towed.

Emergencies Call ℂ **911** or the park's main information number (ℂ **307/344-7381**), which is staffed 24 hours a day.

Gas Stations You can purchase gasoline at Old Faithful, Canyon Village, Grant Village, Lake Village, Mammoth Hot Springs, Fishing Bridge, Bridge Bay, and Tower Junction.

Laundry There are laundry facilities at Lake Lodge, Old Faithful Snow Lodge, Fishing Bridge RV Park, Canyon Village Campground, and Grant Village Campground.

Medical Services There are three **medical clinics** in the park: at Mammoth Hot Springs (ℂ **307/344-7965**), Old Faithful (ℂ **307/545-7325**), and Lake Yellowstone (ℂ **307/242-7241**), where there is a pharmacy and a small hospital. The Lake and Old Faithful clinics are open daily from May to early fall, while the Mammoth clinic is open weekdays year-round and daily in summer.

Permits You can obtain fishing and backcountry permits at most visitor centers. See "Special Permits," in chapter 2, for more information.

Post Offices All the major visitor centers in Yellowstone have post offices (Mammoth, Old Faithful, Grant Village, Lake Village, and Canyon Village).

Supplies Yellowstone Park General Stores are located in all the park villages, with groceries, film and camera supplies, camping gear, and souvenirs.

Weather Updates For weather updates and road conditions, call the park's main information number (ℂ **307/344-7381**), which has recorded information.

2 The Highlights

This is a wonderland that you can return to again and again, sampling a different pleasure each time. All the sites mentioned here are easily accessible along the loop roads of the park. But the farther you get from the pavement, and the farther from July and August you schedule your visit, the more private your experience will be. Behind the wheel, expect to average about 30 mph during peak season.

THE UPPER LOOP

MAMMOTH HOT SPRINGS Here, 5 miles south of the park's north entrance at Gardiner, Montana, you'll find some of the park's spectacular thermal areas, including unique limestone terraces (the

Upper and Lower terraces 🐾🐾, which are described in "Yellowstone: The Extended Tour," later in this chapter). The Albright Visitor Center is here, with some interesting exhibits and a bookstore, as well as the Mammoth Hot Springs Hotel. Your best bet: Follow the interpretive trail through the terraces.

NORRIS GEYSER BASIN 🐾🐾 South of Mammoth Hot Springs, you'll find several impressive **geysers,** geothermal areas of different type and age, as well as two museums. Norris is conveniently close to the west entrance of the park at West Yellowstone. You can follow boardwalks north and south (the south has more activity, but the north takes you across the dramatic Porcelain Basin). Best bet: Tour both boardwalks.

CANYON VILLAGE AREA   East of Norris, the **Grand Canyon of the Yellowstone River** 🐾🐾🐾 provides some of the park's best views. There are hikes of all lengths and for all abilities here. Canyon Village is one of the most developed sections of the park, with lots of facilities and lodging choices. The canyon might not be as big as the Grand Canyon in Arizona, but it's got its own dynamic beauty. Best bet: Hike one of the rim trails.

TOWER-ROOSEVELT AREA   The closest of the major park areas to the northeast entrance (just west of Cooke City, Montana), this is also one of the most easygoing areas of the park, away from the big crowds and a short drive from the **Lamar Valley** 🐾🐾🐾, dubbed "The Serengeti of North America" for its wildlife. The Roosevelt Lodge Cabins are a great budget lodging if you want to rough it without pitching a tent, and **Tower Fall** 🐾 provides a dramatic backdrop for photos. Your best bet: Scope Lamar Valley for wolves and bears; dusk and dawn are optimal times.

THE LOWER LOOP

OLD FAITHFUL AREA   **Old Faithful** 🐾🐾 remains an enduring symbol of Yellowstone, and you'll find standing-room-only crowds at each eruption. The historic **Old Faithful Inn** is located here, and the new **Old Faithful Snow Lodge** is a worthy addition. The most convenient access is from West Yellowstone and the park's west entrance. Boardwalks crisscross the **Upper Geyser Basin,** offering views of numerous geysers other than Old Faithful. Your best bet: Climb to the top of **Observation Point** for a lesser-seen view of Old Faithful's classic burst.

LAKE VILLAGE AREA   On the north shore of Yellowstone Lake you'll find many fishing and boating opportunities, as well as fine dining and lodging choices. The **Lake Yellowstone Hotel** is one of the two best choices in the park. This area is the closest to Yellowstone's east entrance, which is about 50 miles from Cody, Wyoming. The beautiful **Hayden Valley** is nearby. You can rent a boat at Bay Bridge to get out and try to catch one of those elusive lake trout. Best bet: Take a sunset tour from Lake Yellowstone Hotel in one of Xanterra Parks & Resorts' classic 1930s touring buses.

GRANT VILLAGE/WEST THUMB AREAS   Grant Village is the southernmost of the park's developments, a nondescript collection of modern buildings on the south end of Yellowstone Lake. The **West Thumb Geyser Basin** and the Grant Village Visitor Center are nearby. West Thumb has a lakeside boardwalk that allows views of geysers that are on both sides of the water's edge. Best bet: Take an afternoon stroll on the boardwalks and gander at some of the jewels of Yellowstone's geothermal wonders.

3 If You Have Only 1 or 2 Days (the Short Tour)

If you are pinched for time and have only 1 or 2 days to tour Yellowstone, here's an itinerary that highlights the best of the best. If you'll be spending the night, your best bets are to reserve a room at either Old Faithful Inn or the Lake Yellowstone Hotel—if those are booked, try the new Old Faithful Snow Lodge, or get a campsite at Norris or Indian Creek. Other options along the itinerary route are given below.

The quickest route to the inner road loops of the park is by the west entrance road, so come in that way, stopping perhaps for a stroll along the banks of the **Madison River,** where you can see the forest recovering from the 1988 fires. You'll also spot wildlife: ducks and trumpeter swans on the river, and grazing elk and bison. Turn north at Madison Junction to **Norris Geyser Basin,** where there are two boardwalk tours; take the southern one if you're in a hurry.

You're now driving the **upper loop,** which goes north to **Mammoth Hot Springs,** east to **Tower-Roosevelt,** south to **Canyon Village,** and west again to Norris, finally returning to Madison Junction, a circuit of about 85 miles (or 3 hr. of driving minimum). If you go south, rather than west, at Canyon Village, you'll be on the southern loop, which will take you to **Fishing Bridge** and **Lake Village,** then by **West Thumb,** west over Craig Pass to **Old Faithful,** and back to the Madison Junction. The entire lower loop covers 96 miles (another 3 hr. in the car, at the very least).

Altogether, this 2-day circuit is called the **Grand Loop,** taking you through all the major areas of the park except the road between

Norris and Canyon Village. You could do it in a day—it's less than 200 miles long—but you'd scare a lot of other travelers as you sped by.

THE UPPER LOOP If you're pressed for time, the Norris Geyser Basin is a major concentration of **thermal attractions,** and also has a nice museum explaining the park's red-hot underpinnings. Mammoth has one of the park's major attractions, the ever-growing **terraces** of Mammoth Hot Springs. In addition to the natural attraction, the **Albright Visitor Center** provides excellent historical background for everything you see in the park. There is a fine old hotel at Mammoth and lodging just outside the park in Gardiner, too; but I recommend that you continue farther around the loop on your first day.

From Mammoth, the route winds through forested areas that lead to the edge of the **Lamar Valley,** a deep, rounded path for the Lamar River that is a prime haven for wolves, bison, elk, and grizzly bears. Otherwise, you can continue south to Yellowstone's **Grand Canyon,** one of the most dramatic sights in the park.

THE LOWER LOOP This is the better way to go if you have only a day. You'll also see the two largest geyser areas in Yellowstone—**Norris,** to the north, and the park's signature attraction, **Old Faithful,** to the south. On the eastern side of this route, you'll find the **Grand Canyon of the Yellowstone** and **Hayden Valley,** where you'll often find a grazing herd of buffalo. Farther south, the **Yellowstone Lake** offers fishing, boating, and places for picnicking on the shore.

4 Yellowstone: The Extended Tour

Stretching your visit to 4 or 5 days has several advantages. You'll have more time to visit the roadside highlights, plus you can hike a few of the trails and actually learn from the exhibits at the visitor centers instead of just blasting by them.

The **visitor centers** are a good source of information about the volcanic activity, the flora and fauna, and the history of the park; knowledgeable rangers are on hand who can answer your questions. There are 10 centers and information stations (see "Essentials," earlier in this chapter, for a complete list), but some might be closed if you visit the park during the off seasons. The **Albright Visitor Center** is open year-round, and the **Old Faithful Visitor Center** is open during summer months and December to March. The others usually open concurrently with the lodging facilities in their area of the park. Ask the rangers about programs in their area, and check whether any geothermal features have undergone a change in their activity recently—geysers have been known to revive suddenly after years of placidity.

The roads in Yellowstone are organized into a series of interconnecting loops, which you can come into from any of the park's five entrances. To simplify things, I'll discuss attractions and activities going clockwise along each section of the **Grand Loop Road,** beginning at the **Madison Junction.** But you can enter the loop at any point and pick up this tour as long as you are traveling clockwise. I haven't suggested an optimum amount of time to spend on each leg of the loop because that depends on your particular interests. If you want to get away from the crowds, take time to get off the pavement and onto the trails.

WEST YELLOWSTONE TO NORRIS

Closest entrance: West Yellowstone (west entrance)

Distances: 14 miles from West Yellowstone to Madison; 14 miles from Madison to Norris

Because most visitors to Yellowstone enter at the **west entrance,** I'll use that as a jumping-off point to begin an extended tour of the park. As you travel the 14 miles from the gate to **Madison Junction,** you will find the **Two Ribbons Trail,** which offers an opportunity to walk through and inspect the effects of the 1988 fire. The trail head is 3 miles east of the West Yellowstone entrance at a well-marked turnout. Along this .8-mile loop trail, you'll see a mosaic of blackened, singed, and unburned timber—charred snags and green trees side by side among boulders shattered by the heat. A testament to the regenerative effects of fire, millions of bright green saplings have emerged from the soil that surrounds the scraggly, deformed branches and piles of rock.

Park maps don't identify all the observation points and side roads in the area, so now is the time to begin forming the habit of driving off the beaten path, even when you might not know where you're going. Keep a sharp eye peeled for the poorly marked **riverside turnout** on the Madison River side of the road; it's a paved road on the north side of the highway about 6 miles from the entrance. This back road takes you along a river, removed from most traffic, and has a number of turnouts perfectly situated to look for resident swans, enjoy a picnic, or test your fly-fishing ability.

As you continue toward Madison Junction, you'll see more vivid evidence of the 1988 fire and, odds are, a herd of bison that frequents the area during summer months. As frightening as the fire was, it had its good points: There is evidence that the 1988 fire burned hotter here because the old lodgepole pines had been infected by beetles, decimating the trees long before the fires blazed. The good news is that the fire killed the beetles and remineralized the soil. When temperatures exceeded 500°F (260°C), pine seeds were released from fire-adapted pine cones, quickening the rebirth cycle. The shaglike carpet of tiny trees emerging from the soil is evidence that the forest is recovering quickly.

The .5-mile round-trip **Harlequin Lake Trail,** located 1½ miles west of the Madison campground on the West Entrance Road, offers an excellent, easy opportunity to explore the area. It winds through the burned forest to a small lake populated by various types of waterfowl. Despite the lake's moniker, sightings of the rare harlequin ducks are uncommon.

An alternative hike, one of the best in the area, is up the **Purple Mountain Trail,** which begins ¼ mile north of the Madison Junction on the Norris Road. This hike requires more physical exertion because it winds 6 miles (round-trip) through a burned forest to the top of a large hill, with an elevation gain of about 1,500 feet.

Madison Junction is a focal point of the most widely known Yellowstone myth: It is told that in September 1870, Cornelius Hedges and a group of explorers agreed that the land should be protected from those who would exploit its resources, and they began making plans to promote the creation of a national park. In reality, this conversation never happened. Madison Junction is also the confluence of the Gibbon and Firehole rivers, two famous trout streams that meet to form the Madison River, one of three that join to form the Missouri.

The **Madison Campground,** one of the largest and most popular in the park, is situated at the junction, with hiking trails and sites in view of the river. If you're planning a stay here, it's wise to arrive early, or you might be disappointed.

This is where you enter the northern loop toward Norris Junction, along a winding 14-mile section of road that parallels the **Gibbon River.** The river was named for Gen. John Gibbon, who explored here in 1872 but whose main, dubious claims to fame were as the cavalry leader who buried Custer's army and who chased Chief Joseph and the Nez Perce Indians from the park as they attempted to escape to Canada.

At 84-foot **Gibbon Falls,** you'll see water bursting out of the edge of a caldera in a rocky canyon, the walls of which were hidden from view for several hundred years until being exposed by the fire of 1988. There's a delightful **picnic area** just below the falls on an open plateau overlooking the Gibbon River.

Before arriving at Norris Junction, you'll discover the **Artist Paint Pot Trail** ⚎ in Gibbon Meadows, 4½ miles south of the Norris Junction, an interesting, worthwhile, and easy .5-mile stroll that winds through a lodgepole-pine forest to a gurgling mud pot at the top of a hill, passing some small geysers, hot pools, and steam vents along the way.

Across the road from the trail head is **Elk Park,** where you have a good chance of seeing a large herd of the majestic ungulates.

NORRIS GEYSER BASIN
Closest entrances and distances: 28 miles from West Yellowstone (west) entrance; 26 miles from Gardiner (north) entrance

Perhaps more than any other area in Yellowstone, this basin is living testimony to the park's unique thermal activity. It is never the same, changing from year to year as thermal activity and the ravages of wind, rain, and snow create new and different ponds and landscapes. Trees fall, slides occur, and geysers erupt. The **Norris Geyser Basin** ⚎⚎ was named for the second superintendent of the park, the outgoing Philetus Norris, whose name graces many park roads and attractions. It is also the location of one of the park's highest concentration of thermal features, including the most active geysers, with underground water temperatures that reach 459°F (237°C).

There are two loop trails here, both fairly level with wheelchair access, to the Porcelain Basin and the Back Basin. If you complete both of them, you'll see most of the area's interesting thermal features. If you're pressed for time, however, take the shorter **Porcelain Basin Trail,** a .8-mile round-trip that can be completed in 45 minutes. Along this boardwalk are Black Growler Steam Vent, Ledge Geyser, and the descriptively named Whale's Mouth.

The 1.5-mile **Back Basin Loop** is easily negotiable in 1 hour and passes by **Steamboat Geyser,** which has been known to produce the world's highest and most memorable eruptions. However, these 400-foot waterspouts occur infrequently, so it will take some luck to see one—it erupted six times between 2000 and late 2005, and blew only twice during the preceding 12 years. Conversely, **Echinus Geyser,** farther down the trail, erupts several times a day. *Note:* About 1,000 feet of boardwalk have been closed since 2003 due to new thermal activity; call the park service for up-to-date information.

Among the many highlights of the area is the **Norris Geyser Basin Museum,** a beautiful single-story stone-and-log building, the stone archway of which leads to an overlook of the Porcelain Basin. The museum houses several excellent exhibits; with luck, you'll

---

Tips   Watch Your Step!

In thermal areas, the ground might be only a thin crust above boiling hot springs, and there's no way to guess where a safe path is. New hazards can bubble up overnight, and pools are acidic enough to burn through boots; so you must stay in designated walking areas.

---

arrive in time for a ranger-led tour. In the past, ranger programs have been scheduled three times a day; ask at a visitor center for current schedules.

Also nearby is the **Museum of the National Park Ranger,** which is little more than a room full of artifacts in a small building near the Norris Campground (see below).

Both museums open in mid- to late May, weather permitting, and are open until September; hours vary by season, but you can expect the museums to be open from 9 or 10am to 5pm during the busiest times (roughly Memorial Day to Labor Day, but weather is a factor).

The **Norris Campground,** which is just slightly north of the Norris Junction, is another very popular campground, so plan an early arrival or be prepared to look for an alternative site, which isn't easy during the peak season.

NORRIS TO MAMMOTH HOT SPRINGS

Closest entrances: Norris is 28 miles from the West Yellowstone (west) entrance; Mammoth Hot Springs is 5 miles from the Gardiner (north) entrance

Distance: 21 miles from Norris to Mammoth Hot Springs

From Norris Geyser Basin, it's a 21-mile drive north to Mammoth Hot Springs, past the **Twin Lakes,** beautiful, watery jewels surrounded by trees. During the early months of the park year, the water is milky green because of the runoff of ice and snow. This is an excellent place to do some bird-watching.

This stretch of road between Norris Junction and Mammoth Hot Springs presents yet another excellent opportunity to see the effects of the 1988 fire. Try to use one of the turnouts to avoid blocking the roads. The large **meadow,** on the west side of the highway, which begins 3 miles from Norris, is popular with moose, thanks to water from bogs, marshes, and a creek. As you travel alongside **Obsidian Creek,** you'll notice the smell of sulfur in the air, olfactory evidence of thermal vents.

On the east side of the road, 4 miles from Norris, is **Roaring Mountain,** a patch of ground totally devoid of brush and plant life, covered with trees and stumps from the fire. Its bareness is attributed to the fact that, as steam vents developed here, the ground became hot and acidic, which bleached and crumbled the rock, taking the undergrowth with it. Historians say that the noise from the Roaring Mountain was once so loud that it could be heard several miles away; these days, it is silent.

Just 2 miles up the road is the **Beaver Lake Picnic Area,** an excellent little spot for a snack. Keep an eye out for moose.

As you wend your way a half-mile to **Obsidian Cliff,** the terrain changes quickly and dramatically, and you'll find yourself driving through a narrow valley bisected by a beautiful green stream. Obsidian Cliff is where ancient peoples of North America gathered to collect obsidian, a hard black rock that was used to make weapons and tools.

If you didn't stop at Beaver Lake, consider taking time for a short (3-min.) detour on the road to **Sheepeater Cliffs** (unless you're driving an RV or pulling a trailer), which, like most park attractions, is in a well-marked area just off the pavement. Though close to the main road, this quiet, secluded spot sits on the banks of the Gardner River, beside a cliff of columnar basalt rock that was formed by cooling lava following a volcanic eruption. This area, once inhabited by the Sheepeater Indians, is now home to yellow-bellied marmots (nicknamed "whistle pigs") that live in the rocks, safe from flying predators and coyotes.

As you travel the final few miles to Mammoth Hot Springs, you'll be in an area with especially interesting geologic diversity. You'll see evidence of the fire, large springs and ponds, and enormous glaciated rock terraces and cliffs.

Exiting the valley, head north onto a high plateau, where you'll find **Swan Lake,** flanked by Little Quadrant Mountain and Antler Peak to the west, and Bunsen Peak to the north.

At the northernmost edge of the Yellowstone Plateau, you'll begin a descent through **Golden Gate.** This steep, narrow stretch of road was once a stagecoach route constructed of wooden planks anchored to the mountain by a massive rock called the **Pillar of Hercules,** the largest rock in an unmarked pile that sits next to the road.

Beyond Hercules are **The Hoodoos,** an ominous-looking jumble of travertine boulders on the north side of the road, which have tumbled off the mountainside above to create a pile of unusual formations.

From the 45th parallel parking area on the North Entrance Road, north of Mammoth Hot Springs, a short hike leads to the **Boiling River** 🐾🐾. Here you can take a dip during daylight hours, where a hot spring empties into the Gardner River. The best time to soak is just before sunset, tending to muscles made sore by hiking; and you'll get a dramatic demonstration by the hordes of bats in the area. As far as facilities go, there is only a restroom with pit toilets here.

MAMMOTH HOT SPRINGS
Closest entrance and distance: 5 miles from the Gardiner (north) entrance

This area might offer the best argument for getting off the roads, out of your car, and into the environment. Although it's possible to see most of the wildlife and the major thermal areas from behind car windows, your experience of the park will be multiplied tenfold through the expenditure of a small amount of energy. Most people in average shape are capable of negotiating the trails here, a significant percentage of which are level or only moderately inclined boardwalks. Even the more challenging trails frequently have rest areas where you can catch your breath or, more important, stop and absorb the magnificent views.

One of Yellowstone's most unique, beautiful, and fascinating areas is the **Upper and Lower terraces** 🐾🐾. Strolling among them, you can observe Mother Nature going about the business of mixing and matching heat, water, limestone, and rock fractures to sculpt the area. This is one of the most colorful areas in the park; its tapestries of orange, pink, yellow, green, and brown, formed by masses of bacteria and algae, seem to change colors before your eyes.

The mineral-rich hot waters that flow to the surface here do so at an unusually constant rate, roughly 750,000 gallons per day, depositing almost 2 tons of limestone every 24 hours. Contours are constantly changing in the hot springs as formations are shaped by large quantities of flowing water, the slope of the ground, and trees and rocks that determine the direction of the flow.

On the flip side of the equation, nature has a way of playing tricks on some of her creatures: **Poison Spring** is a sinkhole on the trail, so named because carbon dioxide collects there, often killing creatures that stop for a drink.

The **Lower Terrace Interpretive Trail** is one of the best ways to see this area. The trail starts at 6,280 feet and climbs another 300 feet along rather steep grades through a bare, rocky, thermal region to a flat alpine area and observation deck at the top. A park guide

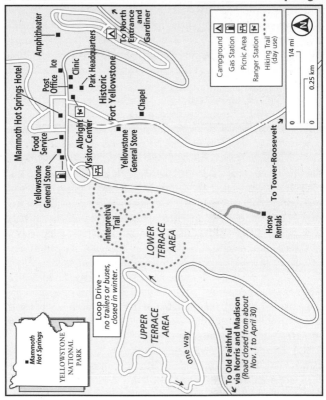

Amphitheater

To North Entrance and Gardiner

Park Headquarters

Ice

Clinic

Post Office

Mammoth Hot Springs Hotel

Historic Fort Yellowstone

Chapel

Food Service

Albright Visitor Center

Yellowstone General Store

Yellowstone General Store

Interpretive Trail

LOWER TERRACE AREA

Horse Rentals

To Tower-Roosevelt

Loop Drive - no trailers or buses, closed in winter.

UPPER TERRACE AREA

one way

To Old Faithful via Norris and Madison (Road closed from about Nov. 1 to April 30)

Mammoth Hot Springs

YELLOWSTONE NATIONAL PARK

Campground · Gas Station · Picnic Area · Ranger Station · Hiking Trail (day use)

1/4 mi

0   0.25 km

says that the 1.5-mile round-trip walk to the Upper Terrace and back normally takes 2 hours, but it can be done in less time.

Liberty Cap is a 37-foot-tall dome at the entrance to the interpretive trail. Once the site of a percolating hot spring, the domed Cap deposit is the result of 2,500 years of continuous gushing. The Hayden Expedition named it as such because of its resemblance to hats worn by Colonial patriots during the French Revolution.

After passing **Palette Spring,** where bacteria create a collage of browns, greens, and oranges, you're on your way to **Cleopatra and Minerva terraces.** Minerva is a favorite of visitors because of its bright colors and travertine formations, the product of limestone deposits. In nature's way, these attractions occasionally become unruly and spray water and mineral deposits large enough to bury the boardwalk.

The hike up the last 150 feet to the Upper Terrace Loop Drive is slightly steeper, although there are benches at frequent intervals. From here you can see all the terraces and several springs—**Canary Spring** and **New Blue Spring** being the most distinctive—and the red-roof buildings of **Fort Yellowstone,** which is now the park headquarters.

Near Fort Yellowstone is the large **Albright Visitor Center** (✆ **307/ 344-2263**), which has more visitor information and publications than other centers, along with significant exhibits telling the story of the park from prehistory through the creation of the National Park Service. It's open daily from 8am to 7pm during peak season. Enclosed in floor-to-ceiling glass cases are uniforms, furniture, side arms, and memorabilia that reflect the park's varied human history. There are excellent photography exhibits, with much of the work by the first park photographer, William Henry Jackson. A second level is filled with displays of the wildlife that inhabits the park, including wolves, mountain lions, waterfowl, and other birds. Films on the park's origin and the art that it has inspired are shown throughout the day.

You can continue walking along **Upper Terrace Loop Drive,** which is also accessible by car. The Upper Terrace has its own unique attractions, including **New Highland Terrace,** which is a forest of tree skeletons engulfed by travertine, and **Angel Terrace,** known for its pure white formations.

Just steps from the lower terrace is the trail head for the **Beaver Ponds Loop Trail,** a 5-mile round-trip jaunt through fir and spruce, then sagebrush and aspen, along a trail that follows **Clematis Gulch.** The ponds are about 2.5 miles from the trail head, after a moderate elevation gain, where the resident toothy engineers are most active early in the morning and at night. The area is also a hangout for elk and bears, and can be closed early in the summer season.

MAMMOTH HOT SPRINGS TO TOWER JUNCTION

Closest entrance: Mammoth is 5 miles from the Gardiner (north) entrance
Distance: 18 miles from Mammoth to Tower

Heading east from Mammoth on Tower Road, a 6-mile drive will bring you to the **Forces of the Northern Range Self-Guiding Trail,** a flat, easy stroll along a boardwalk that offers an excellent opportunity to educate yourself about the effects of the fire on the environment.

Two miles later is **Blacktail Plateau Drive,** a 7-mile, one-way dirt road that offers great wildlife-viewing opportunities and a bit more solitude. You'll be more or less following the route of the Bannock

Trail, made by the long-vanished Indian inhabitants of the area. For centuries, the trail was used by Bannock Indians as they trekked from Idaho to buffalo hunting grounds in eastern Montana; scars in the land made by their travois—twin poles tied to a horse that were used as a luggage rack—are still evident along the trail. You'll emerge back onto Mammoth-Tower Road, about a mile west of the turnoff to the Petrified Tree.

Turn right onto this half-mile-long road to the **Petrified Tree,** a redwood that, while standing, was burned by volcanic ash more than 50 million years ago. If you have the time and energy, park your car at the base of the road after you turn off Mammoth-Tower Road and hike up because the parking area is often congested. After your stop, continue on to Tower Junction.

TOWER-ROOSEVELT
Closest entrances and distances: 23 miles from the Gardiner (north) entrance; 29 miles from the Cooke City (northeast) entrance

Just beyond the Petrified Tree, you'll come to **Tower-Roosevelt,** the most relaxed of the park's villages and a great place to take a break from the more crowded attractions. Even if you aren't going to stay, you might want to make a quick stop at the **Tower Soldier Station,** now the ranger residence at Tower Junction, one of three surviving outposts from the era of U.S. Cavalry management of the park. Also here is **Roosevelt Lodge,** a rustic building that commemorates President Theodore Roosevelt's camping excursion to this area of the park, in 1903. It now serves as a dining hall, bar, and registration area for visitors staying at nearby frontier cabins. You can get into the cowboy spirit by taking a guided trail ride, a stagecoach ride, or a wagon ride. A more adventurous alternative to the rather rustic dining-room atmosphere at Roosevelt Lodge is the lodge's Old West cookout, to which you will arrive by either horseback or wagon for a hearty meal (see "Where to Dine in Yellowstone," in chapter 7, for more details). There's a range of other services in this spot, including a Yellowstone Park General Store if you need to buy provisions, and a gas station.

At **Specimen Ridge,** 2½ miles east of the Tower Junction on the Northeast Entrance Road, you'll find a ridge that entombs one of the world's most extensive fossil forests. Between 45 million and 50 million years ago, the mature forest that stood here was engulfed by deep volcanic ash some 27 times; subsequent erosion has exposed more than 100 different fossilized species in an area that spans 40 square miles.

A DETOUR: THE CHIEF JOSEPH HIGHWAY
Closest entrance and distance: 29 miles to the Cooke City (east) entrance

Because all the major attractions in Yellowstone are located on the loop roads, some of the park's most beautiful and secluded areas go unnoticed by travelers. If you have an additional day or two, I suggest that you head for the eastern entrances on another loop tour. From Tower Junction, go east to Cooke City and then continue to Cody; or, from Fishing Bridge, head across Sylvan Pass to Cody. If you hurry, you can complete the trip in a day, although you'll miss the Cody rodeo.

From **Tower Junction,** you'll traverse the **Lamar Valley** ✦✦✦, one of the prettiest and wildest areas of the park. This area was covered with a thick crust of ice during the last ice age, which began 25,000 years ago and ended 10,000 years later, leaving a valley shaped by melting glaciers that is dotted by glacial ponds and strewn with boulders dropped by moving ice. Before the ice came a volcanic eruption, 50 million years ago. Volcanic ash from the explosion engulfed the mature forest that once stood here, the results of which you can view at the Specimen Ridge wayside (see above). In addition to the region's natural beauty, it's the new home of packs of transplanted wolves and offers excellent fishing in the Lamar River and its numerous tributaries.

Cooke City might best be described as an outpost that provides essential services including restaurants, motels, gas stations, and grocery stores, but it's a long way from being as developed as its sister gateway cities. See chapter 8, "Gateways to Yellowstone & Grand Teton National Parks," for more information about lodging and dining here.

Fourteen miles outside of Cooke City, take the **Chief Joseph Scenic Highway** ✦✦ (Wyo. 296), which connects to Wyo. 120 into Cody. This highway, also called the Sunlight Basin Road, offers great opportunities for viewing deer, coyotes, and other wildlife.

Cody is the quintessential Western town. Folks are friendly, accommodations are well turned out and moderately priced, and there are enough tourist attractions—the nightly rodeo and the impressive Buffalo Bill Historical Center are most famous—to make it worth the detour. See chapter 8 for more details.

From Cody, return to Yellowstone's east entrance on U.S. Hwy. 12/16/20. After you reenter the park, you'll cross 8,541-foot **Sylvan Pass** and travel through the Absaroka mountain range, estimated to be 50 million years old. Driving along the shores of Yellowstone

Lake, you'll pass **Mary Bay,** yet another crater created by a volcanic explosion. You'll return to the main area of the park at **Fishing Bridge Junction,** where you can rejoin the Grand Loop Road and continue your tour.

FROM TOWER JUNCTION TO THE GRAND CANYON OF THE YELLOWSTONE

Closest entrances: 23 miles from the Gardiner (north) entrance; 29 miles from the Cooke City (northeast) entrance

Distance: 19 miles from Tower Junction to Canyon Village

A few minutes' drive from the Tower area is the **Calcite Springs Overlook.** A short loop along a boardwalk leads to the overlook at the rim of **The Narrows,** the narrowest part of this northern section of the Grand Canyon. You can hear the river raging through the canyon some 500 feet below and look across at the canyon walls comprising rock spires and bands of columnar basalt. Just downstream is the most prominent feature in this area of the canyon, **Bumpus Butte.** More noticeable than majestic, it is a box-shape outcropping between Rainy Lake and Calcite Springs.

A few steps from the general store, you'll find a trail to the 132-foot **Tower Fall** and an overlook that is typically crowded with sightseers. You'll have a more interesting and photogenic view if you continue past the overlook on the fairly steep path to the base of the falls where Tower Creek flows into the Yellowstone River.

Continuing south, you'll travel through the **Washburn Range,** an area in which the 1988 fires burned especially hot and fast. The terrain changes dramatically as the road climbs along some major hills toward **Mount Washburn.** The kinkiest section of this road is the aptly named **Mae West Curve.** Just before the curve, one stretch of this highway overlooks stands of aspen trees, a favorite summer haunt of the grizzly bear. Other sections are covered with sagebrush. During the fire, the sagebrush was incinerated, but roots were uninjured; so it now grows vigorously in soil that is fertilized by ash leached into the earth by snowmelt, another example of nature's artful ways.

There are trail heads for the **Mount Washburn Trail** 🦶🦶🦶, one of my favorites, on each side of the summit. One is at the end of Old Chittenden Road (the turnoff to this road from the Tower-Canyon Rd. is well marked); the other begins at Dunraven Pass, about a mile farther down the highway. Both hikes take 2 to 3 hours to complete, but because Old Chittenden has the larger parking lot, it might be more crowded; it's also more scenic (although steeper).

As you approach **Dunraven Pass** (8,859 ft.), keep your eyes peeled for the shy bighorn sheep because this is one of their prime habitats.

One mile farther south is the **Washburn Hot Springs Overlook,** which offers sweeping views of the canyon. On a clear day, you can see 50 to 100 miles south, beyond Yellowstone Lake. Get out of the car and take a look.

CANYON VILLAGE

Closest entrances and distances: 40 miles from West Yellowstone (west) entrance; 38 miles from Gardiner (north) entrance; 48 miles from the Cooke City (northeast) entrance; 43 miles from the east entrance

You're in for yet another eyeful when you reach the **Grand Canyon of the Yellowstone** ✹✹✹, which offers a vivid example of nature unleashing its destructive power to create indescribable beauty.

The canyon has its geologic origins in the same volcanic eruptions that created Yellowstone Lake. As lava flows created lakes that overflowed their banks, walls of granite-like rock remained while softer minerals eroded. This process carved the canyon, which was subsequently blocked by glaciers. Eventually, when the ice melted, floods recarved each end of the canyon, deepening it and removing sand and gravel.

The result: a 24-mile crevasse that at some points is 1,200 feet deep and 4,000 feet wide, and two waterfalls, one of which is twice as high as Niagara Falls. Even the most reluctant hiker will be rewarded with sites as colorful as those seen in "the other canyon." Compared to the Grand Canyon of Arizona, Yellowstone's Grand Canyon is relatively narrow; it's equally impressive, though, because of the steepness of the cliffs, which descend hundreds of feet to the bottom of a gorge where the Yellowstone River flows. It's also equally colorful, with displays of orange, red, yellow, and gold. And you won't find thermal vents in Arizona, but you will find them here, a constant reminder of ongoing underground activity.

You should plan on encountering crowds when you reach **Canyon Village,** where you'll find many necessary services: a post office, a trio of restaurants, and two stores stocked with groceries, gear, and souvenirs. Accommodations are in cabins and a large campground. Concessionaires offer horseback trail rides from a nearby stable and other guided tours. See chapter 7 for more details about lodging and dining in the area.

The snazzy **Canyon Visitor Center** (✆ **307/242-2550**) is the place to go for books and excellent exhibits on the park's geology, with

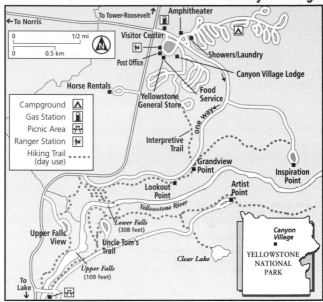

a focus on the underlying super-volcano and receding glaciers. It's also staffed with friendly rangers used to dealing with the crowds here.

An auto tour of the canyon follows **North Rim Drive,** a two-lane, one-way road that begins in Canyon Village, to your first stop, Inspiration Point. On the way, you'll pass a 500-ton **glacial boulder** that was deposited by melting ice more than 10,000 years ago. Geologists estimate that ice floes carried this chunk of rock 40 miles to its present location.

At **Inspiration Point,** a moderately strenuous descent down 57 steps takes you to an overlook with views of the Lower Falls and canyon. (At 8,000 ft., the hike will cause your pulse rate and blood pressure to rise, so it's wise to pause for a few extra minutes before making the return.) Evidence of current earthquake activity is beneath the soles of your shoes. The viewing platform once extended 100 feet farther over the canyon; on June 30, 1975, it was shattered by an earthquake and tumbled into the canyon. There are several other viewpoints you can stop at along North Rim Drive before you reconnect with the main Canyon Village–Yellowstone Lake Road, which will take you down to South Rim Drive.

Along the way, you can also stop at **Grand View** overlook, where the river flows some 750 feet below the observation platform. During summer months, Grand View is an excellent spot from which to view ospreys, which normally nest in this area and can be seen riding the thermals. **Lookout Point** provides a better view of the Lower Falls; however, the observation deck is at the end of a steep, 150-foot trail. Going down is the easy part; the return trip is not recommended for those with heart or lung problems.

For the adventurous, an alternative to driving from one overlook to another is to negotiate the **North Rim Trail** ☆☆, which is 2.3 miles long, beginning at Inspiration Point. This trail ends at the Upper Falls parking area, where the Upper Falls Trail begins; it's another .8 mile to the bridge that connects the North and South rims. Unfortunately, the North Rim Trail is not a loop, so if you take the hike, you'll have to backtrack to get your car at Inspiration Point. The footpath brings you closer to what you want to see, and you won't be fighting for elbowroom like you will at the overlooks that are a stone's throw from the road.

Whether you drive or walk, you should go down to the **Upper Falls View,** where a .3-mile trail leads down from the parking lot to the **Brink of the Upper Falls,** an overlook within splashing distance of the rushing river and the waterfall. At this point you won't just hear the power of the river, you'll feel it as it begins its course down the canyon.

The **South Rim Road** ☆ leads to several overlooks and better views of the Lower Falls. The most impressive vantage point is from the bottom of **Uncle Tom's Trail** ☆☆, a steep 500-foot steel trail to an unbeatable vantage point that begins at the first South Rim parking lot. The trail is named after Tom Richardson, an adventuresome turn-of-the-20th-century guide who led travelers to the base of the falls with ropes and ladders; these days, the trip is down 328 steps of a steel staircase attached to the canyon wall and paved inclines. The trail is rather steep, but can be negotiated in about an hour, although it will be challenging for the neophyte hiker.

South Rim Road continues to a second, lower parking lot and a trail that leads to **Artist Point** ☆☆. The view here is astounding—one of my favorites in the park—and is best in the early morning. It was at this point that Thomas Moran was inspired to create his famous painting of the falls, reproductions of which are seen in galleries and print shops throughout the world. This is one of the most photogenic (and most photographed) tableaux in the country—almost every visitor snaps a shot or two.

> *Tips* **Photo Tip**
>
> The Hayden Valley offers excellent opportunities to photograph **bison**. They are less harassed by tourists here and less confined.

The **South Rim Trail** is an alternative to viewing the Lower Falls and the canyon from wooden observation decks. From the first South Rim parking lot, which is just beyond the South Rim Drive Bridge, follow trail markers to the partially paved trail and then 1.8 miles to Artist Point. (The trail follows the canyon for 3.3 miles beyond Artist Point, to **Point Sublime,** where you must double back along the same route.) You'll have several different views of the falls, and you can always hop off to access Uncle Tom's Trail, Artist Point, and **Lily Pad Lake.** Neither Point Sublime nor Lily Pad Lake is accessible by car.

CANYON VILLAGE TO FISHING BRIDGE

Closest entrances: 27 miles to the east entrance; 43 miles to the south entrance

Distance: 16 miles from Canyon Village to Fishing Bridge

The road from Canyon Village winds through the **Hayden Valley,** which is a vast expanse of beautiful green meadows accented by brown cuts where the soil is eroded along the banks of the Yellowstone River. Imagine this: Ten thousand years before Ferdinand V. Hayden led the survey expedition of 1871, the entire Hayden Valley, except for the tallest peaks that surround it, was covered with a 4,000-foot-thick layer of ice. The valley is now a wide, sprawling area where bison play, and trumpeter swans, white pelicans, and Canada geese float along the river. This is also a prime habitat for the grizzly, so during early-spring months, pay close attention to binocular-toting visitors grouped beside the road.

Nature is at her acidic best at the **Sulphur Caldron** and **Mud Volcano** areas, 12 miles south of the Canyon Junction, which were described by writer Edwin Stanley as "unsightly, unsavory, and villainous." While Stanley anthropomorphized natural phenomena, his appraisal is fairly accurate, so you'll certainly want to explore this area. There's nothing quite like the sound of burping mud pots.

Vapors from Sulphur Caldron (on the east side of the road) had rotted the overlook's foundation, and it collapsed in 1984. The acidity of the caldron is twice that of battery acid; if you stepped in one of these pools, your shoes would be reduced to ashes.

At **Dragon's Mouth Spring,** escaping steam and sulfurous gases propel turbid water from an underground cavern to the surface, where it colors the earth with shades of orange and green. The belching of steam from the cavern and the associated sound, which is caused by the splash of 180°F (82°C) water against the wall in a subterranean cavern, creates an aura of fantasy and medieval times; hence, the name of the spring. Nearby **Mud Volcano** is a murky mud spring, the product of vigorous activity caused by escaping sulfurous gases and steam. The youngest feature in the area is **Black Dragon's Caldron,** which is often referred to as "the demon of the backwoods"—and rightly so. The caldron emerged from its subterranean birthplace for the first time in 1948, when it announced its presence by blowing a hole in the landscape, scattering mature trees hundreds of feet in all directions. Since then, continual seismic activity and intermittent earthquakes in the area have caused it to move several hundred feet south of its original position.

Le Hardy Rapids, a shaded area 2 miles farther south, is an ideal spot for a stroll along the river. This is a prime route for cutthroat trout in the early summer on their way to spawn. It is also popular with the shy harlequin ducks and bald eagles. The scary side of the equation is that this innocent-looking stretch of water flows across a fault in the earth. Some geologists believe that this will be the spot where the next major eruption will occur and that it will be as large as, or larger than, the eruption that created the Yellowstone caldera 600,000 years ago. Their guess: The next explosion will likely occur in the next 100,000 years. In the near term, however, a sluggish lava flow is much more likely than a catastrophic explosion.

The road across the Yellowstone River at **Fishing Bridge** was once the only eastern exit in the park, the route leading over Sylvan Pass to Cody, Wyoming. The bridge, which was built in 1937, spans the Yellowstone River as it exits Yellowstone Lake and is another prime spawning area for native trout. As a consequence, it became so popular that as many as 50,000 fishermen would beat the water into froth every year. To protect the trout, fishing was banned in the 1960s, but the bridge remains a great vantage point from which to watch them as they head upstream. It's also an excellent spot for observing the white pelicans and Canada geese that inhabit the area.

The **Fishing Bridge Visitor Center** (© **307/242-2450**), which is open daily from 8am to 7pm, has an excellent wildlife display. The nearby Yellowstone Park General Store sells provisions as well as liquor. The Fishing Bridge **RV Park** is restricted to hard-sided vehicles only because this is a prime grizzly habitat. You'll find an excellent hiking trail, **Elephant Back Loop Trail** *⚔*, leading off the short strip of high-way between Fishing Village and the Lake Village area. The 2-mile loop leads to an overlook with panoramic views of Yellowstone Lake and its islands, the Absaroka Range, and Pelican Valley to the east. Instead of taking the entire loop around to the overlook, you can shorten the hike a half-mile by taking the left fork approximately 1 mile from the trail head and doubling back after you get to the overlook.

YELLOWSTONE LAKE AREA

Closest entrances: Approximately 27 miles from Fishing Bridge to the east entrance; approximately 43 miles from Fishing Bridge to the south entrance

Distances: The lakefront from Fishing Bridge to the West Thumb Geyser Basin is 21 miles

As if the park didn't have enough record-setting attractions, at 7,773 feet, **Yellowstone Lake** *⚔⚔* is North America's largest high-altitude lake. It is 20 miles long and 14 miles wide, contains 110 miles of shoreline, has depths ranging to 390 feet, and is *very* cold. Because the surface freezes by December, and remains crusted until late May, the temperature at the bottom stays at 39°F (4°C) year-round, and the surface temperature isn't a lot warmer. Considering its size relative to the entire volcanic caldera, the lake is considered by many to be just a puddle. At one point in its history, the entire area was filled with ice, most of which has since melted, so the lake relies on 124 tributaries, including the Yellowstone River, to maintain its present level.

The lake exhibits its multifaceted personality every day, which ranges on an emotional scale from a placid, mirror-like surface to a seething tantrum of 3- to 4-foot waves. Boaters should be especially cautious because of the number of boat-related fatalities resulting from hypothermia. Compelling evidence of the ongoing changes occurring in the park as a consequence of subsurface thermal activity is the fact that the lake bottom is rising and tilting about 1 inch per year, a veritable sprinter's pace in geologic time. Trees on the south end of the lake drown as new beaches come into being on the north end, and existing beaches are expanding.

Because the lake has the largest population of native cutthroat trout in North America, it makes an ideal fishing spot in summer. (See chapters 2 and 4 for information on fishing regulations.) The lake is also an ornithologist's paradise; the skies are filled with osprey, bald eagles, white pelicans, and cormorants. On the shore, moose and grizzly bear are especially prevalent during the trout runs in spring.

Lake Village, on the northwest shore of the lake, offers a wide range of amenities, the most prominent of which is the regal facade of the Victorian **Lake Yellowstone Hotel.** You'll find food in the fine-dining restaurant, as well as in a little deli and the adjacent general store. Lodging is in the hotel, its motel-style annex, and the surrounding yellow cabins, and at **Lake Lodge** in modestly priced, frontier-style cabins. See chapter 7 for more details.

Just south of Lake Village is the **Bridge Bay Marina,** the center of the park's water activities. Here you can arrange for guided fishing trips or small boat rentals, or learn more about the lake during an informative and entertaining 1-hour narrated boat tour. The views are magnificent, and the skipper shares fascinating facts about the area's history. The marina is usually open from mid-June to mid-September.

Campers will find a large **campground** here with sites for RVs and tent campers. Trees surround the campground area, which has been cleared, so campsites here have very little privacy.

Although the **Natural Bridge,** near Bridge Bay, is well marked on park maps, it's one of the park's best-kept secrets, and you might end up enjoying it by yourself. The mile-long path down to the bridge, a geologic masterpiece consisting of a massive rock arch, soaring 51 feet overhead and spanning Bridge Creek, is an excellent bike route.

Looking for a picnic area? Keep a sharp eye out for an inconspicuous paved road on the lake side of the highway, 13 miles west of Fishing Bridge, which leads down to a secluded spot near **Pumice Point.**

The **West Thumb** area, along the western shoreline, is the deepest part of Yellowstone Lake. Because of its suspiciously crater-like contours, many scientists speculate that this 4-mile-wide, 6-mile-long, water-filled crater came to be when a secondary caldera within the primary Yellowstone caldera ferociously burped some 125,000 years ago.

The **West Thumb Geyser Basin** ☆☆ is notable for a unique series of geysers. Some are situated right on the shores, some overlook the lake, and some can be seen *beneath* the lake surface. Three of the shoreline geysers, the most famous of which is **Fishing Cone,** are occasionally marooned offshore when the lake level rises. (Fishing Cone was named for the park's early fishermen who used it as a combination casting spot/kitchen by immediately cooking their catch, hook still in mouth.) Fortunately, a half-mile of boardwalks crisscrosses the area, so it's easy to negotiate.

Yellowstone Lake: Fishing Bridge to Bridge Bay

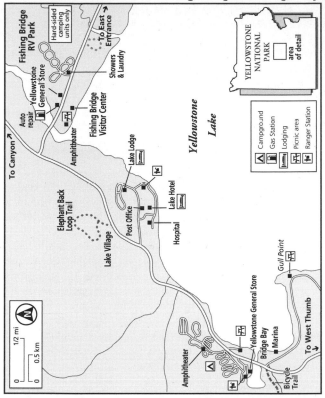

Near the center of an area that is totally surrounded by healthy trees is a **tree graveyard.** These pale, limbless trees were killed when thermal activity caused hot water to move toward them. When their roots absorbed the hot water, the trees were cooked from the inside out.

Details about the area, books, and maps are available at the **West Thumb Information Station,** housed in a log structure that functioned as the original West Thumb Ranger Station. The center is open daily 9am to 5pm from late May to September.

As you depart the West Thumb area, you are presented with two choices: either to head south, toward Grand Teton National Park, or to head west, across the **Continental Divide** at Craig Pass, en route to Old Faithful.

GRANT VILLAGE TO THE SOUTH ENTRANCE
Closest entrance and distance: 22 miles from Grant Village to the south entrance

Located on the southern shore of Yellowstone Lake, Grant Village offers dramatic views of summer squalls and one of Yellowstone's most inspiring sunrises. Perhaps the primary appeal of the village, the southernmost outpost in the park, is its location as a jumping-off place for travelers leaving for Grand Teton National Park, or as a place for them to spend their first night in Yellowstone. Named for President Ulysses S. Grant, the village was completed in 1984. It's the newest of Yellowstone's villages and home to the park's most modern facilities.

The **Grant Visitor Center** (✆ **307/242-2650**) has information, publications, a slide program, and a fascinating exhibit examining the effects of fire in Yellowstone. A video about the fires of 1988 is shown daily.

The **Grant Village Dining Room** is a good restaurant with views of the lake. Reservations are recommended. Nearby is **Lake House,** which serves less expensive pizza and pasta dinners in an informal dining room right on the shoreline. Guest accommodations are in a motel-style building. Other services include a general store that serves light meals and fast food, a modest gift shop, and a service station. For more details about dining and accommodations in the area, see chapter 7. Given a choice, I'd head north to a different destination or continue south to Grand Teton.

In contrast to this forgettable village is the beautiful 22-mile drive to **Grand Teton** along high mountain passes and **Lewis Lake.** The lake, which is 108 feet deep, is the third largest in the park and is connected to Shoshone Lake by a narrow channel populated by German brown trout. After the lake loses its winter coat of ice, it is a popular spot for early-season anglers who are unable to fish streams that are clouded by the spring runoff.

Beyond the lake, the road follows the Lewis River through an alpine area and along the **Pitchstone Plateau,** a pile of lava more than 2,000 feet high and 20 miles wide that was created some 500,000 years ago. A high gorge overlooking the river provides views that are different from, but equally spectacular to, those in other sections of the park. At its highest point, the road winds across a plateau that is accented with forests of dead, limbless lodgepole pine—remnants of the 1988 fire.

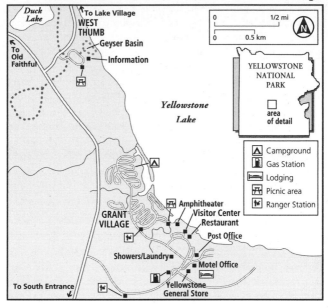

Yellowstone Lake: West Thumb to Grant Village

Duck Lake

To Lake Village
WEST THUMB
Geyser Basin
Information

To Old Faithful

Yellowstone Lake

0   1/2 mi
0   0.5 km

YELLOWSTONE NATIONAL PARK

area of detail

Amphitheater
Visitor Center
Restaurant

GRANT VILLAGE

Post Office

Showers/Laundry

Motel Office

To South Entrance

Yellowstone General Store

Campground
Gas Station
Lodging
Picnic area
Ranger Station

WEST THUMB TO OLD FAITHFUL
Closest entrance: 22 miles from West Thumb to the south entrance

Distance: 17 miles from West Thumb Geyser Basin to Old Faithful area

Craig Pass is an important geologic landmark because it is here, at the Continental Divide in the Yellowstone-Teton area, that the headwaters of two major rivers are formed, one emptying into the Pacific Ocean, the other into the Gulf of Mexico. The Snake River winds from Grand Teton through Idaho to meet the Columbia River in Oregon and then drains into the Pacific Ocean at Astoria, Oregon. The Yellowstone River, which begins south of Yellowstone Park, drains into the Missouri River, which drains into the Mississippi, which empties into the Gulf of Mexico.

An interesting phenomenon takes place on the Old Faithful route at **Isa Lake** atop Craig Pass. Unlike most lakes and streams, it has both eastern and western drainages and ends up in both the Pacific Ocean and the Gulf of Mexico. Amazingly, as a consequence of a gyroscopic maneuver, the outlet on the *east* curves *west* and drains to the Pacific, and the outlet on the *west* curves *east* and drains to the Gulf.

Before you reach the Old Faithful geyser area, two additional detours are recommended. About 3 miles south of Old Faithful is an overlook at the spectacular **Kepler Cascades,** a 150-foot stair-step waterfall on the Firehole River.

Near that parking lot is the trail head for the second detour, the 4.5-mile round-trip **Lonestar Geyser Trail** 𝔊𝔊. The geyser erupts every 3 hours, sending steaming water 30 to 50 feet from its 12-foot cone. The trail, which gently winds along the Firehole River through pastoral meadows and a forest, is a must-do; hiking, biking, and cross-country skiing are all popular. Even when others are on the trail, the area exudes a solitary air because it is possible to abandon the trail, follow the meandering stream, and find flat, open places to relax or picnic.

OLD FAITHFUL AREA
Closest entrance and distances: 16 miles from Old Faithful geyser to Madison Junction, then another 14 miles to West Yellowstone (west) entrance

Despite the overwhelming sight of the geysers and steam vents that populate the Old Faithful area, I suggest that you resist the temptation to explore until you've stopped at the **Old Faithful Visitor Center** (✆ **307/545-2750**). A film describing the park's geothermal features is shown throughout the day in an indoor auditorium that provides relief from hot July afternoons. Various park publications and an informative seismographic exhibit are added attractions. You will also want to check the information board for estimated times of geyser eruptions, and plan your time accordingly. (At press time, the visitor center was housed in a temporary structure near Old Faithful Lodge with construction underway on a cutting-edge facility that will better blend into the architectural motif of the Old Faithful Inn and Snow Lodge; park officials hope to open the new building in 2009.)

The Yellowstone Association's guides for **Old Faithful** and the **Fountain Paint Pots** include complete maps and explanations of the 150 geysers and many hot springs in the area, which happen to be a quarter of the world's total. Priced at 50¢, the guides are a bargain.

The number and variety of accommodations here are greater than at any other park center. The **Old Faithful Inn** is said to be the largest log structure in the world, seven stories underneath an 80-foot ceiling. The inn was finished in 1904 and is a National Historic Landmark. There are two other accommodations in this bustling center of activity: **Old Faithful Lodge,** with rustic frontier cabins for rent, and **Old Faithful Snow Lodge,** which was rebuilt in 1998 and has garnered awards for its rustic, environmentally friendly design.

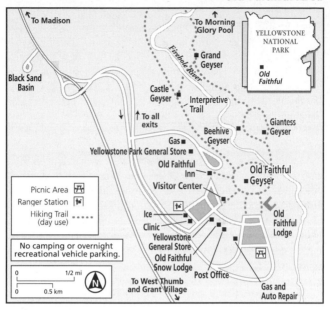

Several **dining** choices are available, the nicest of which is the upscale dining room in the inn, where three meals are served daily; the requisite deli is situated off the lobby. Another good eatery is situated in Snow Lodge, as is a fast-food restaurant; a cafeteria with food to satisfy various ethnic palates and an ice-cream stand are in the Lodge, as is a large gift shop. Nearby are a gas station, an auto repair shop, a post office, a medical clinic, and a Yellowstone Park General Store, with various provisions and souvenirs. For more information about dining and lodging in the area, see chapter 7.

The Old Faithful area is generally divided into four sections: **Upper Geyser Basin,** which includes Geyser Hill, **Black Sand Basin, Biscuit Basin,** and **Midway Geyser Basin.** Paved trails and roads connect all of these areas. If time allows, go on a hike here; it's fairly level, and distances are relatively short. Between the Old Faithful area and Madison Junction, you'll also find the justifiably famous **Lower Geyser Basin,** including Fountain Paint Pot and the trails surrounding it. You can see some of these geysers on Firehole Lake Drive.

Although **Old Faithful** ☝☝ is not the largest geyser in the park, and seems less inclined these days to be as faithful as it once was, its image has been on everything from postage stamps to whiskey bottles.

It acquired its name when the Washburn Expedition of 1870 observed its predictable pattern of eruptions. Seismic activity has wrought changes in the geyser's habits, but it's still the most predictable geyser on the planet, erupting with an average interval of 92 minutes, although it can vary about 30 minutes in either direction. A typical eruption lasts 1½ to 5 minutes, during which 3,700 to 8,400 gallons of water are thrust upward to heights up to 180 feet. For the best views and photo ops of the eruption in the boardwalk area, plan on arriving at least 15 minutes before the scheduled show, to ensure a first-row view.

An alternative to a seat on the crowded boardwalk is a stroll from the Old Faithful Geyser up the **Observation Point Trail** to an observation area that provides better views of the entire geyser basin. The path up to the observation point is approximately a half-mile, and the elevation gain is only 200 feet; so it's an easy 15-minute hike. The view of the eruption of the geyser is more spectacular from here, and the crowds are less obtrusive; watch out for bison and give them a wide berth.

From the vantage point of the Observation Point Trail, you'll have a different perspective of the entire **Upper Geyser Basin;** it's possible to see most of the major geysers as well as inaccessible steam vents in the middle of wooded areas. On clear, sunny days, sunbeams highlight the colors of the ponds and geysers in the valleys below. Interested in continuing your hike? From the top of the boardwalk, continue to the **Solitary Geyser** on a loop that leads back to the inn, adding only 1 mile to the trip on a mostly downhill trail.

Accessible by walkways from Old Faithful Village, the **Upper Geyser Basin Loop** is referred to as Geyser Hill on some maps. The 1.3-mile loop trail winds among several thermal attractions. **Anemone Geyser** might offer the best display of the various stages of a typical eruption as the pool fills and overflows, after which bubbles rising to the surface begin throwing water in 10-foot eruptions, a cycle that is repeated every 7 to 10 minutes.

The **Lion Group** consists of four geysers that are interconnected beneath the surface. The eruptions of the **Lion Geyser,** the largest of the quartet, are usually preceded by gushes of steam and a deep roaring sound, from which it derives its name. **Doublet Pool** is especially popular with photographers who are attracted by a complex series of ledges and deep blue waters. Farther along the trail is **Giantess Geyser,** known for its violent eruptions, which cause the surrounding area to shake and quake as underground steam explodes

Impressions

[W]e beheld one of the grandest displays of the kind we had ever beheld—a perfect geyser—an immediate volume of clear, hot water projected into the air one-hundred and fifty vertical feet, attended with dense volumes of steam rising upward for many hundred feet, and floating away in clouds . . .
　　　　　　—Edwin Stanley, from *Rambles in Wonderland,* 1878

before reaching the surface, where it can burst to heights of 200 feet. It erupts infrequently, at unscheduled intervals, so you should check with rangers to see if it's active.

Two other stars of the show in the Upper Geyser Basin are **Castle Geyser** 🌟🌟 and **Grand Geyser** 🌟🌟. Castle Geyser, which has the largest cone of any geyser in the park, currently erupts for 20 minutes every 10 to 12 hours, after which a noisy steam phase could continue for half an hour. Grand Geyser, the tallest predictable geyser in the world, usually erupts every 7 to 15 hours with powerful bursts that produce streams of water that can reach 200 feet in height.

The **Riverside Geyser** 🌟🌟 is situated on the bank of the Firehole River, near **Morning Glory Pool.** One of the most picturesque geysers in the park, its 75-foot column of water creates an arch over the river two to three times daily. **Morning Glory Pool** was named, in the 1880s, for its likeness to its namesake flower, but has since lost some of its beauty. Vandals have tossed so much debris into its core over the years that it now suffers from poor circulation and reduced temperatures, which are causing unsightly brown and green bacteria to grow on its surface.

The **Black Sand Basin** is a cluster of especially colorful hot springs and geysers located 1 mile north of Old Faithful. It is interesting primarily because of its black sand, a derivative of obsidian. The colors of **Emerald Pool** algae—blues, greens, yellows, and oranges—are an excellent example of the effects of water temperature and sunlight on what are actually unexpected living organisms. **Biscuit Basin,** located 2 miles farther up the road, was named for biscuit-like deposits that surrounded colorful **Sapphire Pool** until a 1959 earthquake caused the pool to erupt, sending them skyward. Both the Black Sand Basin and the Biscuit Basin are easily viewed from flat boardwalks.

The **Midway Geyser Basin** extends for about 1 mile along the Firehole River. The major attractions here are the **Excelsior Geyser,** the third-largest geyser in the world and once the park's most powerful geyser, and the well-known **Grand Prismatic Spring,** the largest hot spring in Yellowstone and the second largest in the world. A boardwalk leads to Excelsior, which, in the 1880s, erupted to 300 feet, creating a 300-foot-wide crater in the process. Just beyond is Grand Prismatic Spring. Those colorful bands of yellow, red, and green are thermal algae.

OLD FAITHFUL TO MADISON JUNCTION

Closest entrances: 30 miles from Old Faithful area to the West Yellowstone (west) entrance; 39 miles to the south entrance

Distance: 16 miles from Old Faithful area to Madison

Believe it or not, there are other superb geysers and hot springs on **Firehole Lake Drive,** all viewable without leaving your vehicle. The turnoff for Firehole Lake Drive is about 8 miles north of the Old Faithful area. There are three geysers of particular interest on this road. The largest is **Great Fountain Geyser,** which erupts every 8 to 12 hours, typically spouting water some 100 feet high for periods of 45 to 60 minutes. Lucky visitors might even see the occasional "superburst" that reaches heights of 200 feet or more.

Estimates are that **White Dome Geyser** has been erupting for hundreds of years. Unfortunately, the age and height of this massive cone are not matched by spectacular eruptions. The vent on top of the cone has been nearly sealed with deposits of geyserite, so eruptions now reach only 30 feet. However, the sight of the cone itself is worth a trip down this road.

Farther on, **Pink Cone Geyser** couldn't be closer to the road, the builders of which cut into the geyser's mound during construction.

About a quarter-mile north of where Firehole Lake Drive rejoins the Grand Loop Road is the **Fountain Paint Pots** ☞ area. This is a popular spot, so you might be forced to wait for a parking place. Although it's not large or spectacular, it's one of the most interesting areas in the park. All the various types of thermal activity are on display here, so as you stroll along the easy, .5-mile boardwalk, you'll be in an area that might have six geysers popping their lids at the same time. Though less impressive than other basins, these ponds, pots, and vents are among the most active in the park.

The first part of this natural exhibit offers an excellent example of how algae and bacteria are at work in these thermal areas. The centerpiece, literally, of this region is **Fountain Paint Pot,** which changes character as summer temperatures increase, causing once thin, watery mud to become very thick. The mud is composed of

---

Fun Fact **Know Your Bacteria**

Even the most casual visitor can do some scientific sleuthing at the **Fountain Paint Pots** ⚗, learning to identify water temperature by observing the colors in the pots. The colors result from different types of bacteria that survive at specific water temperatures. Some turn yellow until temperatures reach 161°F (72°C), above which the yellow bacteria cannot live. As temperatures approach boiling—199°F (93°C) at this elevation—pinks begin to appear.

---

clay and particles of silica that are trapped in the paint pots. (If you see a bubble forming on the surface, be prepared for a burst that could throw mud over the guardrail.) **Leather Pool** has undergone a transformation since the 1959 Hebgen Lake earthquake. It was once a warm, 143°F (62°C) pool lined with leather-like algae, but its temperature increased so dramatically after the quake that the algae were killed. **Red Spouter** changes its temperament with the seasons as its water table changes. During summer months, when the water table is low, it is a fumarole; from late fall through the winter, it spouts red water and mud. The Fountain Pots themselves are very colorful, with orange, yellow, blue, and green pots surrounded by bleached mud, gurgling like experiments in high-school chemistry labs. All in all, it takes roughly 20 minutes to do the whole tour. Before departing, take a look across the large grassy area called **Fountain Flat.**

As you continue toward the Madison Junction, consider a detour along **Fountain Flat Drive,** a left turn about 2 miles beyond Fountain Paint Pot. This scenic paved road ends ¼ mile north of Ojo Caliente, after which it is open only to hikers and bikers. One mile south of the Firehole River bridge, you'll find the **Imperial Meadows Trailhead.** Park the car and head up the 3.8-mile trail to the 200-foot **Fairy Falls.** This trail gets less traffic than the popular Lonestar and Dunraven trails.

Although a detour along **Firehole Canyon Drive** will require backtracking when you're approaching Madison from the south, the trip is worth the time you'll spend. There are great views of the canyon and **Firehole Falls.** The 2-mile, one-way road, which is a left turn off the Grand Loop Road just before you get to the Madison Junction, skirts 800-foot lava cliffs as it meanders along the canyon of the Firehole River in the shadow of National Park Mountain before rejoining the Grand Loop Road. Like much of the park, the 1988 fire scorched this area, so it offers excellent opportunities to see how quickly new growth is reconstituting the forest.

There are excellent views of the beautiful Firehole River as it rages through this narrow canyon, highlighted by a close-up of Firehole Falls. Be sure to bring a camera. Near the end of this 2-mile road is a popular **swimming hole** ✿ complete with restrooms for changing. There are several places to soak weary feet during the hot days of July and August, and scuba enthusiasts have flocked to the spot to view the life beneath the surface in a 45-foot-deep channel. For those without diving gear, bodysurfing the rapids is a popular endeavor.

5 Self-Guided Driving Tours

Depending on your driving skills and your tolerance for large numbers of cars, RVs, and auto-towed trailers, there is no substitute for a self-driven tour of the park. Although roads are narrow, there are hundreds of turnouts that afford opportunities to take in the views. On the downside, the roads twist, turn, and change elevation frequently, so freeway speeds are out of the question.

For $35 a day, gadget fiends can rent dashboard-mounted GPS units with prerecorded audio keyed to waypoints in both Yellowstone and Grand Teton from **GaperGuide,** 145 W. Gill Ave., Jackson, WY 83001 (✆ **307/733-4626;** www.gaperguide.com).

6 Organized Tours

A number of tour companies offer bus and van tours of the park originating in gateway communities: **Yellowstone Alpen Guides** (✆ **800/858-3502;** www.yellowstoneguides.com) takes travelers around the park from West Yellowstone. Salt Lake City–based **AdventureBus** (✆ **888/737-5263;** www.adventurebus.com) takes groups to Yellowstone and Grand Teton between June and August. If you are looking for specialized guided trips—such as photo safaris—contact the chambers of commerce in the gateway community where you want to begin (see "Getting Started: Information & Reservations," in chapter 2, for contact information).

Within the park, the hotel concessionaire, **Xanterra Parks & Resorts** (✆ **307/344-7311;** www.travelyellowstone.com), has a variety of general and specialized tours. Five different motorcoach tours are available from all of Yellowstone's villages. For $55, you can explore the **Circle of Fire** (Old Faithful, Yellowstone Lake, the Hayden Valley); you can cruise to the southern neighbor of Grand Teton for $58 on **Teton Vista Rendezvous;** or, for about $60, you can do the **Yellowstone in a Day** tour. These are full-day tours, with stops at all the sights and informative talks by the guides. In 2007, eight restored **Old Yellow Buses** that roamed the Yellowstone roads here in the first half of the 20th century went back into service for Xanterra. Tours in the buses range from 1 hour to all day ($30–$87). Other specialty trips include custom van tours, photo safaris, wildlife trips up the Lamar Valley, and Yellowstone Lake sunset tours in historic buses from the 1930s.

At Bridge Bay Marina, 1-hour **Scenicruiser tours** (© 307/344-7311) depart throughout the day from June to the end of September for a trip around the northern end of giant Yellowstone Lake. You view the Lake Yellowstone Hotel from the water and visit Stevenson Island while a guide fills you in on the history, geology, and biology. Fares are $11 for adults and $7 for children ages 2 to 11. Guided fishing trips on 22-foot and 34-foot cabin cruisers are also available at Bridge Bay ($70 and $90 per hour, respectively), and you can rent smaller outboards and rowboats.

Buses are replaced in the winter by **snowcoach tours.** These are closer in size to a van than a bus, mounted on tank treads with skis in front for steering. The snowcoach can pick you up at the south or west entrances, or at Mammoth, and take you all over the park. You can spend a night at Old Faithful and then snowcoach up to Mammoth the next night, or do round-trip tours from the gates or wherever you're staying in the park. One-way and wildlife-watching trips range from $30 to $60, while round-trips cost $100 to $120. **Yellowstone Alpen Guides** (© 800/858-3502; www.yellowstoneguides.com) offers snowcoach trips and tours from West Yellowstone for $99.

Guided horseback trail rides lasting from 1 to 2 hours are available at Roosevelt Lodge and Canyon Village. Children must be at least 8 years old and 48 inches tall; adults cannot exceed 240 pounds. Tour prices are $35 for a 1-hour ride and $54 for a 2-hour ride (no discount for children). Check any activity desk for times and dates. Reservations are recommended and can be made at **Xanterra Parks & Resorts** activity centers in the hotels, although not before you leave home.

The **Yellowstone Association Institute** ☆☆☆ (© 307/344-2293; www.yellowstoneassociation.org) offers a slew of guided classes, from daylong hikes to multiday backcountry adventures, often with a historical or scientific bent. The Institute has teamed with Xanterra Parks & Resorts to offer visitors days spent exploring trails with guides and nights at the comfortable lodgings throughout the park. These **Lodging and Learning** packages are excellent options for those who want to delve into the park without too much of the traditional "roughing it." Rates (starting at about $600 per person) include box lunches, breakfast, and in-park transportation. Contact **Xanterra Parks & Resorts** (✆ **307/344-5566;** www.travel yellowstone.com).

In September, the Institute takes over **Roosevelt Lodge** with the **Roosevelt Rendezvous,** a series of 4-day educational experiences with a daily menu of different field trips led by park experts. There are also evening programs. Rates start at $629 per person, including a cabin and three meals a day.

7 Ranger Programs

Yellowstone National Park continues to offer free **ranger-led educational programs** that will significantly enhance a visitor's understanding of the area's history, geology, and wildlife. Most programs run from early June to early September. Detailed information on locations and times is listed in the park newsletter, which is distributed at the entrance gates. On a more informal basis, you'll run into ranger-naturalists roaming the geyser basins and along the rim of the Grand Canyon in Yellowstone, and in areas where wildlife gather in both parks, leading informative walks and answering questions from inquisitive visitors.

Evening campfire programs are presented nightly in the summer at Mammoth, Norris, Madison, Bridge Bay, Grant, and Canyon. Many of these activities are accessible to those with disabilities. It's a good idea to bring a flashlight, warm clothing, and rain gear. Rangers also conduct walking, talking, and hiking programs throughout the park, including half-day "Adventure Hikes" that cost $15.

As one would expect, there are quite a few programs in the **Old Faithful** area. The topics of the guided walks, which can run as long as 1½ hours, usually focus on the geysers, their fragile plumbing, and their role in the Yellowstone ecosystem. There is a slide-show program in the auditorium in the evening.

Beginning in June, daily hikes in the **Canyon** area skirt along the rim of the Grand Canyon; a ranger talk on the art inspired by the falls is held several times a day at the lower platform of Artist Point. An explanation of the origins of the hot pools and mud pots is conducted twice daily beginning in June as part of a walk of the Lakeshore area of the **West Thumb Geyser Basin.** The **Lake Village/Fishing Bridge** agenda includes walking tours of the Mud Volcano area and the shores of Yellowstone Lake. There is an afternoon talk at the Fishing Bridge Visitor Center about such wildlife as grizzlies and wolves, and a discussion concerning the native cutthroat is held on the west end of the Fishing Bridge.

Mammoth Hot Springs is host to several interesting ranger-led programs, including talks on the park's natural and cultural wonders and a historical tour of the original site of Fort Yellowstone, established more than 125 years ago. There is also a guided tour of the hot springs terraces. The hottest, most dynamic, and oldest geyser basin in the park is at **Norris,** where a popular 1½-hour tour begins at the Norris museum on a daily basis in season.

Many changes are made annually in these presentations; consult the park newsletter that is distributed at the entrance gates.

4

Hikes & Other Outdoor Pursuits in Yellowstone National Park

Those who complain that Yellowstone's three million annual visitors have compromised the park's wilderness should park their car and tackle a trail: There's plenty of extremely wild country here.

There are short hikes on which you never lose sight of the road, moderate hikes on which you might spend an afternoon penetrating the forest to visit a spot of secluded beauty, and overnight trips on which you can hike and camp for days without running into another visitor.

In fact, there's so much to see and do in Yellowstone that it's easy to get overwhelmed. I've tried to make it easier by describing my favorite day hikes, backcountry experiences, and park activities.

1 Day Hikes

Below is a small selection of good hikes, long and short. The **Continental Divide Trail (CDT)** links many of these individual hikes together as part of a continuous trail from Mexico to Canada, roughly following the spine of the continent. The Yellowstone Backcountry Office maintains a guide to CDT trails. The **Howard Eaton Trail** system once went all through the park but was largely supplanted by the Grand Loop Road. Sections of the old trail are still maintained and will be found in trail guides, although some of them closely parallel park roads.

Wherever you go, if you're planning to hike for more than 30 minutes, be sure to carry a supply of water and rain gear. Bear spray is also recommended; hiking alone is not.

WEST YELLOWSTONE TO MADISON

Artist Paint Pot Trail (ℝ (Kids) Free of heavy foot traffic, this interesting and easy .5-mile path winds through a lodgepole forest in Gibbon Meadows to the Amazonia Mud Pot atop a small hill. This thermal area contains some small geysers, hot pools, and steam vents, colored by hues of orange, bright red, and rust.

1 mile round-trip. Easy. Access: Trail head is 4½ miles south of Norris Junction in Gibbon Meadow.

Harlequin Lake Trail   You'll get a good look at the interior of a burned forest en route to a small lake that is populated by various types of waterfowl, although few of the harlequin ducks that inspired its name remain. Short and level, this hike is a good diversion for those who don't want to divert too much from the road. Be sure to bring your insect repellent.

.5 mile round-trip. Easy. Access: Trail head is 1½ miles west of the Madison Campground on West Entrance Rd.

Purple Mountain Trail   This hike requires more physical exertion because it winds almost 3 miles through a burned forest to the top of what many consider only a tall hill with an elevation gain of 1,500 feet.

5.2 miles round-trip. Easy. Access: Trail head is ¼ mile north of the Madison Junction on the Madison-Norris Rd.

Two Ribbons Trail   This trail offers an opportunity to inspect the effects of the 1988 fire. Along the boardwalk, you'll see evidence of not only the blaze that ravaged the area but also the beginning of a new cycle of life in the dense green shag of lodgepole saplings. You'll also see some of the calling cards of bison in wallows, patches of rubbed-raw earth once used to scratch an itch.

1.5 miles round-trip. Easy. Access: Trail head is 5 miles east of the west entrance at an unmarked turnout on the north side of the road.

NORRIS GEYSER BASIN

Back Basin Loop ☞   This level boardwalk is easily negotiable in an hour and passes by **Steamboat Geyser,** which has been known to produce the world's highest eruptions. How often? About once a decade, with an impressive spurt of activity from 2000 to mid-2005: six eruptions—and counting. Wait instead by **Echinus Geyser** because its colorful pool fills and erupts several times a day.

1.5 miles round-trip. Easy. Access: Trail head is located at Norris Geyser Basin.

Porcelain Basin Trail   You'll share this boardwalk with other folks, but it takes you across a broad, flat basin where steaming water makes colorful trails. You can complete the walk in less than an hour, but you'll probably stop to look closely at some of these geothermal features, a few of which periodically spit and rumble in small eruptions.

.5 mile round-trip. Easy. Access: Trail head is located at Norris Geyser Basin.

MAMMOTH HOT SPRINGS AREA

Beaver Ponds Loop Trail   Start at Clematis Gulch and make your way to a series of beaver ponds. Your best chance of seeing the big-tailed beasts is early morning or late afternoon, and you might spot a moose, pronghorn, or elk on the way. There are some good views, including Mount Everts.

5 miles round-trip. Easy. Access: Trail head is located at Mammoth Hot Springs Terrace.

Bunsen Peak Trail 🐾🐾 *(Finds)*   This trail takes you up 1,300 feet in 2 miles to the 8,564-foot summit. Make the hike early, and you can watch the morning sun strike Electric Peak; then leave your thoughts in a rusted lockbox packed with the notes of thousands of past hikers. You can take an alternate route back down to the Osprey Falls Trail (see below).

4.3 miles round-trip. Moderate. Access: Trail head across the road from the Glen Creek Trailhead, 5 miles south of Mammoth on Mammoth-Norris Rd.

Forces of the Northern Range Self-Guiding Trail *(Kids)*   This fully accessible trail along a boardwalk presents an excellent opportunity to learn about the effects of fire on the environment. Signposts encourage kids to get down and dirty to examine the indications of the forest's rejuvenation.

.8 mile round-trip. Easy. Access: Trail head is on Tower Rd., about 6 miles east of Mammoth Hot Springs.

Lower Terrace Interpretive Trail 🐾   This interpretive trail is one of the best ways to see Mammoth Hot Springs. The boardwalk begins at 6,280 feet and climbs another 300 feet along marginally steep grades through a bare, rocky, thermal region to a flat alpine area and observation deck at the top; it's not a difficult climb in exchange for some splendid views. A park guide says the 1.5-mile round-trip walk to the Upper Terrace and back takes 2 hours, but it can be done in less.

1.5 miles round-trip. Easy. Access: Trail head is south of the village on the road to Norris.

Osprey Falls Trail 🐾🐾   The first 3.3 miles of this hike lead along an old, bike-friendly roadbed at the base of Bunsen Peak. From the Osprey Falls Trail turnoff, it's another 1.5 miles through a series of steep switchbacks in Sheepeater Canyon to a secluded waterfall on the Gardner River.

9.3 miles round-trip. Moderate. Access: Trail head is at Bunsen Peak Trailhead, 5 miles south of Mammoth Hot Spring on Mammoth-Norris Rd.

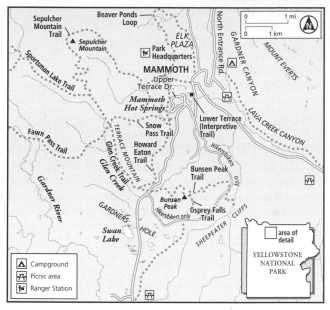

Sepulcher Mountain Trail 🚲🚲   The Glen Creek Trailhead presents hikers with several alternative paths through the Sepulcher Mountain area. During the early summer, this plateau is a beautiful, wide open area that follows the base of Terrace Mountain. With huge expanses of sagebrush and pines interspersed with the brilliant yellows and blues of wildflowers, this is an excellent place to escape the crowds. You will also get a feel for the real park in this wilderness area without making much of a physical commitment. Because the trail is in the Gallatin Bear Management Area, you'll want to make noise or tie a bell to a shoe while hiking here.

   Three miles from the trail head, you'll arrive at a fork in the trail. Now you have to make a choice: Continue another 2 miles up the steeper option to the mountain's summit, continue on to the east on the Terrace Mountain loop of the **Snow Pass Trail,** or retrace your steps to the trail head. If you're continuing, I recommend the former. It's a moderate hike that climbs 2,300 feet as the trail winds through a diverse selection of wildlife and scenery.

6–12 miles round-trip. Easy to moderate. Access: Glen Creek Trailhead, 5 miles south of Mammoth on Mammoth-Norris Rd.

Trout Lake Trail 🐾 A short, somewhat steep hike through spruce and fir, this trail's destination is the small Trout Lake, which is encircled by a footpath. The lake, nestled between dramatic cliffs and Druid and Baronette peaks, is a favorite fishing hole and one of the best places in the park to witness the fascinating cutthroat spawn. Because of the density of the fish, the lake once served as a major source of food for Cooke City and continues to attract otters, beavers, and bears.

1.3 miles round-trip. Easy. Access: 10 miles west of the northeast entrance, at the trail head 1 mile west of Pebble Creek campground.

GRAND CANYON OF THE YELLOWSTONE RIVER AREA

Clear Lake and Ribbon Lake Loop Trail 🐾 The hike to Clear Lake is 1.5 miles, a gradual climb across a high plateau, with Ribbon Lake less than 2 miles beyond it. Views of the plateau improve with each step until you find yourself surrounded by the mountains of the Canyon area. Clear Lake itself is intimately small and gives you the opportunity to see subsurface activity of the thermal areas below the lake. On a circumnavigation of the lake along a trail, you will see and smell vented gas making its way to the surface; in some spots, the lake looks like a small boiling pot. There is bear activity in this area early in the year, so check with rangers for current conditions before heading out.

6 miles round-trip. Moderate. Access: Wapiti Trailhead, across the street from the South Rim parking lot.

Howard Eaton Trail Both the Clear Lake and Ribbon Lake trails give access to the Howard Eaton Trail, the means to an arduously lengthy hike to Fishing Bridge and Yellowstone Lake. You'll see some riverside thermal features and waterfowl on the way, and pass a ford favored by bison crossing the Yellowstone River. There is bear activity in this area early in the year; check with rangers for current conditions before heading out.

15 miles one-way. Moderate to difficult. Access: Wapiti Trailhead across the street from the South Rim parking lot.

Mount Washburn Trail 🐾🐾🐾 This is a relatively short hike to panoramic views, with wildflowers decorating the way and nonchalant bighorn sheep browsing nearby. You might also see marmots and red fox; for a few years, grizzly bears were regulars in a nearby meadow. Trail heads are located at the summit of Dunraven Pass (elevation 8,895 ft.) and on Old Chittenden Road, where there's more parking. Either hike is 6 miles round-trip with an elevation

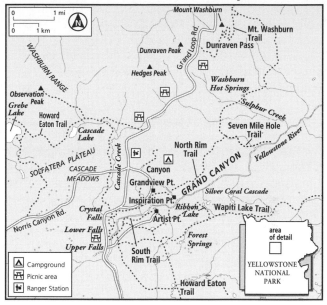

Canyon Area Trails

gain of 1,400 feet. However, the climbs are fairly gradual and interspersed with level stretches: You can reach the summit in an easy 90-
minute walk if you keep a steady pace. From the summit, the park
will lie before you like a map on a table: You'll see the Absaroka
Mountains to the east, Canyon and Yellowstone Lake to the south,
and the Gallatin Mountains to the west and north. The summit is
over 10,000 feet, so bring warm clothing to fend off the wind that
whips at the top. There's a warming hut in the ranger lookout, with
pay telescopes and restrooms.

6 miles round-trip. Moderate. Access: Trail heads at the end of Old Chittenden Rd.
and at Dunraven Pass.

North Rim Trail 🐾   This trail, which is described more fully under
"Canyon Village," in chapter 3, offers better views of the falls and
the river than you'll get from the parking areas. It's a nice way to see
a longer stretch of the canyon.

4 miles round-trip. Easy. Access: Trail head at Inspiration Point.

Seven-mile Hole Trail   You'll see the Silver Cord Cascade from
the rim and then descend to the river after a couple of miles in an

area where the canyon widens enough for trees. There are a few active hot springs along this hike, and it is popular with fishermen because of its river access. This is quite a drop (1,400 ft.), and novice hikers should remember that whatever goes down must come up.

11 miles round-trip. Moderate to difficult. Access: Trail head off North Rim Trail.

South Rim Trail ✿   As with the North Rim Trail, there are more and better views of the canyon and river here than you can see from a vehicle. It's easy and not long, yet you'll have it mainly to yourself because most folks are in and out of the bus at the parking lots.

6 miles round-trip. Easy. Access: Trail head at the parking lot just beyond South Rim Dr. bridge.

Uncle Tom's Trail ✿✿   The short trip is down 328 stairs and paved inclines that lead to an incredible perspective on Lower Falls. The staircase (shackled to the canyon's wall) and trails here are rather steep but can be negotiated in an hour, although it will be challenging for the neophyte hiker. Take your time, enjoy a break on the way back up, and watch for ice on cold mornings.

1 mile round-trip. Moderate. Access: Trail head is located at the South Rim parking lot.

YELLOWSTONE LAKE AREA

Elephant Back Loop Trail ✿   Here's an opportunity to look down on (literally!) the island-dotted expanse of Yellowstone Lake, the Absaroka Mountains, and the Pelican Valley. This is a great photo opportunity and a fairly easy hike for a novice.

4 miles round-trip. Easy. Access: From the east, the trail head is on the right side of the road, just before the turnoff for the Lake Yellowstone Hotel.

Pelican Valley Trail   Take this loop through a marsh- and meadow-dotted area north of the lake loaded with elk, bison, sandhill cranes, trout, eagles, grizzly, and the new kids on the block, wolves. You can take hikes of different lengths, up to a 16-mile loop, but a lot of folks, having had their fill of wildflowers and beasts, go no farther than Pelican Creek Bridge, about 3.5 miles in. If you continue on, you'll pass through forest and "bear meadows," where you should be watchful and respectful of wildlife. This is a daytime-only hiking area, and it's closed in the early summer until July 4 because of bear activity.

7–16 miles round-trip. Moderate. Access: Trail head is across from Yellowstone Lake's north shore.

Storm Point Trail ✿   The Storm Point Trail follows a level path that terminates at a point jutting into the lake, offering a rocky viewpoint of the lake, Stevenson Island, and the mountains beyond. (On a clear day, you'll see as far south as the Tetons.) It begins near Indian Pond, a favorite hangout for bison. During spring months, this is a popular spot with grizzlies, so the trail might be closed; however, even when it's open, check with rangers regarding bear activity.

2 miles round-trip. Easy. Access: Trail head is 3½ miles east of Fishing Bridge, directly across from the Pelican Valley Trailhead (on the lake side of the road).

OLD FAITHFUL AREA

Fairy Falls Trail 🐾   Though longer than the Mystic Falls Trail, the Fairy Falls Trail is popular because it leads to a taller waterfall, which drops 200 feet. The level hike begins at the Imperial Meadows Trailhead, 1 mile south of the Firehole River Bridge on Fountain Flat Drive. After following an old roadbed that winds through an area populated by elk along Fairy Creek, you'll pass the Imperial Geyser. From here, the trail joins Fairy Creek Trail and travels east to the base of the falls. (You can also access the falls via this trail, which is ultimately a shorter trip but less scenic.) The total gain in elevation is only 100 feet.

7.5 miles round-trip. Moderate. Access: Trail head located at Imperial Meadows in Biscuit Basin.

Fountain Paint Pot Trail 🐾 *(Kids)*   This is a very accessible, popular area, so you might be forced to wait for a parking place. All types of thermal activity are on display, so as you stroll along the boardwalk, you'll be distracted at every turn by another bubbling pool or colorful mud pot.

.5 mile round-trip. Easy. Access: Trail head begins at Fountain Paint Pot parking lot.

Geyser Hill Loop 🐾   One of the most interesting, and easiest, loops in the area, this trail winds among several thermal attractions. Anemone Geyser puts on a good display of the various stages of a typical eruption as the pool fills and overflows; the Lion Group consists of four geysers interconnected beneath the surface; Doublet Pool is popular with photographers who are attracted by a complex series of ledges and deep blue waters; and Giantess Geyser is known for its violent eruptions.

1.3 miles round-trip. Easy. Access: Trail head at Old Faithful boardwalk.

Lonestar Geyser Trail 🐾   The popularity of this trail detracts from the pleasure of walking a fairly level, forested trail along the Firehole River, interrupted now and then by broad riverbank meadows. The geyser itself sits in a meadow pocked by steam vents and thermal features. About every 3 hours, it spouts water some 50 feet in the air from a vanilla-and-chocolate-colored cone. The path is partially paved and open to bicycles as far as the geyser (hikers can go farther, over Grants Pass). In the winter, this is a popular route for cross-country skiers.

4.3 miles round-trip. Easy. Access: Trail head at the parking lot opposite Kepler Cascades.

Mystic Falls Trail   This trail leads to a waterfall on the Little Firehole River that drops more than 100 feet, one of the steepest in the park. The trail starts at Biscuit Basin, crosses the river, and then disappears into the forest. The total distance to the base of the falls is only 1 mile; there's a trail to the top, and if you want to take a different way home, connect with the **Little Firehole Meadows Trail,** with long-distance views of Old Faithful, back to Biscuit Basin.

3 miles round-trip. Easy. Access: Trail head located at Imperial Meadows in Biscuit Basin.

Observation Point Trail–Solitary Geyser 🐾🐾 *(Moments)*   For a spectacular view of Old Faithful and the geyser basin from above, take this 2-mile loop. While it requires a bit more planning than watching Old Faithful from the bleachers, you'll have a totally different perspective from that of the masses below. The path up to the observation point is just half a mile, and the elevation gain is only 200 feet, an easy 15-minute hike. From the top, you can see most of the major geysers, as well as inaccessible steam vents located in the middle of wooded areas. From the top of the boardwalk, continue to the Solitary Geyser on a downhill slope that leads past the geyser, through the basin, and back to the Old Faithful Inn, which completes the loop.

2 miles round-trip. Easy. Access: Trail head at Old Faithful boardwalk.

2 Exploring the Backcountry

The backcountry of Yellowstone is the real thing: a domain of free-roaming wildlife and natural treasures predominately untouched by the hand of man. The National Park Service, through its system of permits, designated camping areas, and rules (for more on these, see below), has managed to preserve a true wilderness. Yellowstone has more than 1,200 miles of trails (most of which are in the backcountry) and 300 backcountry campsites.

For general information on backpacking and safety, see chapter 2.

Old Faithful Area Trails

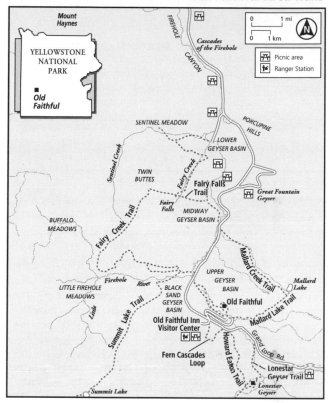

INFORMATION BEFORE YOU GO Contact the **Yellowstone Backcountry Office,** P.O. Box 168, Yellowstone National Park, WY 82190 (© **307/344-2160;** www.nps.gov/yell/planyourvisit/ backcountrytripplanner.htm), and someone there will send you the useful *Backcountry Trip Planner* with a detailed map showing where the campsites are, how to make reservations, and how to prepare.

BACKCOUNTRY PERMITS Backcountry permits are free, but you have to have one for any overnight trip, on foot, on horseback, or by boat. Camping is allowed only in designated campsites, many of which are equipped with food-storage poles to keep wildlife out of your stores. Some are also equipped with pit toilets. These sites are primitive and well situated, and you won't feel like you're in a campground.

⌐Tips Planning Ahead

You can pick up a permit the day before beginning a trip, but if you'll be traveling during peak season, try to make a reservation in advance. If you don't, and someone else has reserved the campsites in the area you want to go, you're out of luck. It costs $20 to hold a site, and you can begin making reservations for the upcoming year on April 1.

Caution: The reservation is just that, a reservation; upon your arrival at the park, you'll need to secure the permit, which is valid only on the dates for which it is issued.

Pick up your permit in the park within 48 hours of your departure at one of the following stations any day of the week during the summer: Bechler, west entrance, or south entrance ranger stations (no phones); or Canyon, Mammoth, Old Faithful, Tower, Grant Village, Lake, or Bridge Bay visitor centers (see "Essentials," in chapter 3, for phone numbers and information).

WHEN TO GO   Many of the trails into the park backcountry remain covered with snow and become muddy in the first weeks of melt, well into June. At the higher elevations, over 9,000 feet, summer doesn't truly begin until early July, and even then the weather is precarious at best. Trail maintenance in the backcountry is much less thorough than on the more public trails near the roads: Creeks and streams described as "intermittent" during summer months might be filled with snowmelt that converts them to impassable, swiftly running rivers, often drenching trails and converting them to mud. Look in the *Backcountry Trip Planner* for approximate dates when specific campsites will be accessible and habitable.

MAPS   Park rangers suggest using the "Yellowstone Series" of maps produced by Trails Illustrated. Each of the four maps in the collection covers about nine of those produced by the U. S. Geologic Survey and is printed on durable plastic; the maps also show backcountry campsite locations. For more information, contact **Trails Illustrated** (© 800/962-1643; http://maps.nationalgeographic.com), or the **Yellowstone Association** (© 307/344-2293; www.yellowstoneassociation.org).

OUTFITTERS   An alternative to going on your own is to go with an outfitter. Outfitters provide most equipment, which can offset the cost of their services, which might include setting up tents and making meals.

Based in Emigrant, Montana, **Big Wild Adventures** (② 406/848-7000; www.bigwildadventures.com) offers guided trips into Yellowstone's backcountry with a focus on a specific topic, like waterfalls or wolves. The trips usually last 5 days to a week and cost $1,300 to $1,600. **Yellowstone Llamas** (② 866/586-1155 or 406/586-1155; www.yellowstonesafari.com) offers an excellent compromise: beasts of burden that carry the heavy gear, leaving you free to wander the trails. The trips typically cover 3 to 6 miles per day in the park, and gourmet meals are served at the end of the day along with stream-chilled bottles of wine. The rate is $200 per person per day.

THE YELLOWSTONE BACKCOUNTRY

If you just can't get your fill of geysers, or if you've had your fill of people, several trails lead to more isolated backcountry. The **Shoshone Geyser Basin** and **Heart Lake Geyser Basin** contain active geysers, as do **Ponuntpa Springs** and the **Mudkettles** in the Pelican Valley area, **Imperial Geyser** in the Firehole area, and the **Highland Hot Springs** on the Mary Mountain Trail. If you head in these directions, be careful about walking on unstable surfaces: A young man died in 1988 when he fell into a superheated pool.

SHOSHONE LAKE

Shoshone Lake is the largest backcountry lake in the Lower 48 and a popular spot for backcountry hikers. The shortest route to the lake is via the **Delacy Creek Trail,** which begins 8 miles east of Old Faithful on Old Faithful–West Thumb Road. From here, the trail winds 3 miles along Delacy Creek through moose country and the edge of the forest at the lake. At this point, it's a tossup: You can head around the lake in either direction. Assuming that you take a clockwise track around the lake—a distance of 18 miles—you'll continue 4.5 miles on the Delacy Creek Trail to its intersection with **Dogshead Trail,** and then head west on the **Shoshone Lake Trail** until it intersects with the **North Shoshone Trail** and returns to your starting point.

A detour: At the western end of the lake, you'll arrive at the 1-mile **Shoshone Geyser Basin Trail** ❀❀, which loops through a number of geysers, hot springs, and meadows that, during spring months, are ankle-deep in water and mud. Union Geyser, which erupts sporadically, is impressive because eruptions occur from three vents simultaneously. Because the crust of the earth is so thin here,

Tips **Wilderness U: Guided Backpacking with the Yellowstone Association Institute**

The **Yellowstone Association Institute (YAI)** uses the park's backcountry as a 2.2-million-acre classroom for many of its 400 annual classes. In fact, a number of courses are guided backpacking trips into the Yellowstone wilderness.

I went on a YAI expedition with about 10 other customers in August 2004, following the same route the Nez Perce Indians took through Yellowstone in summer 1877 while evading the U.S. Army. Our 4-day adventure—which was preceded by a day in an indoor classroom in Gardiner—traversed 40 miles under the leadership of an experienced backcountry guide and park historian, Lee Whittlesey, whose wry humor nicely complemented his historical insight.

We learned about the obstacles the Nez Perce faced en route to their ultimate surrender in Montana. Led by Chief Joseph, 600 to 800 people, including a good number of children and elderly persons, evaded capture from June into October, cutting through a slice of the fledgling national park known as Yellowstone.

We learned about the rugged terrain the Nez Perce crossed, and about differing accounts of their exact path through the park. We learned about wolf tracks, as well as

your footsteps might sound like thumping on a hollow gourd.

As you travel the lake's loop trail along the **Delacy Creek Trail,** you'll have views of the lake at the top of a 100-foot rise. Then, on the **Shoshone Lake Trail,** you'll cross the Lewis Channel, which can have thigh-high water as late as July. Beyond that, the trail is a series of rises that are easily negotiable by the ordinary hiker, passing across shallow Moose Creek and through meadows where you might spot deer or moose early in the morning or evening.

The 8.5-mile **North Shoshone Trail** winds through a lodgepole-pine forest, over numerous ridges up to 200 feet high. The best views of the lake are from the high points on this trail. The loop trail is especially popular with overnighters because there are 26 campsites on the loop, the largest of which has space for eight campers. (Some of the sites are accessible by paddlers only, however.)

about the "Leave No Trace" etiquette upheld by backcountry enthusiasts.

Most of all, we learned that the flight of the Nez Perce has been the key event in the tribe's history since 1877. The 5-month ordeal haunts many of its members to this day. The contemporary Nez Perce are a nostalgic tribe, still focused on the events of summer 1877, and thus—for better or for worse—they are quite different from the typically modern people of the United States.

The "Flight of the Nez Perce" backcountry course has become a staple in the YAI catalog, along with guided back-packing classes about wolves, grizzly bears, waterfalls, photography, and the microbes that inhabit the park's thermal features. Taking a course is a great way to educate yourself and to learn the ins and outs of backpacking; plus you meet a bunch of like-minded Yellowstone lovers in the process. Trips typically last 4 days to a week and cost $400 to $700 per person. You need to bring most of your own gear. Call 𝄐 307/344-2294 or visit www.yellowstoneassociation.org for a course catalog and other information.

THE BECHLER REGION

This area in the park's southwest section is often referred to as Cascade Corner because it contains a majority of the park's waterfalls. It escaped the fires of 1988 and offers great opportunities to view thermal features. Many backpacking routes cut through this region, including one that leads to Old Faithful on the **Bechler River Trail** 𝄐.

To begin your hike, drive into the park from Ashton, Idaho, and check in at the Bechler Ranger Station. To reach the ranger station, drive east 17 miles from Ashton on the Cave Falls Road; 3 miles before reaching Cave Falls, you'll find the ranger station turnoff. The ranger station is 1½ miles down the gravel road.

The **Bechler Meadows Trail** 𝄐 takes you into this southwest corner, rich in waterfalls, cascades, and thermal areas that rarely have human visitors. About 6 miles into the journey, the trail fords the river several times as it enters Bechler Canyon, where it passes Colonnade and Iris falls. There are places on this trail where you can view the Tetons in the distance and the hot springs that warm the creeks. You can cover a good 30 miles in 3 or 4 days, depending on what turns you take. It's a camping trip best made late in the summer, to avoid high water during creek crossings. For a shorter trip, hike 3.5 miles along the **Bechler River Trail** to the **Boundary Creek Trail,** and then return to the station via the **Bechler Meadows Trails,** a round-trip of 7 miles.

The most adventurous and scenic route takes you 30 miles from the ranger station to the end of the trail at the **Lonestar Geyser Trailhead,** near Old Faithful. Beyond Iris Falls and then Ragged Falls, you'll reach a patrol cabin at Three Rivers Junction at the 13-mile mark, a popular camping area. If you continue toward Old Faithful, you'll intersect the **Shoshone Lake Trail** at the 23.5-mile mark and exit 6.5 miles later. Hikers should be able to cover from 6 to 12 miles a day, depending on experience.

HEART LAKE LOOP

Heart Lake is another popular backcountry lake that attracts plenty of paddlers and anglers—not to mention wildlife. It's a 7.5-mile hike on the **Heart Lake Trail** 🥾 to the lakeshore, where numerous campsites are nestled near the forested banks. There is a 32-mile loop around the lake, with long stretches in a burn area well away from the water, but it makes for an excellent 3- to 4-day backpack, or a great destination without circumnavigation. Day hikers can tack on the hike up Mount Sheridan, which looms above the lake with a fire lookout at its summit, 10,308 feet above sea level—about 3,000 feet above the lake via a strenuous 3.9-mile trail.

THOROFARE AREA

When you enter this country in the park's southeast corner, you're venturing into the most remote, roadless area in the lower 48. You can make a round-trip of around 70 miles deep into the wilderness, or you can take shorter hikes, such as a trip from the park's East Entrance Road to the Yellowstone River inlet on Yellowstone Lake's southeast arm. The remoteness of this country discourages many hikers, so you'll have it mostly to yourself. Along the way, tepee rings and lean-tos are reminders that Indians once used this trail as the main route between Jackson Hole and points north.

The **Thorofare Trail** 🥾 follows first the eastern shore of Yellowstone Lake and then the Yellowstone River up into some of the most remote and beautiful backcountry in the Rockies. It's a lot of miles and a lot of climbing, but you'll be rewarded with spectacular views of the Upper Yellowstone Valley and Two Oceans Plateau, and there's a good chance of seeing some wildlife. You'll reach the Park Service's Thorofare Ranger Station at 32 miles, and a few miles farther you'll come to Bridger Lake, outside the park, and a gorgeous alpine valley with a ranger station known as Hawk's Rest. Fishermen love this area, as do grizzly bears, especially during the cutthroat trout spawning season in early summer. You'll be a good 35 miles from the trail head at the lake, and even the most capable hikers should consider riding with an outfitter. You can cut 9 miles off the trip by getting a boat shuttle (about $300 round-trip, with a maximum capacity of six people) to the mouth of the lake's southeast arm (call the **Bridge Bay Marina** at © 307/344-7311), or you can come in through Bridger-Teton National Forest to the south (check with the forest's **Blackrock Ranger Station** in Moran, Wyoming; © 307/543-2386). Other than bears, the major obstacle to early-season trips in the Thorofare is water; you'll encounter knee-deep water at **Beaverdam Creek** and at **Trapper Creek** as late as July.

THE SPORTSMAN LAKE TRAIL

This trail begins near Mammoth Hot Springs and extends west toward U.S. Hwy. 191 to Sportsman Lake: a moderate, 14-mile trail that displays a diverse combination of flora and fauna. From the Glen Creek Trailhead, 5 miles south of Mammoth Hot Springs, you'll spend 2 miles on the Glen Creek Trail as you traverse a mostly level, wide open plateau covered with sagebrush that is the home of herds of elk and a bear-management area. At the 3-mile mark of the **Sepulcher Mountain Trail** 🐾🐾, the terrain becomes steeper as you continue northwest on the **Sportsman Lake Trail.** The trail eventually enters the forest and descends to a log that is used to cross Gardner River. Then it's uphill for another 4 miles to **Electric Divide,** another 2,000-foot gain in elevation. From there, the trail descends 2,100 feet in 3 miles to Sportsman Lake, which is located in an area burned by the 1988 conflagration. The lake, which sits in a meadow populated by moose and elk, is teeming with cutthroat trout. Two campsites provide overnight spaces for a total of 30 visitors.

THE SLOUGH CREEK TRAIL

Beginning in the Lamar Valley of the park's northeast corner, the **Slough Creek Trail** 🐾🐾 takes hikers through some of the best wildlife habitat in the park. You can see elk, bison, trumpeter swans, sometimes grizzly bears, and now wolves that have quite happily taken up residence among abundant prey. The presence of wolves has made this area much more popular, and the trail is also used by horse-packers. The trail starts from the road to Slough Creek campground, following the creek's valley north, and then crosses a ridge to a second valley. You can hike a few miles or take your camping gear and head for the park boundary, 11 miles to the north.

3 Other Activities

BIKING   Considering the vast expanse of real estate that the parks cover, the challenging terrain, and the miles of paved roads and trails, a cyclist might conclude that the parks are prime areas for biking, on or off the roads.

It looks good on paper, but the reality is more harrowing. The roads are narrow and twisty; there are no bike lanes, so bikers continually fight for elbowroom with wide-bodied RVs and trailers, some of which have side-view mirrors designed to decapitate bicyclists. Off-road opportunities are limited because of the small number of trails on which bikes are allowed.

Nevertheless, plenty of bicyclists take the challenge. The following trails are available, but you'll be sharing them with hikers. The **Mount Washburn Trail,** leaving from Old Chittenden Road, is a strenuous trail that climbs 1,400 feet. The **Lonestar Geyser Trail,** accessed at Kepler Cascade near Old Faithful, is an easy 1-hour ride on a user-friendly, partly paved road. Near Mammoth Hot Springs, **Bunsen Peak Road** and **Osprey Falls** trails present a combination ride/hike: The first 3 miles travel around Bunsen Peak; getting to the top requires a hike. A hike down to Osprey Falls adds another 2.8 miles to the journey.

Bike rentals are available in the gateway towns of West Yellowstone at **Yellowstone Bicycles** (© **406/646-7815;** www.cycle yellowstone.com) and Jackson at **Hoback Sports** (© **307/733-5335;** www.hobacksports.com). Rental fees for a full-suspension mountain bike are about $20 to $40 a day.

BOATING   The best place to enjoy boating in Yellowstone is on **Yellowstone Lake,** which has easy access and beautiful, panoramic views. The lake is also one of the few areas where powerboats are allowed. Rowboats and outboard motorboats can be rented at **Bridge Bay Marina** (© **307/344-7311**). Cost for rowboats is $43 per day or $9.50 per hour; an outboard, with room for six, rents for $45 per hour. Sea kayakers and canoeists should stay close to the

Kids   Especially for Kids

You might find that several of the ranger programs will appeal to kids. Yellowstone has a **Junior Ranger Program** for kids ages 5 to 12. For $3, you get a special activity paper, *Yellowstone's Nature.* (Sign up at any visitor center.) Kids get a Junior Ranger badge for completing certain activities.

There's also a unique residential-education program for kids in fourth through eighth grades at Yellowstone called *Expedition: Yellowstone!* This residential program takes place in the spring and fall, with sessions lasting 4 to 5 days. For more information, write *Expedition: Yellowstone!* **Coordinator,** P.O. Box 168, Yellowstone National Park, WY 82190-0168 (www.nps.gov/yell/planyourvisit/expeditionyell.htm).

shore on Yellowstone Lake because of high winds that can easily capsize a small craft. Motorboats, canoes, and kayaks can be used on Lewis Lake as well.

FISHING   Seven varieties of game fish live in the parks: native cutthroat, rainbow, brown, brook, lake trout, grayling, and mountain whitefish. Of the trout, only the cutthroats are native, and they are being pressured in the big lake by the larger lake trout. As a result, you can't keep any pink-meat cutthroat caught anywhere in Yellowstone, and you *must* keep every single lake trout. This catch-and-release policy has done little to discourage fly-fishing purists who are more interested in the sport than in its spoils.

The Yellowstone season typically opens on the Saturday of Memorial Day weekend and ends on the first Sunday in November. Yellowstone Lake has a slightly shorter season, and the lake's tributaries are closed until July 15 to avoid conflicts between humans and grizzly bears, both of which are attracted to spawning trout.

Many fine anglers come to Yellowstone, and they are well informed about which seasons are best on which stretches of river. In June, try the **Yellowstone River** downstream of Yellowstone Lake, where the cutthroat trout spawn. In July, fish the **Madison River** near the west entrance, and fish again in late fall for rainbow and some brown trout. In late summer, you can try to hook the cutthroats that thin out by September on the **Lamar River,** in the park's beautiful northeast corner.

Fishing on **Yellowstone Lake** has been popular until recent years, when regulations designed to bring back the waning population of cutthroat trout began to send some of the trolling powerboats elsewhere. The problem is the introduced lake trout, which compete with, and eat, the cutthroat. If you catch a lake trout, you *must* kill it, and if you catch a cutthroat, you *must* throw it back. Certain areas of the lake, such as the southeast arm, are closed to motorized boats—this makes the Yellowstone River inlet a wonderful area to canoe, camp, and fish.

You can fish the **Yellowstone River** below the Grand Canyon by hiking down into **Seven-mile Hole,** a great place to cast (not much vegetation to snag on) for cutthroat trout from July to September. You'll have the best luck around Sulphur Creek.

Other good fishing stretches include the **Gibbon and Firehole rivers,** which merge to form the Madison River on the park's west side, and the 3-mile **Lewis River Channel** between Shoshone and Lewis lakes during the fall spawning run of brown trout.

There is access on the **Madison River** for anglers with disabilities, 3½ miles west of Madison Junction at the Haynes Overlook, where you'll find a wheelchair-accessible fishing platform overhanging the river's edge along 70 feet of the bank.

Suggested Reading Two reference guides present excellent information about park fishing opportunities and requirements: *Fishing Yellowstone National Park,* by Richard Parks (Falcon Press, 2003), and *The Yellowstone Fly-Fishing Guide,* by Craig Mathews and Clayton Molinero (Lyons Press, 1997). Both can be purchased from the **Yellowstone Association** (© 307/344-2293; www.yellowstone association.org).

Permits Park permits are required for Yellowstone anglers ages 16 and older; the permit costs $15 for 3 days, $20 for 7 days, and $35 for the season. Youths 12 to 15 years of age also must have a permit, but it's free. Children younger than 12 years old may fish without a permit. Permits are available at any ranger station, any visitor center, Yellowstone General Store, and most fishing shops in the gateways. The season usually begins on the Saturday of Memorial Day weekend and continues through the first Sunday in November. Exceptions to this rule are Yellowstone Lake, its tributaries, and sections of the Yellowstone River.

Supplies & Fishing Guides If you need supplies or a guide in Gardiner, stop at **Parks' Fly Shop,** 202-A Hwy. 89 (© **406/848-7314**). In West Yellowstone, check **Bud Lilly's Trout Shop,** 39 Madison Ave. (© **406/646-7801**). Full-day trips typically cost about $375 for two people.

Also, several Jackson, Wyoming–based fishing guides lead trips into Yellowstone. See "Fishing," in the "Other Activities" section of chapter 6.

HORSEBACK RIDING People who want to pack their gear on a horse, llama, or mule must either get permits to enter the Yellowstone backcountry or hire an outfitter with a permit (see below). Other visitors who want to get in the saddle but not disappear in the wilderness can put themselves in the hands of the concessionaire, **Xanterra Parks & Resorts** (© **307/344-7311;** www.travel yellowstone.com). Stables are located at Canyon Village and Roosevelt Lodge. Choices are 1- and 2-hour guided trail rides (the prices are $35 and $54, respectively) aboard well-broken, tame animals. Wranglers refer to these as "nose-and-tail" tours, and an experienced rider is likely to find them awfully dull.

If you're looking for a longer, overnight horse-packing experience, contact the park and request a list of approved concessionaires who lead backcountry expeditions. Most offer customized, guided trips, with meals, horses, and camping and riding gear provided. Costs run from $250 to $500 per day per person, depending on the length of the trip and number of people. In Livingston, at the north entrance to the park, **Wilderness Pack Trips** (© **406/333-4655;** www.ab yellowstone.com) offers horseback-riding trips in the park for groups of four or more; rates begin at $240 per day for guided day rides, more for overnight trips. Another good outfitter is **Rockin' HK Outfitters** (© **307/333-4505;** www.rockinhk.com), offering 3- to 10-day trips for about $450 per person per day.

4 Winter Sports & Activities

The average snowfall in a Yellowstone winter is about 50 inches, creating a beautiful setting for sightseers and a wonderful resource for outdoor winter recreation. The steaming hot pools and geysers generate little islands of warmth and clear ground, attracting not just tourists but wildlife as well. Nearby trees are transformed into "snow ghosts" by frozen thermal vapors. Bison become frosted, shaggy beasts, easily spotted as they take advantage of the more accessible vegetation on the thawed ground. Yellowstone Lake's surface freezes to an average thickness of 3 feet, creating a vast ice sheet that sings and moans as the huge plates of ice shift. But the ice is thinner where hot springs come up on the lake bottom, and you'll see otters surfacing at the breaks in the ice. Waterfalls become astounding pieces of frozen sculpture. Snow-white trumpeter swans glide through geyser-fed streams under clear-blue skies of clean, crisp mountain air.

Only two of the park's hostelries, **Mammoth Hot Springs Hotel** and the **Old Faithful Snow Lodge,** provide accommodations from December to March (see chapter 7 for more information). The only road that's open for cars is **Mammoth Hot Springs–Cooke City Road.** Most visitors these days come into Yellowstone in winter from the west or south by snowcoach or snowmobile.

For additional information on all of the following winter activities and accommodations, as well as snowcoach reservations, contact **Xanterra Parks & Resorts** (© **307/344-7311;** www.travelyellow stone.com). There are also many activities, outfitters, and rental shops in the park's gateway towns.

The **Yellowstone Association Institute** ✩✩✩ (© **307/344-2294;** www.yellowstoneassociation.org) offers winter courses at various park locations. Past offerings have included 3-day classes devoted to wintertime photography in the park, cross-country skiing, and the ecology of wolf reintroduction.

CROSS-COUNTRY SKIING There are 64km (40 miles) of cross-country trails in the Old Faithful area, including the popular **Lonestar Geyser Trail,** a 13km (8-mile) trail in a remote setting that starts at the Old Faithful Snow Lodge, and the **Fern Cascades Trail,** which winds for 5km (3.1 miles) through a rolling woodland landscape on a short loop close to the Old Faithful area. In the Mammoth area, try the **Upper Geyser Basin and Biscuit Basin Trail** (about 10km/6.2 miles), which some say is the best in Yellowstone, although it might take an entire day to negotiate.

Equipment rentals (about $15 per day), ski instruction, ski shuttles to various locations, and guided ski tours are all available at the **Old Faithful Snow Lodge** and the **Mammoth Hot Springs Hotel,** the park's two winter lodging options. Discounts are available for multiday rentals of skis or snowshoes. Ski instruction costs around $30 per person for a 2-hour group lesson; a full-day guided excursion costs $65 to $115 per person (lunch may or may not be included). Guided snowshoe trips are about $30 and 3 hours.

> ## (Tips) **Winter Road Conditions**
>
> Due to the high elevation and the abundance of snow,
> most of the roads in Yellowstone are closed to all wheeled
> vehicles during winter. The only major park area that is
> accessible by car is Mammoth Hot Springs; cars are allowed
> to drive in the village at Mammoth Hot Springs. Signs will
> alert you as to how far south into the park you can actu-
> ally go from here (usually to Tower Junction, 18 miles
> away). From Tower Junction, it's another 29 miles to the
> northeast entrance. This entrance is open but not accessi-
> ble from Red Lodge, Montana, and points east (because
> the Beartooth Hwy. is closed in winter). You can go only as
> far as Cooke City, Montana, and the roads are kept open
> specifically so that the folks in Cooke City aren't totally
> stranded during the long winters. **Snowmobiles, snow-
> coaches,** and **cross-country skiers,** however, use park roads
> regularly throughout the winter season. For up-to-the-
> minute information on weather and road conditions, call
> © **307/344-7381.**
>
> Basing yourself in **West Yellowstone** is another option.
> From the West Yellowstone entrance, you're only 14 miles to
> the Madison Junction, which presents opportunities to head
> south to Old Faithful or north to the Grand Canyon and
> Mammoth Hot Springs. Because this is the most popular way
> to access the park, plan on making reservations early.

ICE-SKATING   The Mammoth Hot Springs ice rink is located
behind the Mammoth Hot Springs Recreation Center. On a crisp
winter's night, you can rent a pair of skates ($1 per hour, $4 per day)
and glide across the ice while seasonal melodies are broadcast over
the PA system. It's cold out there, but there's a warming fire at the
rink's edge. Plans for an Old Faithful rink were in the works at press
time. Call © **307/344-7311** for more information.

SNOWCOACH TOURS   It is possible to enjoy the sights and
sounds of Yellowstone without raising a finger—except to write a
check or sign a credit card voucher—by taking one of the scenic
snowcoach tours that originate at the south and west entrances, as

well as at Mammoth and Old Faithful. One-way and wildlife-watching trips range from $35 to $70, while round-trips cost about $100 to $130.

If you've never seen a snowcoach, you're in for a treat. Don't be fooled into thinking that this distinctively Yellowstone mode of transportation is merely a fancy name for a bus that provides tours during winter. Imagine instead an Econoline van with tank treads for tires and water skis extending from its front, and you won't be surprised when you see this unusual-looking vehicle. The interiors are toasty warm, with seating for a large group, and they usually allow each passenger two bags. They aren't the fastest, smoothest, or most comfortable form of transportation, but they do allow large groups to travel together, and they're cheaper and warmer than snowmobiles. They're also available for hire by groups at many snowmobile locations. Guides provide interesting and entertaining facts and stories of the areas as you cruise the park trails, and they give you opportunities to photograph scenery and wildlife.

For snowcoach information, contact **Xanterra Parks & Resorts** (© **307/344-7311**). Out of West Yellowstone, **Yellowstone Vacations** (© **800/426-7669** or 406/646-9564; http://snowcoachyellowstone.com) and **Yellowstone Alpen Guides** (© **800/858-3502** or 406/646-9591; www.yellowstoneguides.com) provide service as well.

SNOWMOBILING   This is an excellent way to sightsee at your own pace, but note that the courts are still debating long-term snowmobile policies for the parks. A driver's license and guide are required for rental at **Mammoth Hot Springs Hotel** or **Old Faithful Snow Lodge.** Day tours cost $215 for a single rider or $235 double; custom tours are also available, but considerably more costly. A helmet is included with the snowmobile, as is a clothing package for protection against the bitter cold. **Warming huts** are located at Mammoth, Indian Creek, Canyon, Madison, West Thumb, and Fishing Bridge. They offer snacks, a hot cup of coffee or chocolate, and an excellent opportunity to recover from a chill.

Snowmobile rentals are also available in the **gateway communities** of Gardiner, Cooke City, and West Yellowstone. In West Yellowstone, try **Yellowstone Arctic/Yamaha,** 208 Electric St. (© **406/646-9636;** www.yellowstonearcticyamaha.com), or **Yellowstone Adventures,** 131 Dunraven Ave. (© **800/231-5991** or 406/646-7735; www.yellowstoneadventures.com). Most rental shops accept reservations weeks in advance, so reserving at least 2 weeks ahead of time is a good idea.

For snowmobile rentals in Jackson, contact **Leisure Sports,** 1075 S. Hwy. 89 (© **307/733-3040;** www.leisuresportsadventure.com), which charges $145 and up per day. For a guided trip, call **Wyoming Adventures,** 1050 S. Hwy. 89 (© **800/637-7147** or 307/733-2300; www.wyomingsnow.com), which offers three different loop trips through Yellowstone for $230 to $300.

5

Exploring Grand Teton National Park

Although Grand Teton National Park is much smaller than Yellowstone, there is much more to it than just its peaks, a dozen of which climb to elevations greater than 12,000 feet. The park's size— 54 miles long, from north to south—allows visitors to get a good look at the highlights in a day or two. But you'd be missing a great deal: the beautiful views from its trails, an exciting float on the Snake River, the watersports paradise that is Jackson Lake.

Whether your trip is half a day or 2 weeks, the park's proximity to the town of Jackson allows for an interesting trip that combines the outdoors with the urbane. You can descend Grand Teton and be living it up at the Million Dollar Cowboy Bar or dining in a fine restaurant that evening. The next day, you can return to the peace of the park without much effort at all.

1 Essentials

ACCESS/ENTRY POINTS Grand Teton National Park runs along a north-south axis, bordered on the west by the Teton Range. Teton Park Road, the primary thoroughfare, skirts along the lakes at the mountains' base. From the **north,** you can enter the park from Yellowstone National Park, which is linked to Grand Teton by an 8-mile stretch of highway (U.S. Hwy. 89/191/287) running through the **John D. Rockefeller Jr. Memorial Parkway,** along which you might see some bare and blackened trees from the 1988 fires. If you enter this way, you will already have paid your entrance fee to both parks, but you can stop at the park information center at Flagg Ranch, just outside Yellowstone, to get Grand Teton information. From December to mid-March, Yellowstone's south entrance is open only to snowmobiles and snowcoaches.

You can also approach the park from the **east,** via U.S. Hwy. 26/ 287. This route comes from Dubois, 55 miles east on the other side of the Absaroka and Wind River mountains, and crosses **Togwotee**

Pass, where you'll get your first (and one of the best) views of the Tetons towering over the valley. Travelers who come this way can continue south on U.S. Hwy. 26/89/191 to Jackson without paying an entrance fee, although they are within the park boundaries, and enjoy spectacular mountain and Snake River views.

Finally, you can enter Grand Teton from Jackson in the **south,** driving about 12 miles north on U.S. Hwy. 26/89/191 to the Moose Junction turnoff and the park's south entrance. Here you'll find the park headquarters and the Craig Thomas Discovery and Visitor Center, plus a small community that includes dining and shops.

VISITOR CENTERS & INFORMATION There are three visitor centers in Grand Teton National Park. Opening in August 2007, the dazzling, $22-million **Craig Thomas Discovery and Visitor Center** (© 307/739-3399) is a half-mile west of Moose Junction at the southern end of the park; it's open daily 8am to 7pm from June to Labor Day, and daily from 8am to 5pm the rest of the year. The **Colter Bay Visitor Center** (© 307/739-3594), the northernmost of the park's visitor centers, is open daily from 8am to 8pm from early June to Labor Day, and from 8am to 5pm after Labor Day through early October. There is also **Jenny Lake Visitor Center** (© 307/739-3343), open daily 8am to 7pm from early June to Labor Day, and daily from 8am to 5pm after Labor Day through early October. Maps and ranger assistance are available at all three centers, and there are bookstores and exhibits at Moose and Colter Bay. Finally, there is an information station at the **Flagg Ranch** complex (© 307/543-2861), which is located approximately 5 miles north of the park's northern boundary.

To obtain park maps before your arrival, contact **Grand Teton National Park,** P.O. Drawer 170, Moose, WY 83012-0170 (© 307/739-3300; TDD 307/739-3400; www.nps.gov/grte).

FEES There are no park gates on U.S. Hwy. 26/89/191, so you can get a free ride through the park on that route; to get off the highway and explore, you'll pay $25 per automobile for a 7-day pass (admission is good for both Yellowstone and Grand Teton). If you expect to visit the parks more than once in a year, buy an annual pass for $50. And if you visit parks and national monuments around the country, purchase an **Interagency Annual Pass** for $80 (good for 365 days from the date of purchase at nearly all federal preserves). Anyone age 62 or older can get an **Interagency Senior Pass** for a one-time fee of $10, and people who are blind or who have a permanent disability can obtain an **Interagency Access Pass,** which

Grand Teton National Park

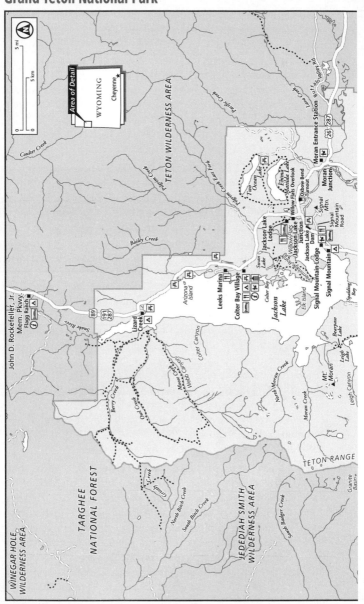

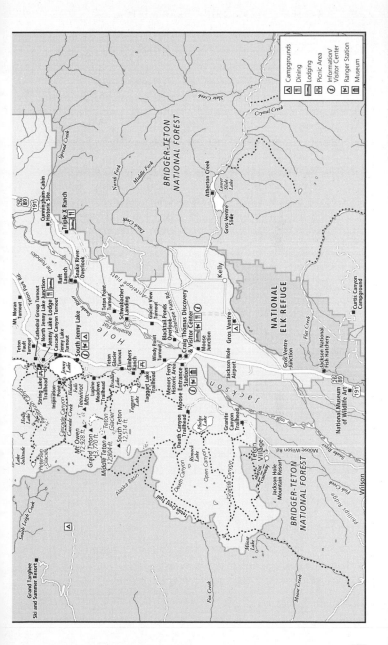

costs nothing. All passes are available at any entrance point to the parks. While the Interagency Senior and Interagency Access passes must be purchased in person (to verify age or disability), Interagency Annual Passes are also available online at **store.usgs.gov/pass**.

Most of the money from entrance fees goes back into the park where it was collected, so consider it a contribution worth making: In Grand Teton, this revenue has been spent on renovating the Jenny Lake Overlook, maintaining trails, and restoring the lakeshore at Jenny Lake, among other things.

Fees for **tent camping** are $17 to $19 per night at all the park campgrounds ($5 for hike- and bike-in sites). For recorded information on campgrounds, call ☏ **307/739-3603.** For more information on camping, see "Where to Camp in Grand Teton," in chapter 7. It is not possible to make advance reservations at campgrounds in Grand Teton.

SPECIAL REGULATIONS & WARNINGS   See chapter 3 for a summary of the major park regulations, which are generally similar in both parks.

FAST FACTS: Grand Teton

ATMs There are three ATMs in the park: at the Jackson Lake Lodge, at the Dornan's Store in Moose, and at the general store in Colter Bay Village.

Car Trouble & Towing Services There are no towing services inside the park; if you are not a member of an automobile club, try one of the services in nearby Jackson, Wyoming. The park's main information number is ☏ **307/739-3300.**

Emergencies Dial ☏ **911**, or dial 307/739-3301 and ask for park dispatch.

Gas Stations Gasoline is available at Flagg Ranch, Colter Bay Village, Jackson Lake Lodge, Signal Mountain Lodge, and Dornan's Store in Moose.

Laundry There are laundry facilities at the Colter Bay Village.

Medical Services There is a medical clinic at Jackson Lake Lodge (☏ **307/543-2514** daily before 10am or after 6pm), open late May to early October, and a hospital in Jackson, Wyoming (☏ **307/733-3636**).

Permits Boating permits and backcountry permits can be obtained at the Colter Bay and Moose visitor centers and at the Jenny Lake Ranger Station. For recorded information on climbing, call © 307/739-3604.

Post Offices There are post offices in Moose (© 307/733-3336) and Moran (© 307/543-2527).

Supplies You'll find well-stocked general stores in the Dornan's complex at Moose Village and in Colter Bay Village; there are convenience stores at Flagg Ranch, Signal Mountain Lodge, and South Jenny Lake.

Weather Updates Call © 307/739-3611 for weather information.

2 The Highlights

No matter what you do in Grand Teton, you are nearly always in view of the big granite peaks dominating the western skyline. They define the park and, therefore, deserve top billing of all of its highlights.

THE PEAKS The **Cathedral Group** 𝕬𝕬𝕬 comprises **Grand Teton** (elevation 13,770 ft.), **Mount Owen** (elevation 12,928 ft.), and **Teewinot** (elevation 12,325 ft.). Nearby, almost as impressive, are **South Teton** (elevation 12,514 ft.) and **Middle Teton** (elevation 12,804 ft.). To the north, **Mount Moran,** at 12,605 feet, is the fourth largest of the Tetons (on a clear day, though, you can take a great photograph of this peak all the way from Colter Bay to North Jenny Lake Junction). If you come from the east, you will pass no tollbooths on your way south on U.S. Hwy. 26/89/191, but there are frequent pullouts on the west side of the road that give you a panoramic overview of the Snake River and the Tetons. For that matter, you get a more distant but equally spectacular perspective of the mountains coming over **Togwotee Pass** on U.S. Hwy. 26/287. **Signal Mountain,** reached off Teton Park Road by Jackson Lake, is less a peak to look at than to look off—you can drive or hike to the top for a grand view.

COLTER BAY At the north end of the park, alongside Jackson Lake, Colter Bay offers a busy mix of information, services, activities on and off the water, and shopping. The visitor center provides wildlife videos, slide programs, natural history hikes, and evening amphitheater programs. Most remarkable is the **Indian Arts Museum** 🏵, which houses a collection of American Indian crafts, clothing, and beadwork, covering rooms on two floors.

JACKSON LAKE 🏵 The biggest of the park's lakes was dammed to provide more water for potato farmers in Idaho, but that also makes it a good place to sail, fish, and ride around on powerboats. Several lodges dot its shores, but the one that bears its name, **Jackson Lake Lodge,** is set back from the lake, bordered by Willow Flats and marshlands—prime moose habitat. The views are striking, and some good hikes begin here.

Signal Mountain Area 🏵 The **Signal Mountain campground** is a favorite of park visitors, conveniently located on the lakeshore for folks with watercraft, and the **Signal Mountain Lodge** is a fine place to stop for a meal with a view or a room for the night. Across the road, you can climb the mountain, by foot or car, and get a panoramic view of the valley and mountains—the best way to get a perspective on the glacier-carved area known as Jackson Hole.

Jenny Lake 🏵🏵 A loop off Teton Park Road takes you close to String and Jenny lakes and the exclusive **Jenny Lake Lodge** (home to what is probably the finest restaurant in any national park). Day visitors can go to the south end of the lake, the point of origin of both boat rides and the popular trail to **Inspiration Point and Hidden Falls** 🏵, on the west side of the lake. There's also a small store. If you've got your wide-angle lens handy, stop at the **Cathedral Group Turnout,** a terrific spot for photographers.

MOOSE You'll find plenty of services and shops here—even a fine wine store—and the **park headquarters** and a **visitor center.** It's been a service area since the days of Bill Menor, who ran a river ferry and a country store here a century ago. Half a mile from the park offices, the store and ferry have been re-created at the **Menor/Noble Historic District.** The nearby **Chapel of the Transfiguration** is a log church built in 1925. The altar window frames a view of the Grand Teton.

SNAKE RIVER 🏵🏵 Below Jackson Lake Dam, the Snake River winds its way east and south, eventually turning west toward Idaho in the Snake River Canyon. There are beautiful stretches of river in the park, such as Oxbow Bend, where trumpeter swans and moose appear, which make it a destination for canoeists and kayakers. To the east and up on the flats, U.S. Hwy. 26/89/191 follows the river from Moran Junction to Jackson, with several pullouts and overlooks.

3 If You Have Only 1 Day

A 1-day trip around this park is not unreasonable, given its size, and you can do a loop where you see many major attractions without having to retrace your steps. For more complete information on what you'll see along the way, read the next section on touring the park. Although this 1-day itinerary assumes that you are entering Grand Teton from the north, after visiting Yellowstone, you could just as easily begin your itinerary in Jackson, which is 8 miles south of the Moose Entrance Station.

Begin at the south entrance of Yellowstone National Park, driving through the **John D. Rockefeller Jr. Memorial Parkway** (U.S. Hwy. 89/191/287) south past **Flagg Ranch** and to the park. As you drive south, you'll find yourself skirting the northern shore of Jackson Lake, with a view of **Mount Moran** to the west, and, farther south, the stunning **Cathedral Group.**

On the northeast shore, **Colter Bay Village** is one of the park's busiest spots. You can rent boats, take scenic cruises, embark on guided fishing trips, buy fishing licenses and supplies, rent a cabin, or camp. Several popular hiking trails start here. If you turn right at Colter Bay Junction, you'll be at the **Colter Bay Visitor Center** a half-mile later; stop here to take in the **Indian Arts Museum** ⊛.

The **Lakeshore Trail** begins at the marina entrance and runs along the harbor for an easy 2-mile round-trip. It's level, paved, shady, and wheelchair accessible; it's the best opportunity for a hike in this area if you don't have much time. Nearby, on the shore of the lake, is an amphitheater where ranger-naturalists conduct evening programs. The Douglas firs and pine trees here are greener and healthier than the lodgepole pines that you see at higher elevations in Yellowstone.

A few minutes' drive south of Colter Bay, you'll pass Jackson Lake Lodge (you might want to look in the lobby and out the big picture window) and then **Jackson Lake Junction,** where a right turn puts you on **Teton Park Road,** the beginning of a 43-mile loop tour. You'll be driving parallel to the mountain range, with Grand Teton as the 13,770-foot centerpiece. You'll see lakes created by glaciers thousands of years ago, bordering a sagebrush valley inhabited by pronghorn and elk.

Just 5 miles down the road along Jackson Lake, a left (east) turn will take you up **Signal Mountain,** where you'll have a 360-degree view of the valley. Then continue down Teton Park Road to **South Jenny Lake,** where there is a huge parking area (which fills quickly in

---

Tips **The LSR Preserve**

In 2007, the Rockefeller family donated to the National Park Service their former private retreat, the 1,106-acre JY Ranch, on the shore of Phelps Lake in the southern reaches of the park. The buildings were demolished as part of a restoration effort, and a trail system was developed, as well as a staffed "reflection center" to allow visitors to make a personal connection with nature. The new facility and trail system was expected to open in 2008; contact the park for current information.

---

peak season) for the many people who stop to either hike around the lake or take a boat ride across. If you have time, get to the other side (it's a 2-mile hike) and make the short climb to **Hidden Falls** *⊀*. Another good day hike in this area is the **Taggart Lake Trail** (p. 132).

When you leave South Jenny Lake, you'll drive along a flat, sagebrush-dotted stretch to Moose, the southernmost of the park's service centers. A half-mile before Moose Junction is the **Craig Thomas Discovery and Visitor Center,** which features exhibits of the Greater Yellowstone area's rare and endangered species, a video room, and an excellent bookstore. While you're in Moose, you might want to visit the **Menor/Noble Historic District** and the **Chapel of the Transfiguration.**

Coming out of Moose, take a left (north) turn on U.S. Hwy. 26/89/191, which crosses the open flats above the Snake River to Moran Junction. The best views along this road are the **Glacier View Turnout** and the **Snake River Overlook** *⊀*, both of which are right off the road and well marked. At Moran Junction, turn left for a final 5-mile drive back to Jackson Lake Junction, past **Oxbow Bend,** a great spot for wildlife-watching.

Worn out? Catch the dramatic sunset behind the Tetons, and then head for your campsite (if you're tenting, stake out a spot early) or room, either in the park or in Jackson, Wyoming.

4 Touring Grand Teton

A 1-day whirlwind tour of Grand Teton is far from ideal. Like Yellowstone, this park demands a visit of 2 days or more. An extended stay allows for some relaxed hiking, picnicking, and sightseeing—you'll gain a greater appreciation for the park and the area's culture and history. A day at the Jenny Lake area, for instance, will provide awe-inspiring views of the peaks and a chance to walk the trails around the lake, to Inspiration Point or beyond up Cascade Canyon. You could also easily spend a day in the Jackson Lake Lodge area, where there are several wildlife viewing spots, trails, and places for a secluded picnic.

As with the short tour in the previous section, I begin at the northern end of the park, but you could just as easily start exploring from the southern end near Jackson. From Jackson, it's about 13 miles to the Moose Entrance Station, another 8 miles to the Jenny Lake Visitor Center, another 12 miles to the Jackson Lake Junction, and 5 more miles to Colter Bay.

JACKSON LAKE & THE NORTH END OF THE PARK

Many people enter Grand Teton National Park from the north end, emerging from Yellowstone's south entrance with a 7-day park pass that is good for admission to Grand Teton as well. Yellowstone is connected to Grand Teton by a wilderness corridor called the **John D. Rockefeller Jr. Memorial Parkway** that runs north-south for 8 miles past meadows sometimes dotted with elk, over the Snake River, above Jackson Lake, and through forests that in some places still show the mosaic burns of the 1988 fires.

Along the parkway, not far from Yellowstone, you'll come to the recently modernized **Flagg Ranch** (see chapter 7), with gas, restaurants, lodging, and other services.

Giant **Jackson Lake** ✮, a vast expanse of water filling a deep gouge left 10,000 years ago by retreating glaciers, dominates the north end of the park. While it is a natural lake, it was dammed nearly a century ago, encroaching the surrounding forest and dismaying conservationists. It empties cast into the Snake River, curving around in the languid **Oxbow Bend**—a favorite wildlife-viewing float for canoeists. The water eventually turns south and then west through Snake River Canyon and into Idaho. Stream flow from the dam is regulated both for potato farmers downstream in Idaho and for rafters in the canyon. Elsewhere on the lake, things look quite natural, except when water gets low in the fall.

As the road follows the east shore of the lake from the north, the first development that travelers encounter is **Leeks Marina,** where boats launch, gas up, and moor from mid-May to mid-September. A casual restaurant here serves pizza during the summer, and there are also numerous scenic pullouts along the lake that are good picnic spots.

Just south of Leeks is **Colter Bay,** a busy outpost of park services where you can get groceries, postcards and stamps, T-shirts, and

Jackson Lake: Colter Bay Area

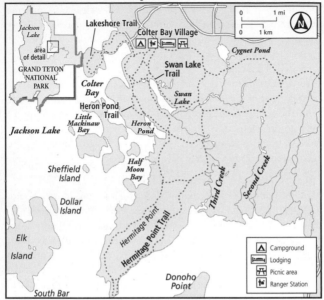

advice. At the **Colter Bay Visitor Center,** you can view park and wildlife videotapes and attend a park orientation slide program throughout the day. Ranger-led activities include museum tours, park-orientation talks, natural-history hikes, and evening amphitheater programs. Colter Bay has plenty of overnight options, from cabins and old-fashioned tent camps to a trailer park and campground (see chapter 7). There are also a general store, a laundry facility, two restaurants, a boat launch and boat rentals, and tours. You can take pleasant short hikes in this area, including a walk around the bay or out to **Hermitage Point** (see chapter 6).

The **Indian Arts Museum** ⚑ (✆ **307/739-3594**) at the Colter Bay Visitor Center is worth a visit, although it is not strictly about the Native American cultures of this area. The artifacts are mostly from Plains Indian tribes, but there are also some Navajo items from the Southwest. The collection was assembled by David T. Vernon and includes pipes, shields, dolls, and war clubs sometimes called "skull crackers." There are large historic photos in the exhibit area. Visiting Indian artists work in the museum all summer long and sell their wares on-site. Admission is free.

Jackson Lake: Signal Mountain Area

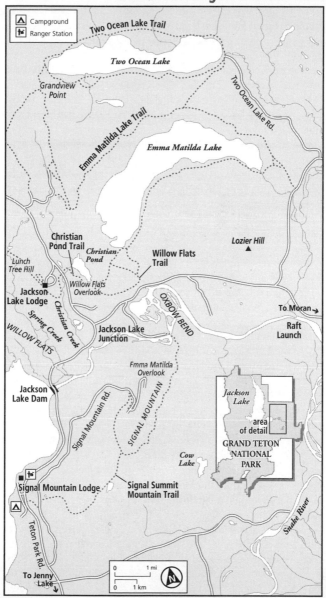

From Colter Bay, the road curves eastward and then south again, passing **Jackson Lake Lodge** (see chapter 7), a snazzy 1950s-style resort with a great view of the Tetons and brushy flats in the foreground where moose and coyotes often roam. Numerous trails emanate from here, both to the lakeshore and east to **Emma Matilda Lake** (see chapter 6). The road then comes to **Jackson Lake Junction,** where you can either continue west along the lakeshore or go east to the park's Moran entrance station. If you exit via the Moran entrance, you are still in the park, and can turn south on U.S. Hwy. 26/89/191 and drive along the Snake River to Jackson, making most of your journey within the park's borders. However, you're probably here to enjoy the park, so you should turn right (west) on **Teton Park Road** at Jackson Lake Junction. After only 5 miles, you will arrive at **Signal Mountain.** Like its counterpart at Colter Bay, this developed recreation area, on Jackson Lake's southeast shore, offers camping sites, accommodations in cabins and multiplex units, two restaurants, and a lounge with one of the few televisions in the park. If you need to stock up on gas or food, do so at the small convenience store here. Boat rentals and scenic cruises of the lake are also available.

If you turn east instead of west off Teton Park Road at Signal Mountain, you can drive up a narrow, twisty road to the top of the mountain, 700 feet above the valley, where you'll have a fine view of the ring of mountains—Absarokas, Gros Ventres, Tetons, and Yellowstone Plateau—that create Jackson Hole. Clearly visible are the "Kettles": potholes in the valley's hilly moraines that are the mark of long-gone glaciers. Below the summit, about 3 miles from the base of the hill, is **Jackson Point Overlook,** a paved path 100 yards long leading to the spot where legendary photographer William Henry Jackson shot his famous landscapes of Jackson Lake and the Tetons in the 1870s—proof to the world that such spectacular places really existed.

Looking for a hideaway? On the right (west) side of the road between Signal Mountain and North Jenny Lake Junction, approximately 2 miles south of the Mount Moran turnout, is an unmarked, unpaved road leading to **Spalding Bay.** It's a sheltered little campsite and boat launch area with a primitive restroom. There isn't much space if others have beaten you there, but it's a great place to be alone with spectacular views of the lake and mountains. If you decide to camp, a park permit is required. An automobile or SUV will have no problem with this road, but speed had better not be of the essence to you. Passing through brush and forest, you might just spot a moose.

JENNY LAKE & THE SOUTH END OF THE PARK

Continuing south along Teton Park Road, you move into the park's southern half, where the tallest peaks rise abruptly above a succession of small, crystalline lakes—**Leigh Lake,** the appropriately named **String Lake,** and **Jenny Lake** ⊛⊛, beloved by many visitors. At North Jenny Lake Junction, you can take a turnoff west to **Jenny Lake Lodge** (see chapter 7). The road then continues as a one-way scenic loop along the lakeshore before rejoining Teton Park Road about 4 miles later.

In summer, beautiful **Jenny Lake** attracts its share of crowds—hikers who circumnavigate the lake on a 6-mile trail, as well as more sedentary folks who pay for a boat ride across the lake to Hidden Falls and the short steep climb to Inspiration Point (see chapter 6). The parking lot at **South Jenny Lake** is often jammed, and there can be a long wait for the boat ride; so you might want to get there early in the day. Or you can save your money by taking the 2-mile hike around the lake—it's level and easy. There are also a tents-only campground, a visitor center, and a general store stocked with a modest supply of prepackaged foods and even less fresh produce and vegetables. You'll have to buy a ticket and wait in line for the trip across the lake in a powerboat that holds about 30 people. Contact **Jenny Lake Boating Company** (⊛ **307/734-9227;** www.jennylakeboating.com); round-trips cost $9 for adults and $5 for children 5 to 12.

South of the lake, Teton Park Road passes through wide-open sagebrush plains with immaculate views of the mountains. You'll pass the **Climbers' Ranch**—an inexpensive dormlike lodging alternative for climbers, run by the American Alpine Club (⊛ **307/733-7271;** www.americanalpineclub.org)—and some trail heads for enjoyable hikes to a handful of pristine alpine lakes. Look closely in the sagebrush for the shy pronghorn, more commonly (and incorrectly) labeled antelope. This handsome animal, with tan cheeks and black accent stripes, can spring up to 60 mph. Badgers also roam the brush here; you might encounter one of the shy-but-ornery creatures in the morning or at twilight.

The **Teton Glacier Turnout** presents a view of a glacier that grew for several hundred years until, pressured by the increasing summer temperatures of the past century, it reversed course and began retreating.

The road arrives at the park's south entrance at Moose, home to the stunning new **Craig Thomas Discovery and Visitor Center,** as well as park headquarters. If you are approaching the park from the south rather than the north, this is where you'll get maps, advice, and some interpretive displays.

Jenny Lake Area & Trails

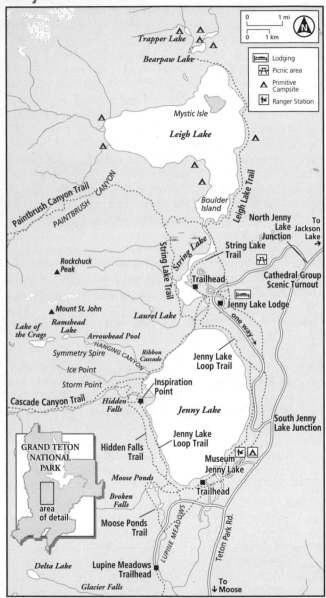

Trapper Lake

Bearpaw Lake

Mystic Isle

Leigh Lake

Paintbrush Canyon Trail

PAINTBRUSH CANYON

Boulder Island

Leigh Lake Trail

North Jenny Lake Junction

To Jackson Lake

String Lake Trail

Rockchuck Peak

String Lake Trail

String Lake

Trailhead

Cathedral Group Scenic Turnout

Mount St. John

Laurel Lake

Jenny Lake Lodge

one way

Lake of the Crags

Ramshead Lake

Arrowhead Pool

HANGING CANYON

Ribbon Cascade

Jenny Lake Loop Trail

Symmetry Spire

Ice Point

Storm Point

Cascade Canyon Trail

Inspiration Point

Hidden Falls

Jenny Lake

South Jenny Lake Junction

Hidden Falls Trail

Jenny Lake Loop Trail

GRAND TETON NATIONAL PARK

area of detail

Moose Ponds

Broken Falls

Museum Jenny Lake

Trailhead

Moose Ponds Trail

LUPINE MEADOWS

Teton Park Rd.

Delta Lake

Lupine Meadows Trailhead

To ↓ Moose

Glacier Falls

0   1 mi
0   1 km

N

Lodging
Picnic area
Primitive Campsite
Ranger Station

Just behind the visitor center is **Menors Ferry.** Bill Menor had a country store and operated a ferry across the Snake River at Moose back in the late 1800s. The ferry and store have been reconstructed, and you can buy items like those once sold here. Nearby is a historic cabin where a group of locals met in 1923 and planted the seed for the protection of the natural and scenic quality of the area, an idea that eventually led to the creation of the national park.

Also in this area is the **Chapel of the Transfiguration.** In 1925, this chapel was built in Moose so that settlers wouldn't have to make the long buckboard ride into Jackson. It's still in use for Episcopal services from spring to fall and is a popular place for weddings, with a view of the Tetons through a window behind the altar.

Dornan's is a small village area just south of the visitor center on a private holding of land owned by one of the area's earliest home-steading families. There are a few shops and a semigourmet grocery store, a post office, rental cabins, a bar with occasional live music, and, surprisingly, a first-rate wine shop.

THE EAST SIDE OF THE PARK

At Moose Junction, just east of the visitor center, drivers can rejoin the highway and either turn south to Jackson and the Gros Ventre turn or cruise north up U.S. Hwy. 26/89/191 to Moran Junction. This 18-mile trip is the fastest route through Grand Teton National Park and, being farther from the mountains, offers views of a broader mountain tableau.

The junction of U.S. Hwy. 89 with **Antelope Flats Road** is 1¼ miles north of the Moose Junction. The 20-mile route beginning here is an acceptable biking route. It's all on level terrain, passing by the town of Kelly and the Gros Ventre campground before looping back to U.S. Hwy. 26/89/191 at the Gros Ventre Junction to the south. (If you're interested in the area, you might also look at "Far-ther Afield: Southeast of Moose," in chapter 6.) If you continue straight on Antelope Flats Road, you'll reach the **Teton Science Schools** ✿ at the road's end, about a 5-mile trip. The school offers interesting learning-vacation programs, which are described more fully in chapter 2 (see p. 33).

Less than a mile down U.S. Hwy. 26/89/191, on the left, **Black-tail Ponds Overlook** offers an opportunity to see how beavers build dams and the effect these hard-working creatures have on the flow of the streams. The area is marshy early in summer, but it's still worth the .3-mile hike down to the streams where the beaver activity can be viewed more closely.

Two miles farther along U.S. Hwy. 26/89/191 brings you to the **Glacier View Turnout,** which offers views of an area that 140,000 to 160,000 years ago was filled with a 4,000-foot-thick glacier. The view of the gulch between the peaks offers vivid testimony of the power of the glaciers that carved this landscape. Lower **Schwabacher Landing** is at the end of a 1-mile, fairly well maintained dirt road that leads down to the Snake River; you'll see the turnoff 4½ miles north of the Moose Junction. The road winds through an area filled with glacial moraine (the rocks, sand, and gravel are debris left behind as glaciers passed through the area), the remnants of the ice age. At the end of the road is a popular launch site for float trips and for fly-fishing. It's also an ideal place to retreat from the crowds. Don't be surprised to see bald eagles, osprey, moose, river otter, and beaver, all of which regularly patrol the area.

The **Snake River Overlook** ⊛, approximately 4 miles down the road beyond the Glacier View Turnout, is the most famous view of the Teton Range and the Snake River, immortalized by Ansel Adams. From this overlook, you'll also see at least three separate, distinctive 200-foot-high plateaus that roll from the riverbed to the valley floor, leaving a vivid example of the power of the glaciers and ice floes as they sculpted this area. In the early 1800s, this was a prime hunting ground for John Jacob Astor's Pacific Fur Company and a certain David E. Jackson, for whom the lake and valley are named. But by 1840, the popularity of the silk hat had put an end to fur trapping, and the hunters disappeared. Good thing—by the time they departed, the beaver population was almost decimated.

A half-mile north of the Snake River Overlook is the newly repaved road to **Deadman's Bar,** a peaceful clearing on the riverbank. Many float trips launch here (multiday trips also camp in the area), and there is a limited amount of fishing access.

Cunningham Cabin, 1¾ miles north of Deadman's Bar, is a nondescript historic site at which homesteaders Pierce and Margaret Cunningham built their ranch in 1890. By 1928, they had been defeated by the elements and sold out to Rockefeller's Snake River Land Co. You can visit it at any time for a peek into the rough life of early Jackson Hole ranchers.

If you head down the highway in the other direction (south) from Moose Junction, on U.S. Hwy. 26/89/191, you can turn east on the **Gros Ventre River Road** 5 miles before you reach Jackson and follow the river east into its steep canyon; a few miles past the little town of Kelly, you'll leave the park and be in **Bridger-Teton National Forest.** In 1925, a huge slab of mountain broke off the north end of the Gros Ventre Range on the east side of Jackson Hole, a reminder that nature still has an unpredictable and violent side.

The slide left a gaping open gash in the side of Sheep Mountain, sloughing off nearly 50 million cubic yards of rock and forming a natural dam across the Gros Ventre River half a mile wide. Two years later, the dam broke and a cascade of water rushed down the canyon and through the little town of Kelly, taking several lives. Today, the town of **Kelly** is a quaint and eccentric community with a large number of yurts (tentlike homes) and, nearby, the **Teton Science Schools.** Up in the canyon, formed by the Gros Ventre River, there is a roadside display with photographs of the slide area and a short nature walk from the road down to the residue of the slide and **Lower Slide Lake.** Here, signs identify the trees and plants that survived or grew in the slide's aftermath.

5 Organized Tours & Ranger Programs

The **Grand Teton Lodge Company** (℃ **800/628-9988** or 307/543-3100 for reservations, ℃ **307/543-2811** for information; www.gtlc.com) runs half- and full-day bus tours of Grand Teton ($35 adults, $18 children 3–11) and Yellowstone ($65 adults, $40 children 3–11) from late May to early October, weather permitting.

The **Teton Science Schools** ☞☞, 700 Coyote Canyon Rd., Jackson, WY 83001 (℃ **307/733-1313;** www.tetonscience.org), has an excellent curriculum for students of all ages, from integrated science programs for junior-high kids to adult seminars covering everything from botany to astronomy. Classes take place at campuses in Jackson and Kelly, and other locations in Jackson Hole. The school's **Wildlife Expeditions** (℃ **888/945-3567** or 307/773-2623; www.wildlifeexpeditions.org) offers tours that bring visitors closer to the park's wildlife. These trips range from a half-day to a week, covering everything from bighorn sheep to the wolves of Yellowstone.

Within the park, there are several interesting ranger programs. These include a ranger-led 3-mile hike from the Colter Bay Visitor Center to Swan Lake, as well as a relaxed evening chatting with a ranger on the deck of the Jackson Lake Lodge while you watch for moose and birds through a spotting scope. There are numerous events during the summer at Colter Bay, South Jenny Lake, and the Craig Thomas Discovery and Visitor Center at Moose. Check the daily schedules in the park's newspaper, *The Teewinot,* which is available at any visitor center.

From Moose, rangers lead visitors out to the "lek"—the mating ground of the strutting grouse, whose males' displays are dramatic, to say the least, during the springtime mating season. In winter, **guided snowshoe hikes** begin at the visitor center in Moose.

At the Taggart Lake trail head, there are **wildflower walks** led by rangers who can tell you the difference between lupine and larkspur, daily in June and July, and guided morning hikes to Hidden Falls from Jenny Lake (you take the boat across the lake), among other activities.

Youngsters 8 to 12 can join **Young Naturalist programs** at Colter Bay or Jenny Lake and learn about the natural world for 2 hours while hiking with a ranger. Signups are at the visitor centers (the fee is a mere $1), and the kids will need basic hiking gear.

There are also evening campfire gatherings at the Gros Ventre, Jenny Lake, Signal Mountain, Lizard Creek, and Colter Bay campground amphitheaters on a variety of park-related topics.

Hikes & Other Outdoor Pursuits in Grand Teton National Park

Beyond the watersports on its lakes and rivers, Grand Teton National Park is a hiker's dream. The varied trail system—more than 250 miles in all—offers both short, level trails around the valley floor and more demanding trails to the Teton Range that escape the crowds and challenge the body.

For a more extensive and detailed list of trails than what follows here, pick up *Teton Trails,* by Katy Duffy and Darwin Wile. It's available for $6.95 from the Grand Teton Association, P.O. Box 170, Moose, WY 83012 (© **307/739-3403;** www.grandtetonpark.org).

1 Day Hikes

The park's many trails vary greatly in length and level of difficulty, so you'll want to consult with rangers before tackling the trails. They can update you on everything from bear activity to trail damage (such as bridge outages) to weather concerns. Rangers might be able to suggest hikes suitable to your expectations and ability; they also conduct various guided walks.

Below is a fairly broad selection of hikes, ranging from easy to difficult. For those who have only a brief time at Grand Teton, here are two suggestions in the "if you can only do one hike" category: the **Signal Mountain Summit Trail** 𝒜𝒜 and the **Inspiration Point Trail** 𝒜 in the Jenny Lake area. Trails are generally very well marked. Turn to chapter 5 for **maps** of the Colter Bay, Signal Mountain, and Jenny Lake areas that show the major trails described in this section.

And remember, if you are planning to hike for more than 30 minutes, be sure to carry a supply of water and some rain gear.

COLTER BAY AREA

A map showing the trails in this area is found in chapter 5.

Lakeshore Trail This short jaunt starts at the marina and leads out to pebble beaches on the west side of Jackson Lake. The trail is wide and shady, and you can stop to look over the boats moored at the marina. Views of the entire Teton Range leap out at you from across Jackson Lake when you arrive at the end of the trail. The sounds of water lapping at the shore extend a peaceful atmosphere, as traffic and crowd noise are left well behind. The loop can be completed in about 1 hour of brisk walking.

2 miles round-trip. Easy. Access: Trail head located at the Marina entrance.

TRAILS FROM THE HERMITAGE POINT TRAILHEAD

The **Hermitage Point Trailhead,** near the marina, is the starting point for an interesting variety of trips ranging from 1 to 9 miles. With careful planning, it's possible to start the day with a hike beginning at Colter Bay that leads past **Cygnet Lake** across **Willow Flats** to **Jackson Lake Lodge,** where you can stop for lunch. Then, after a break, take the same path and return to Colter Bay in time for the evening outdoor barbecue. All told, that's 10 miles round-trip. The numerous trail options here can be confusing, so carry a map.

Hermitage Point Loop ⚑ From the trail head, this footpath heads through a thickly forested area to the isolated Hermitage Point, a peninsula jutting into Jackson Lake. Beyond the timber, the terrain consists of gently rolling hills, passing ponds, streams, and meadows. If you're seeking solitude, this is an excellent place to find it, although you should check with rangers before leaving—this is bear country.

8.8 miles round-trip. Moderate. Access: There are directional signs near the Swan Lake/Heron Pond Trail intersection.

Tips Photo Op

Not far from the trail head, the **Hermitage Point Loop** ⚑ opens to a broad, sagebrush-carpeted meadow. In the summer, the area blooms with wildflowers to offer one of the most impressive views of colossal **Mount Moran,** which is as impressive in its own way as the Grand Teton. To avoid retracing your steps past Heron Pond, bear right at the third creek intersection and continue straight ahead to the corrals at Colter Bay—this route adds no distance to the hike.

Heron Pond Trail   You journey through dense stands of lodgepole pine to this pond, inhabited by beavers most likely to be seen in the early morning. This is bear territory and a haven for Canada geese, trumpeter swans, and moose. Wildflowers are part of the show in the early summer: Look for lupine, *Gilia,* heartleaf arnicas, and the Indian paintbrush. Don't be put off by the fact that the first 200 yards of the trail are steep; after reaching the top of a rise, it levels out and has only moderate elevation gains from that point on. *Note:* Because three trails run through the area, the foliage and terrain for this trail, the Swan Lake Trail, and Hermitage Point Trail are virtually identical.

3 miles round-trip. Easy. Access: Trail head located at Hermitage Point Trailhead, Colter Bay.

Swan Lake Trail   Finding swans at Swan Lake requires a trip to its southern shore, where a small island offers them isolation and shelter for nests. From Swan Lake, it's only .3 mile through a densely forested area to the intersection with the trail to Heron Pond. Hermitage Point is 3 miles from this junction along a gentle path that winds through a wooded area that's popular with bears. If you circumnavigate the lake, expect to spend 2 hours on this hike.

3 miles round-trip. Easy. Access: Trail head located at Hermitage Point Trailhead, Colter Bay.

Willow Flats Trail ☆   An alternative to the park's mountainous, forested trails, this trip from Colter Bay to Jackson Lake Lodge takes you across marshy flats where you'll have an idyllic view of the Tetons and a good chance of seeing a moose. Unfortunately, you begin by skirting the sewage ponds at Colter Bay, but it gets better. Pick up a trail east to Cygnet Lake and, instead of looping back to Colter Bay, you take a spur that crosses Pilgrim Creek going east across the flats. You can hike in either direction, but drop a car at each end if you don't want to double back on foot.

10 miles round-trip. Easy. Access: Horse corrals at Colter Bay.

JACKSON LAKE LODGE AREA

A map showing the trails in this area is found in chapter 5.

Christian Pond Trail   Starting with a half-mile walk through a grassy, wet area to a pond with nesting trumpeter swans and other waterfowl, this is a short trail for all skill levels. If you're more ambitious, you can circumnavigate the pond, adding another 3 miles to the trip. In May and June, this is a great wildflower walk; but the area is also prime habitat for bears, so check with rangers before venturing onto the trail. The south end of the pond is covered with little grassy knolls upon which the birds build their nests and roost, and beavers have constructed a lodge here, too. It's a restful sanctuary, but one that's often infested by gnats and mosquitoes, so be sure to apply a coat of insect repellent.

1 mile round-trip. Easy. Access: The trail head is some 200 yards south of the entrance to Jackson Lake Lodge, most easily accessed from the Jackson Lake Lodge corrals. It's unmarked, so look carefully.

Signal Mountain Summit Trail 🐾🐾 Venturing up this uneven trail will give you a few fine hours of quiet trail time with views of the mountains, wildflowers, and, at the pinnacle, a grand panorama of the glacially carved valley. After negotiating a steep climb at the beginning of the trail, you'll come upon a broad plateau covered with lodgepole pine, grass, and seasonal wildflowers. Cross a paved road to a lily-covered pond, and just beyond you'll come upon two different trails up the mountain—take the right one up (ponds, maybe moose and bear) and the left one down (open ridges with views).

8 miles round-trip. Moderate. Access: The trail head is near the entrance to the Signal Mountain Lodge, or you can drive 1 mile up Signal Mountain Rd. to a pond on the right and pick up the trail there.

TWO OCEAN & EMMA MATILDA LAKE TRAILS

You can arrive at these lakes from the east or west: From the west you begin at the Grand View Point Trailhead, 1 mile north of Jackson Lake Lodge, or at the Christian Pond Trailhead, just east of Jackson Lake Lodge. From the east, you go up Pacific Creek Road, 4 miles east of Jackson Lake Junction on the road to the Moran entrance. There is a pullout for Emma Matilda Lake 2 miles up this road, or you can go a half-mile farther, take a left on Two Ocean Lake Road, and go to the Two Ocean Lake Trailhead parking lot, from which trails lead to both lakes.

(*Tips* **Photo Op**

A wide-open meadow near the summit of Signal Mountain presents an excellent opportunity to look to the west for photos of both **Mount Moran** and the **Teton Range**. The best time to take those photos is before 11am, when the sun will be mostly at your back, or in the early evening, when the sun will be lower in the sky to the west.

Kids **Especially for Kids**

Youthful visitors (ages 8–14) to the park are encouraged to explore and experience Grand Teton as members of the **Young Naturalist** program. To participate, pick up a copy of the Young Naturalist activity brochure at any visitor center, and then complete projects outlined in the booklet during your stay. When you present the completed project (and $1) to a ranger at the Moose, Jenny Lake, or Colter Bay visitor centers, you'll be awarded a Young Naturalist patch.

Two trails within Grand Teton are especially kid-friendly. The **Inspiration Point hike** 👧 is less strenuous if you take the boat shuttle across Jenny Lake. This reduces the hiking distance to less than a mile; at 7 miles round-trip, the entire Jenny Lake Loop Trail is a bit too long for kids, but the terrain is fairly level if you stick to the portion along the eastern shore. Also, the **Christian Pond Trail,** a level, 1-mile round-trip from the corrals at Jackson Lake Lodge, is a nice diversion, offering great views and a chance to see myriad waterfowl.

Emma Matilda Lake Trail   Circumnavigating this lake involves a pleasant up-and-down trek with great views of the mountains and a good chance of seeing wildlife. Emma Matilda Lake was named after the wife of Billy Owen, reputedly the first climber to reach the peak of Grand Teton. The hike winds uphill for a half-mile from the parking area to a large meadow favored by mule deer. The trail follows the northern side of the lake through a pine forest 400 feet above the lake and then descends to an overlook where you'll have inspiring views of the Tetons, Christian Pond, and Jackson Lake. The trail on the south side of the lake goes through a densely forested area populated by Engelmann spruce and subalpine fir. Be watchful and noisy because this is bear country. It's possible to branch off onto the Two Ocean Lake Trail along the northern shore of the lake.

11.8 miles round-trip. Easy to moderate. Access: Emma Matilda Lake Trailhead on Pacific Creek Rd. or trail head off Two Ocean Lake Rd. north of Jackson Lake–Moran Rd.

Two Ocean Lake Trail ⭐ (Finds)   Take your time and take a picnic on this delightful, underused trail around Two Ocean Lake. You can start at either end, but I recommend a side trip up Grand View Point, which will add about 2.5 miles of hiking. You'll be rested for this climb because the walk around the lake is fairly level, and you'll be in a great mood if you've been watching ducks, swans, grebes, and loons on the water. The variety of habitat—marshes, lakes, woodlands, and meadows—means that you'll see birds, wildflowers, butterflies, and possibly bear, beaver, elk, deer, and moose. As usual, awesome views of the Tetons abound; for the best perspective, take the trip up 600 feet to Grand View Point, a somewhat difficult climb through lodgepole and fir en route to a hilltop covered with orange arrowleaf balsamroot. You'll look down on lakes, meadows, and volcanic outcrops, and in the distance, you'll gaze at the Tetons, the Mount Leidy Highlands, and Jackson Lake. It's possible to branch off onto the Emma Matilda Lake Trail at the east end of Two Ocean Lake.

5.8 miles round-trip. Easy to moderate. Access: Two Ocean Lake Trailhead on Two Ocean Lake Rd., or Grand View Point Trailhead.

JENNY LAKE AREA

A map showing the trails in this area is in chapter 5.

Amphitheater Lake Trail ⭐⭐   Here's a trail that can get you in and out of the high mountains in a day, presuming that you're in good shape and acclimated to the altitude—it's a 3,000-foot climb. You'll cross glacial moraines and meadows quilted with flowers, and enter forests of fir and pine (including whitebark pine, a delicacy for bears—be alert!). Finally, you clear the trees and come into a ring of monstrous rock walls topped by Disappointment Peak, with Grand Teton and Teewinot in view. Surprise Lake and Amphitheater Lake sit in this dramatic setting, with a few gnarled trees struggling to survive on the slopes.

9.5 miles round-trip. Difficult. Access: Use the Lupine Meadows Trailhead. From the Moose entrance station on Teton Park Rd., drive 6½ miles to the Lupine Meadows Junction and follow signs to the trail head; if you're coming from Jenny Lake, the trail head is at the end of a road less than 1 mile south of South Jenny Lake.

Cascade Canyon Trail ⭐⭐⭐ (Moments)   Cascade Canyon Trail is the most popular trail in the park for intermediate and expert hikers. You can begin the hike from South Jenny Lake, but you can also shave 2 miles off each way by riding the boat shuttle across the lake and beginning your hike at the boat dock. At this point, you're only a steep mile from Inspiration Point (see "Hidden Falls & Inspiration Point Trail," below), which is as far as most visitors ever get. From here, you make a brief climb up a sharp grade to the glacially rounded canyon. The trail flattens, allowing for a relaxing exploration of a true wonderland of nature: Wildflowers, waterfowl, and busy pikas abound. On a nice day, the warblers will be singing and you could see moose and bear.

If you want to go farther, you have two choices when you reach forks of North and South Cascade Canyon: Follow the South Fork to Hurricane Pass or the North Fork to Lake Solitude. At 23 and 18 miles, respectively, these are overnight trips for most mortals, so you'll need camping gear and a backcountry permit.

A less taxing alternative to the Cascade Canyon trip mentioned above is a detour to **Moose Ponds,** which begins on the Inspiration Point Trail. The ponds, located 2 miles from either west or east boat docks, are near the south end of Jenny Lake and are alive with birds. The stretch near the base of Teewinot Mountain, which towers over the area, is populated with elk, mule deer, black bears, and moose. The trail is flat (at lake level), short, and easy to negotiate in 1 to 1½ hours. The best times to venture forth are early morning and evening.

9 miles round-trip. Moderate to difficult. Access: The trail into Cascade Canyon begins at Inspiration Point.

Hidden Falls & Inspiration Point Trail 🏞 *(Kids*   Many people cross Jenny Lake, either by boat or on foot around the south end, and then make the short, forest-shaded uphill slog to **Hidden Falls** (less than 1 mile of hiking if you take the boat; 5 miles round-trip if you walk around), which tumbles down a broad cascade. Some think that's enough and don't go another steep half-mile to **Inspiration Point.** Up there you get a great view of Jenny Lake below, and you can see the glacial moraine that formed it. If you're going to only these two overlooks, I recommend a relaxed and easy hike around the south end of the lake.

Whichever route you take to Inspiration Point, start early in the day to avoid the crowds. Then pace yourself. And once you've reached Inspiration Point, what's to stop you from proceeding on to Cascade Canyon?

1.8–5.8 miles round-trip. Moderate. Access: Trail heads at East Shore Boat Dock or at West Shore Boat Dock of Jenny Lake (if you take the boat shuttle).

Jenny Lake Loop Trail 🏞🏞   This trail circumnavigates the lake, following the shore. You can cut it in half by taking the Jenny Lake Boat Shuttle from the East Shore Boat Dock to the West Shore Boat Dock. The unblemished lake, which is 2.5 miles long, is in an idyllic setting at the foot of the mountain range, so it presents excellent views throughout the summer.

Keep in mind that Jenny Lake is one of the most popular spots in the park; to avoid the crowds, travel early or late in the day. The trails to Hidden Falls, Inspiration Point, and the Moose Ponds branch off of this trail on the southwest shore of the lake. The trails to String and Leigh lakes branch off this trail on the northern shore of Jenny Lake.

6.5 miles round-trip. Easy to moderate. Access: Trail head at East Shore Boat Dock.

Leigh Lake Trail ⚘   This trail begins at String Lake, which is a small, finger-shape lagoon connecting Leigh and Jenny lakes. The trail for Leigh Lake is well marked and relatively flat, and it goes through a forested area that is always within sight of the lake. Picnickers willing to expend the energy necessary to hike roughly 1 mile from the String Lake picnic area to the end of the lake will find themselves eating in a less congested area with spectacular views of Mount Moran. The trail continues along the eastern shore of Leigh Lake to a meadow with typically wonderful views and then goes on to small Bearpaw Lake. A better option, if time allows, is to return to the picnic area, cross the String Lake inlet, and explore the western edge of Jenny Lake along the trail that circumnavigates its shoreline (see the "Jenny Lake Loop Trail," described above).

7.5 miles round-trip. Easy. Access: The trail head is located adjacent to the String Lake picnic area.

String Lake Trail   This easy hike along the eastern shore of String Lake has two things going for it: It provides easy access to Leigh Lake, and it's in a forest that is a better alternative for a lunch break than the crowded picnic area. You'll wander in the shade of a pine forest along the shore with excellent views of Mount Moran above. However, because this is a heavily trafficked area, you should not count on seeing much wildlife, if any. This is also the starting point for a more ambitious trip up Paintbrush Canyon (see "Exploring the Backcountry," below).

3.3 miles round-trip. Easy. Access: Trail head is located at the Leigh Lake Trailhead.

Taggart and Bradley Lakes Trail ⚘⚘   Want to get away from the crowds on Jenny Lake trails? Just down the road from South Jenny is the trail head to Taggart and Bradley lakes, named for two members of the 1872 Hayden expedition. This hike winds through a burned-out area, in the midst of recovery, to Taggart Lake, which was created by glacial movements. The hike from the parking lot to the lake (where you can fish from the shore) is only 1.5 miles along the southern (left) fork of the trail. Swimming in these cold waters is not recommended. From the lake, you can return by the same trail or continue north to **Bradley Lake** for a round-trip of 5 miles. This route adds 1.8 miles to the trip, and the elevation gain is 467 feet; but the payoff is that, at its highest point, the trail overlooks all of Taggart Lake and the stream flowing from it. Like other hikes in Grand Teton, this one is best made during the early-morning or early-evening hours, when it's cooler and there's less traffic.

5 miles round-trip. Moderate. Access: The trail head is well marked and located west of Teton Park Rd., approximately 6 miles south of Jenny Lake.

FARTHER AFIELD: SOUTHEAST OF MOOSE

Although it is situated near Kelly, outside the park boundaries, the **Gros Ventre Slide area** is an interesting hiking area and historical site. You can get to the slide area by traveling east from the Gros Ventre Junction on U.S. Hwy. 26/89/191, 6 miles north of Jackson; alternately, 1 mile north of the Moose Junction on U.S. Hwy. 26/89/191, take the Antelope Flats Road to the second right turn, then take the second left. (There is a sign.)

It was at this spot, in June 1925, that the side of Sheep Mountain broke loose and created one of the largest earth movements ever observed. Nearly 50 million cubic yards of sandstone formed a dam 225 feet high and ½ mile wide across the Gros Ventre River. Then, in 1927, the upper 60 feet of the dam gave way, creating a raging river that flooded the town of Kelly, 3½ miles downstream.

Informational brochures and maps of this interpretive trail, which is in the Bridger-Teton National Forest, are available from the U.S. Forest Service. Stop in at the **Greater Yellowstone Visitor Center,** at 532 N. Cache St. in downtown Jackson, where you can pick up all the information you'll need to hike in this area, or call the **Forest Service** at (**C**) 307/739-5500.

2 Exploring the Backcountry

Grand Teton might seem small compared to Yellowstone, but there are more than 250 miles of trails in the backcountry and plenty of opportunities for solitude or adventure. As in Yellowstone, a permit is required for camping in the backcountry—the permits are free and are essentially for keeping track of campers and for making sure that no one area is overused. Rather than receiving a specific site reservation, the permits allow you to establish camp in one of several camping "zones," where you'll have a choice of sites.

For **general information** on backpacking and safety, see chapter 2.

INFORMATION BEFORE YOU GO   For background information, write for the *Grand Teton Backcountry Camping* brochure, Grand Teton National Park, P.O. Drawer 170, Moose, WY 83012, or print it out from www.nps.gov/grte. For recorded backcountry information, call © **307/739-3602.**

BACKCOUNTRY PERMITS   Backcountry permits from the Park Service are required to use an overnight campsite; the permits themselves are free, but an advance reservation entails a nonrefundable $25 fee. To avoid the fee, you may pick up a permit the day before you commence your trip. Reservations are accepted only from January 1 to May 15; it's wise to reserve a camp area if you're going in July or August. The permit is valid only on the dates for which it is issued.

   Warning: The reservation is just that, a reservation; upon your arrival at the park, you'll need to secure the permit. Permits are issued at the Moose and Colter Bay visitor centers and at the Jenny Lake Ranger station; you may make reservations by writing the **Permits Office,** Grand Teton National Park, P.O. Drawer 170, Moose, WY 83012, or faxing 307/739-3438. Reservations can also be made online at **www.nps.gov/grte**.

WHEN TO GO   Remember that this region has a short summer and virtually no spring. While the valley floor of the park is open in May, some of the high-country trails might not be clear of snow or high water before late June or early July. Look in the *Backcountry Camping* brochure (see above) for approximate dates when specific campsites are habitable.

MAPS   Topographic maps of Grand Teton are available from the U.S. Geological Survey and Trails Illustrated, as is the *Grand Teton Hiking and Climbing* map, which includes maps of Granite and Moran canyons and a trip planner; it is available from the **Grand Teton Association,** P.O. Box 170, Moose, WY 83012 (© **307/739-3403;** www.grandtetonpark.org).

THE BACKCOUNTRY IN GRAND TETON

The premier backcountry activity in Grand Teton is not hiking but rather **mountain climbing,** which you should not attempt alone unless you are an expert. For a complete discussion of mountaineering possibilities and outfitters in Grand Teton National Park, see "Climbing," below.

   Perhaps the most popular backcountry trail in Grand Teton is the 19.3-mile **Cascade Canyon Loop** ✸✸✸. The loop starts on the west side of Jenny Lake, winds northwest 9.3 miles on the **Cascade Canyon Trail** to Lake Solitude and the Paintbrush Divide, and then returns on the 10-mile-long **Paintbrush Canyon Trail** past Holly Lake, tucked into a cirque including Mount Woodring. While there are longer hikes, this is one of the most rigorous in either park because of gains in elevation—more than 2,600 feet—rocky trails, and switchbacks through loose gravel that can get slippery, especially in years when snow remains until the middle of summer on the north-facing side of Paintbrush Divide.

Rangers recommend the hike for several reasons, the most noteworthy of which is unsurpassed scenery. Moose and black bears call this part of the park home, so hikers are cautioned to be diligent about making noise (strap some bells on your pack). You might also see harlequin ducks, which nest near the trail in Cascade Creek. You'll see many other avians, a whole host of wildflowers, and large stands of whitebark pine trees.

Although it adds 5 miles to the trip (one-way), a detour west from the Cascade Canyon Trail to **Hurricane Pass** will reward you with a view from the foot of **Schoolroom Glacier.** If it's an extended trip you're after, head west into the **Jedediah Smith Wilderness** on a trail that eventually crosses into Idaho. This trail doesn't stop anytime soon—you can actually continue trekking all the way to Alaska.

If you are looking to make a *long* day hike out of this, you can trek 7.3 miles on the Cascade Canyon Trail to **Lake Solitude** and return via the same trail. But you're better off planning for a multiday trip because camping zones are 6 miles west of the trail head on the Cascade Canyon Trail and 8.8 miles northwest on the Paintbrush Canyon Trail at Holly Lake. Be sure to get a reservation.

The quickest way to get up high in these mountains for a backcountry foray is to hitch a ride up **Rendezvous Mountain** *⊛* on the Jackson Hole Ski Resort Tram—but it's being rebuilt and is out of commission until winter 2008. Once it's operational again, hikers can ride it up to 10,450 feet above sea level in **Bridger-Teton National Forest,** just south of the park, and embark north toward the park's Middle Fork Cutoff. From here, you can head down into **Granite Canyon** to Phelps Lake, which has three lakefront campsites—and is the closest backcountry camping zone to civilization. Alternatively, you can hike north through the high country along the **Teton Crest Trail** to Fox Creek Pass (over 8 difficult miles from the tram) and to Death Canyon and beyond.

If you are hardy enough to make it to **Death Canyon Shelf,** a wildflower-strewn limestone ledge that runs above Death Canyon toward **Alaska Basin,** you'll have an extraordinary, high-altitude view of the west side of the Tetons' biggest peaks. If you are on an extended backcountry trip, you can continue north to Hurricane Pass, where you can come back down to the valley floor by way of Cascade Canyon.

This kind of backcountry trip is truly an expedition and requires a certain level of skill and experience. Go over any such plans with park rangers, who can help you evaluate your ability to take on such a challenge.

3 Other Activities

In addition to the activities listed here, check out some of the other options in the Jackson area that are listed in chapter 8.

BIKING   Bikes are banned from all hiking trails in the park, and on the paved roads below. The problem is safety—there are huge RVs careening about, and some roads have only narrow shoulders. Construction has widened Teton Park Road a bit, but traffic on it is still heavy. Instead, road bikers should try **Antelope Flats,** beginning at a trail head a mile north of Moose Junction and going east. Sometimes called **Mormon Row,** this paved route crosses the flats below the Gros Ventre Mountains, past old ranch homesteads and the small town of Kelly. It connects to the unpaved **Shadow Mountain Road,** which actually leaves the park and continues into national forest, climbing through the trees to the summit. After a total distance of 7 miles and an elevation gain of 1,370 feet, you'll be looking at Mount Moran and the Tetons across the valley.

Mountain bikers have a few more options: Try **Two Ocean Lake Road** (reached from the Pacific Creek Rd. just north of Moran Junction) or the **River Road,** a 15-mile dirt path along the Snake River's western bank. Ambitious mountain bikers might want to load their overnight gear and take the **Grassy Lake Road,** once used by Indians, west from Flagg Ranch on a 50-mile journey to Ashton, Idaho.

Books and maps with bicycle routes are available at visitor centers, or from **Adventure Sports,** at Dornan's in the village of Moose (© **307/733-3307**), which is inside the boundaries of Grand Teton National Park. You can also rent mountain bikes here, $32 for a full day and $22 for half a day, as well as road and performance bikes for a few dollars more. Children's bikes are also available.

BOATING   Boaters have more choices in Grand Teton than they do in Yellowstone. Motorboats are permitted on Jenny, Jackson, and Phelps lakes. Bigger boats, even a few yacht-size vessels, find room on Jackson Lake, where powerboats pull skiers, sailboats move noiselessly in summer breezes, and fishermen ply the waters. Those who venture on the big lake need to be aware that the weather can change suddenly, and late afternoon lightning is not uncommon; sailors should be particularly wary of the swirling winds that accompany thunderstorms.

If you bring your own boat, you must register it: For human-powered craft, it's $10 for 7 days, or $20 for a yearlong permit; motorized skippers pay $20 for 7 days and $40 for an annual permit, which you can buy at the Colter Bay and Moose visitor centers. Boat and canoe rentals, tackle, and fishing licenses are available at Colter and **Signal Mountain Lodge** (℃ **307/543-2831**). Rental fees are $28 per hour for motorboats; kayaks, canoes, pontoon boats, and deck cruisers are also available. Signal Mountain also offers guided half-day sailboat tours for $280 for two people.

Motorized boats are allowed on Phelps, Jackson, and Jenny lakes, but on Jenny Lake the motor can't be over 8 horsepower. Only human-powered vessels are permitted on Emma Matilda, Two Ocean, Taggart, Bradley, Bearpaw, Leigh, and String lakes. Rafts, canoes, dories, and kayaks are allowed on the Snake River within the park. No boats are permitted on Pacific Creek or the Gros Ventre River.

Scenic cruises ⚓ of Jackson Lake are conducted daily by the **Grand Teton Lodge Company** (℃ **307/543-2811**; www.gtlc.com). Breakfast cruises run Saturday through Thursday and dinner cruises run Monday, Wednesday, and Friday. Both depart from the **Colter Bay Marina** from May to September. You'll travel to Elk Island, where they cook up a pretty good meal: trout and steak for dinner, and pancakes and eggs for breakfast. The scenic trips are 1½ hours long, and cost $21 for adults and $10 for kids 3 to 11; the meal cruises are twice that length and run $33 (breakfast) or $55 (dinner) for adults, and $21 or $33, respectively, for kids 3 to 11.

Jenny Lake Boating Company (℃ **307/734-9227**; www.jenny lakeboating.com) takes visitors on scenic cruises in Jenny Lake; the cost is $14 adults, $7 children. The tours are scheduled throughout the day and last about an hour. Reservations are strongly recommended. The company also rents kayaks for $12 an hour or $60 a day.

Additionally, you can rent kayaks and canoes at **Adventure Sports** at Dornan's in the town of Moose (℃ **307/733-3307**), which is in the boundaries of Grand Teton National Park. Rentals run $10 an hour or $46 per day.

CLIMBING   Mountaineering in Grand Teton is wildly popular, but it's important to stay within the limits of your skill level. Every single year, there are rescues of climbers who fall or get trapped on Teton rock faces, and many years there are fatalities. Yet the peaks have a strong allure for climbers, even inexperienced ones, perhaps because you can reach the top of even the biggest ones in a single day, albeit not without a serious workout. The terrain is mixed, speckled with snow and ice even in midsummer—knowing how to self-arrest with an ice axe is a must—and the weather can change suddenly. The key is to get good advice, know your limitations, and, if you're not already skilled, take some lessons at the local climbing schools (see paragraph below). If you go without a professional guide, you should have experienced companions who know the mountain.

Climbers who go out for a day do not have to register or report to park officials, but they should be sure to tell friends where they're going and when they'll be back. Overnight climbers must pick up a free permit. Climbing rangers who can lead rescue efforts are on duty at the **Jenny Lake Ranger Station** at South Jenny Lake from late May to late September. The American Alpine Club provides inexpensive dormitory beds for climbers at the **Grand Teton Climbers' Ranch** (© **307/733-7271;** www.americanalpineclub.org). A pair of long-standing operations offer classes and guided climbs of Grand Teton: **Jackson Hole Mountain Guides** in Jackson (© **800/ 239-7642** or 307/733-4979; www.jhmg.com) and **Exum Mountain Guides** ✦ in Moose (© **307/733-2297;** www.exumguides. com). Expect to pay around $500 to $600 for a guided 2-day climb of Grand Teton or $125 to $150 for a class.

The **Jenny Lake Ranger Station** (© **307/733-3392**), which is open only in summer, is the center for climbing information; climbers are encouraged to stop in and obtain information on routes, conditions, and regulations.

FISHING   The lakes and streams of Grand Teton are popular fishing destinations, loaded with lively cutthroat trout, whitefish, and mackinaw (lake) trout in Jackson, Jenny, and Phelps lakes. Jackson has produced some monsters weighing as much as 50 pounds, but you're more likely to catch fish under 20 inches, fishing deep with trolling gear from a boat during hot summer months.

The Snake River runs for about 27 miles in the park and has cutthroat and whitefish up to about 18 inches. It's a popular drift-boat river for fly fishermen. If you'd like a guide who knows the holes, try **Jack Dennis Sports** (© **800/570-3270** or 307/733-3270; www.jackdennis.com), **Triangle X Float Trips** (© **307/733-2183;**

www.trianglex.com), or **Westbank Anglers** (☏ 800/922-3474 or 307/733-6483; www.westbank.com). The going rate is $425 for a full day for two people. **Signal Mountain Lodge** (☏ 307/543-2831) offers guided half-day trips on motorized craft in **Jackson Lake** for one or two people for $250. As an alternative, stake out a position on the banks below the dam, where you'll have plenty of company and just might snag something. While special fishing permits are issued by the Park Service in Yellowstone, a **Wyoming fishing license** is required of anglers in Grand Teton (nonresident $11 for 1 day, $76 for season; $3 per day, $15 per season for youngsters 14–18; no license required for kids under 14). An $11 Conservation Stamp is also required for all licenses except the 1-day variety.

FLOAT TRIPS   The upper end of the Snake River in the park can be deceptive—its smooth surface runs fast during the spring, and there are deadly snags of fallen trees and other debris. Without a local guide or past experience, you might want to think twice about dropping your personal raft in. Check in with rangers, and let them discourage you if they think your skills might not match the river. There are plenty of commercial-rafting outfitters that will help you get acquainted (see paragraph below). If you want white water, there are a dozen commercial outfitters offering white-water trips down Snake River Canyon, outside the park (see "Jackson, Wyoming," in chapter 8).

The park's 27-mile stretch of river attracts all sorts of wildlife, with moose, eagles, and other animals coming to the water's edge. There are many commercial float operators in the park that generally run trips from mid-May to mid-September (depending on weather and river flow conditions). These companies offer 5- to 10-mile scenic floats, some with early-morning and evening wildlife trips. Try **Solitude Float Trips** (☏ 888/704-2800 or 307/733-2871; www.grand-teton-scenic-floats.com), **Barker-Ewing Float Trips** (☏ 800/365-1800 or 307/733-1800; www.barkerewingscenic.com), **Grand Teton Lodge Company** (☏ 307/543-2811; www.gtlc.com), or **Signal Mountain Lodge** (☏ 307/543-2831; http://signalmountain lodge.com). Scenic float trips cost about $50 for adults, with discounts for children under 12.

HORSEBACK RIDING   Horseback riding is as popular in Grand Teton as it is in Yellowstone. The **Grand Teton Lodge Company** (☏ 307/543-2811; www.gtlc.com) offers tours from corrals at Colter Bay and Jackson Lake Lodge. Guided trail rides run $33 to $48; breakfast or dinner rides are $63 per adult and $53 per child.

An experienced rider might find these tours too tame; wranglers refer to them as "nose and tail" tours. The names of several other companies that organize horseback trips are under "Jackson, Wyoming," in chapter 8.

4 Winter Sports & Activities

Park facilities pretty much shut down during the winter, except for a skeleton staff at the Moose Visitor Center, and the park shows no signs of becoming a winter magnet, a la Yellowstone. That may be just as well—you can enjoy some quiet, fun times in the park without the crowds.

WINTER ROAD CONDITIONS Teton Park Road opens to conventional vehicles and RVs around May 1. The **Moose-Wilson Road** opens to vehicles about the same time. Park roads close on November 1 for the winter season. They are open to snowshoers and cross-country skiers after mid-December.

SPORTING GOODS & EQUIPMENT RENTALS Jackson has enough sporting equipment places to keep everyone in Wyoming outfitted. The **Jack Dennis Outdoor Shop,** on the south side of Town Square (© **800/570-3270** or 307/733-3270; www.jack dennis.com), has all the skis and outdoor clothing you can possibly need. **Teton Mountaineering,** 170 N. Cache St. (© **800/850-3595;** www.tetonmtn.com), is the equipment shop of choice for the knowledgeable and advanced skier or ice climber; **Hoback Sports,** 520 W. Broadway Ave. (© **307/733-5335;** www.hobacksports. com), is another good option. **Skinny Skis,** at 65 W. Deloney Ave. off the Town Square (© **888/733-7205** or 307/733-6094; www.skinnyskis.com), is a year-round specialty sports shop focusing on Nordic skiing. For a great supply of seconds (same quality of material as "firsts"), stop at **Moosely Seconds** (© **307/739-1801**) in Moose.

CROSS-COUNTRY SKIING You can ski flat or steep in Grand Teton; the two things to watch out for are hypothermia and avalanches. As with climbing, know your limitations, and make sure you're properly equipped. Check with local rangers and guides for trails that match your ability. Among your options is the relatively easy **Jenny Lake Trail,** starting at the Taggart Lake Parking Area, about 13km (8 miles) of flat and scenic trail that follows Cottonwood Creek. A more difficult ski is the **Taggart Lake–Beaver Creek Loop,** a 5km (3.1-mile) route that has some steep and icy pitches coming back. About 6.5km (4 miles) of the **Moose-Wilson Road**— the back way to Teton Village from Moose—is unplowed in the winter and is an easy trip through the woods. You can climb the windy unplowed road to the top of **Signal Mountain**—you might encounter snowmobiles—and have some fun skiing down. There is an easy ski trail from the Colter Bay Ranger Station area to **Heron Pond**—about 4km (2.5 miles), with a great view of the Tetons and Jackson Lake. Get a ski trail map from the visitor centers.

SNOWMOBILING   Snowmobiling is a popular winter option. The main roads in Grand Teton are groomed, providing access to trails in the nearby **Bridger-Teton National Forest,** the area to the immediate east of Grand Teton National Park, and to the **Continental Divide Trail,** which runs 320 miles through the Rockies.

7

Where to Stay & Dine in the Parks

Before picking up the phone to make a reservation, take some time to study maps of the parks (see our maps in chapters 3 and 5). While the parks are small enough that you can drive practically anywhere in a day, you'll want to be acquainted with the locations of the park attractions that you most want to see and their proximity to accommodations. For instance, if you want to see Old Faithful at all different hours of the day and night, or if you want to hike the Lonestar Geyser Trail, try to get a room at the Old Faithful Inn or the Snow Lodge. If you find big bodies of water soothing, check in at the Lake Yellowstone Hotel or Colter Bay.

Also keep in mind that the characteristics of the lodgings vary considerably, and request specific information about the type of rooms available before making a reservation. If you are bedding down in one of the historic hotels or cabins in the parks, be aware that they offer fewer modern conveniences than your typical commercial motel.

One final bit of advice: Try to spend at least 2 nights within park boundaries, whether you prefer campgrounds or hotels. When the sun dips below the horizon, you'll see a summer sky that sparkles more brightly than in the gateway cities (weather permitting), and you might hear coyotes and other wildlife. And you will discover that the hours just after daybreak are an ideal time for exploring: The trails are empty, animals go about their early-morning routines oblivious to visitors, and the silence is deafening.

1 Where to Stay in Yellowstone National Park

To book a room within Yellowstone, you need to contact **Xanterra Parks & Resorts,** P.O. Box 165, Yellowstone National Park, WY 82190 (© **866/439-7375** or 307/344-7311; www.travelyellowstone. com). Most Yellowstone accommodations are open from early May to mid-October. During Yellowstone's winter season, which begins in mid-December and runs through early March, accommodations and meals for snowmobilers, cross-country skiers, and other visitors can be found at either Mammoth Hot Springs Hotel or Old Faithful Snow Lodge. There are also special packages in winter and summer that bundle activities and lodging; visit the Xanterra website for current specials. Because these dates are heavily dependent on weather conditions, it's best to call ahead to check the listed dates with the concessionaire.

It's easier to find a vacant room before June 20 and after September 25, and the week before Labor Day weekend is traditionally slow. The more popular lodges and campgrounds in the parks are typically fully booked during the peak season, so reservations should be made a few months in advance. The rates sometimes drop early in the season and in October, and those making reservations before April 1 can also get a significant discount. Both of these specials apply only to Old Faithful Snow Lodge, Lake Yellowstone Hotel, Grant Village, and Mammoth Hot Springs Hotel.

If you want television, air-conditioning, and other modern amenities typical of American hotels, stay in a gateway town rather than in the park. Some of the inns are close to a century old, and the park has encouraged the concessionaires to keep technology to a minimum. Although some of the park lounges now have televisions, and telephones have been added to many rooms, you'll find only two in-room TVs in the entire park (in the suites at Mammoth, but reception wavers). Most of the accommodations do have heat, although, in some cases—the cabins at Roosevelt, for example—it's a wood stove.

MAMMOTH HOT SPRINGS AREA
5 miles from the Gardiner (north) entrance to Yellowstone

This area is open year-round and houses the park headquarters. It's a 5-mile drive from the park's north entrance, and you can often find a room here, even during the height of its peak summer and winter seasons. Besides easy access, the area has quite a bit to offer: the park's best visitor center; colorful, travertine limestone terraces; a historic hotel with one of the park's better restaurants; and a campground.

Mammoth Hot Springs Hotel and Cabins ⚘ Below the steaming terraces of Mammoth Hot Springs, this is one of two Yellowstone hotels open during both summer and winter seasons. (The other is the Old Faithful Snow Lodge.) Established in 1911, the hotel itself is less distinguished than the Lake Yellowstone Hotel or the Old Faithful Inn, but it manages to blend a wide range of rooms into a satisfying whole. Make sure you drift into the **Map Room** (named for the massive inlaid map of the United States on one of the broad paneled walls), a great place to while away an evening reading or listening to a pianist.

The only truly high-end accommodations are the suites. Standard rooms and cabins are arranged around three grassy areas, offering minimal amenities with a fair amount of charm. Some rooms have tubs only, some rooms have showers only, and some share a bathroom down the hall. The cottage-style cabins are clustered in rings adjacent to the hotel, and vary in quality.

At Mammoth Hot Springs, P.O. Box 165, Yellowstone National Park, WY 82190. © 866/439-7375 or 307/344-7311. Fax 307/344-7456. www.travelyellowstone. com. 212 units, including 2 suites. $82–$110 double; $72–$104 cabin; $182 hot tub cabin; $339 suite. AE, DC, DISC, MC, V. Closed Oct to mid-Dec and early Mar to early May. **Amenities:** 2 restaurants; lounge; tour desk. *In room:* No phone (cabins).

CANYON VILLAGE AREA
40 miles from the West Yellowstone (west) entrance; 38 miles from the Gardiner (north) entrance

This is one of the busiest areas in the park because the Grand Canyon of the Yellowstone is, like Old Faithful, on everyone's itinerary. Accommodations here are in lodge rooms, modestly priced cabin units, or a large campground, and there are restaurants and coffee shops that fit most palates and pocketbooks, as well as a visitor center, general store, and post office. With the many amenities available here, it doesn't matter that it's 40 miles from the nearest gateway town.

Canyon Lodge and Cabins   This complex is one of the newer facilities in the park (both Cascade and Dunraven lodges were completed here in the 1990s), but it can't escape the Disneyland-style atmosphere of the sprawling Canyon Village. However, the lodges are located a mere half-mile from the Grand Canyon of the Yellowstone and Inspiration Point, one of the most photographed spots in the park. Cascade Lodge offers simple rooms appointed with tasteful log furnishings in the three-story building; the newer Dunraven is similar, although it is more modern (with an elevator); both are located adjacent to a woodland setting. There are also clusters of cabins scattered throughout the village: clean, motel-style configurations. The cabins are single-story duplex and fourplex structures with private bathrooms that are among the largest in the park. They're a bit weathered but generally acceptable, and, given the sheer number of units involved, this isn't the place to "get away from it all."

In Canyon Village, P.O. Box 165, Yellowstone National Park, WY 82190. © **866/439-7375** or 307/344-7311. Fax 307/344-7456. www.travelyellowstone.com. 605 units.

$155 double; $66–$142 cabin. AE, DC, DISC, MC, V. Closed Oct to late May. **Amenities:** Restaurant; lounge; tour desk; self-serve laundry. *In room:* No phone.

TOWER-ROOSEVELT AREA
23 miles from the Gardiner (north) entrance; 29 miles from the northeast entrance

This is a throwback to the early days of Yellowstone: no big complex of shops and services, and a certain cowboy philosophy. Out of the way and far from the crowds, the lodge here offers easy access to the hiking trails and the beautiful corridor of the Lamar Valley. The basic cabins are an affordable (and apt) choice for families who want to "rough it" without pitching a tent.

Roosevelt Lodge Cabins *(R) (Kids)*   This is considered the park's family hideaway, a low-key operation with dinky, primitive cabins; stables; and a lodge restaurant that feels like a big ranch house. The bare-bones cabins are called Roughriders, and they're furnished with two simple beds, clean linens, a writing table, and a wood stove. A step up, the Frontier cabins have their own bathrooms and showers. The lodge is a rugged-but-charming stone edifice; its large, inviting porch is outfitted with rockers so guests can sit back and watch the world go by. Stagecoach rides, horseback trips, and Western trail cookouts give this place a cowboy flavor, and it's a less hectic scene than the other park villages.

At Tower Junction, P.O. Box 165, Yellowstone National Park, WY 82190. (At junction of Mammoth-Tower Rd. and Tower-Canyon Rd.) *(C)* **866/439-7375** or 307/344-7311. Fax 307/344-7456. www.travelyellowstone.com. 80 cabins, 14 with private bathroom. $64–$104 cabin. AE, DC, DISC, MC, V. Closed early Sept to June. **Amenities:** Restaurant; lounge; tour desk. *In room:* No phone.

LAKE VILLAGE AREA
27 miles from the east entrance; 56 miles from the West Yellowstone (west) entrance; 43 miles from the south entrance

More elegant than the Old Faithful Inn, this cluster of structures on the lake has the feel of a Victorian-era resort. There are accommodations in a historic hotel, motel and cabin units, and waterfront camping sites, all of which provide access to the lake's numerous recreational opportunities and the nearby hiking trails. The hotel's dining room is the finest in the park, although there are also cheaper alternatives in the neighborhood.

Lake Lodge Cabins *(Value)*   These cabins surrounding Lake Lodge stand near the lake, a relatively quiet, traffic-free area just around the corner from the Lake Yellowstone Hotel. The old Western lodge's most attractive feature is a large porch with wicker rockers that invite visitors to sit and gaze out across the waters. The accommodations are in well-preserved, clean, freestanding cabins near a trout stream that threads through a wooded area. (There are nature walks around the lodge, but because this is a trout spawning area, access is usually restricted early in the summer when grizzlies emerge from hibernation.)

These cabins come in two grades: **Western** cabins provide electric heat, paneled walls, two double beds (and, in some cases, an extra twin), and combination bathrooms, while **Pioneer** cabins are smaller and sparsely furnished, with one or two double beds each and small shower-only bathrooms. A number of the cabins here have been recently renovated, making them among the freshest in the park and a good deal for the money. You'll need to head outdoors to enjoy the lake views, as the only things you can see from your cabin are other cabins. Because the dining room here is a tad short on atmosphere, you might want to make the short trek to the Lake Yellowstone Hotel for a more sumptuous meal in a more appetizing setting.

On Yellowstone Lake, P.O. Box 165, Yellowstone National Park, WY 82190. ℂ **866/439-7375** or 307/344-7311. Fax 307/344-7456. www.travelyellowstone.com. 186 cabins. $65 Pioneer cabin; $132 Western cabin. AE, DC, DISC, MC, V. Closed mid-Sept to early June. **Amenities:** Restaurant; lounge; tour desk; self-serve laundry. *In room:* No phone.

Lake Yellowstone Hotel and Cabins ⭐⭐   The Ionic columns, dormer windows, and deep porticos on this classic yellow building faithfully recall the year it was built: 1891. It's an entirely different world from the rustic Western style of other park lodgings. The facility was restored in the early 1990s, and its better rooms are the most comfortable and roomy in the park, with soul-stirring views of the massive lake.

The three- and four-story wings house the hotel rooms, and there's also a motel-style annex and an assortment of cabins. The upper-end rooms here are especially lavish for Yellowstone, with stenciled walls and traditional spreads on one queen-size or two double beds. Smaller rooms in the annex are fitted with two double beds and bring to mind a typical motel chain. The freestanding yellow-clad cabins here are passable, decorated with knotty pine paneling, and furnished with double beds and a writing table. A number of them were nicely renovated in 2004, making them among the best cabins in the park.

On the north side of the lake, P.O. Box 165, Yellowstone National Park, WY 82190. ℂ **866/439-7375** or 307/344-7311. Fax 307/344-7456. www.travelyellowstone.com. 300 units, including 1 suite. $139–$211 double; $111 cabin; $525 suite. AE, DC, DISC, MC, V. Closed early Oct to mid-May. **Amenities:** 2 restaurants; lounge; tour desk; self-serve laundry. *In room:* No phone (cabins).

GRANT VILLAGE AREA

22 miles from the south entrance; 47 miles from the West Yellowstone (west) entrance

This relatively modern addition doesn't have the romantic ambience of the Old Faithful Inn or Lake Yellowstone Hotel. Regardless, it's reasonably priced and has a good location, on the south shores of beautiful Yellowstone Lake near West Thumb, with a good visitor center and access to various sights.

Grant Village   The southernmost of the major overnight accommodations in the park, Grant Village was completed in 1984 and is one of the more contemporary choices in Yellowstone. It's not as architecturally distinctive as the Old Faithful options, consisting of six condo-style units (with motel-style rooms), but it's also less touristy and more isolated. Rooms are tastefully furnished, most outfitted with light wood furniture, track lighting, electric heat, and laminate counters. Nicer and more expensive rooms affording lake views have mullioned windows, one queen-size or one or two double beds, and full bathrooms.

On the West Thumb of Yellowstone Lake, P.O. Box 165, Yellowstone National Park, WY 82190. (℃ **866/439-7375** or 307/344-7311. Fax 307/344-7456. www.travel yellowstone.com. 300 units. $125–$130 double. AE, DC, DISC, MC, V. Closed late Sept to late May. **Amenities:** Restaurant; lounge; tour desk.

OLD FAITHFUL AREA

30 miles from the West Yellowstone (west) entrance; 39 miles from the south entrance

Despite the crowds, the Old Faithful area is probably the best spot to center a hotel-based visit to the park. First of all, you'll spend a night in the midst of the most famous geyser basin in the world. You'll also have more choices of rooms, restaurants, and services—including a visitor center, a gas station, and a large Yellowstone General Store—than anywhere else in the park. And, from a logistical point of view, you'll have excellent access to attractions in every direction.

Old Faithful Inn ✮✮✮   There are three hotels within viewing distance of the geyser, including a very nice new one, but this is undoubtedly the crown jewel of Yellowstone's man-made wonders. Seven stories tall with dormers peaking from a shingled, steep-sloping roof, it's an architectural wonder that was designed by Robert Reamer to blend into the natural environment—and it's been the place to stay in Yellowstone for a century, first welcoming guests in 1904.

The cavernous, log-laden lobby is striking, with an ambience that is half elegant palace and half rugged wilderness lodge. You can climb the stairs to its internal balconies, but seismic activity eventually closed the crow's nest, where a chamber orchestra initially performed for the well-dressed guests below. Only 30 miles from the west entrance and 40 miles from the south entrance, this is the first place visitors think of when they want a bed for the night, so make reservations far ahead during the busy summer months.

Guest rooms are in the main building and in wings that flank the main lodge. Original rooms are basic, appointed with conservative fabrics and park-theme art, but they don't all have private bathrooms; the wing rooms offer better facilities and more privacy.

At Old Faithful, P.O. Box 165, Yellowstone National Park, WY 82190. © 866/439-7375 or 307/344-7311. Fax 307/344-7456. www.travelyellowstone.com. 327 units, including 6 suites. $117–$198 double with private bathroom; $91 double with shared bathroom; $344–$457 suite. AE, DC, DISC, MC, V. Closed mid-Oct to mid-May. **Amenities:** 2 restaurants; lounge; tour desk. *In room:* No phone.

Old Faithful Lodge Cabins *Value*   These are the leftovers from the days when crude cabins littered the landscape around the world's most famous geyser. The ones closest to the geyser were hauled away years ago, but you still get a sense of what tourism was like in the park's early days, especially if you rent one of the **budget cabins,** which are only slightly less flimsy than tents and have basic beds and sinks, no more. Showers and restrooms are a short walk away. **Frontier cabins** are the better units, adding a private bathtub to other amenities. If amenities are irrelevant, these rustic, thin-walled cabins are an economical way to put a roof over your head in the park. The lodge is perhaps the busiest spot in the geyser area, featuring several snack shops and a huge cafeteria dishing up varied fast food.

At Old Faithful, P.O. Box 165, Yellowstone National Park, WY 82190. © 866/439-7375 or 307/344-7311. Fax 307/344-7456. www.travelyellowstone.com. 96 cabins, some with shared bathroom. $67–$104 double. AE, DC, DISC, MC, V. Closed mid-Sept to mid-May. **Amenities:** 2 restaurants; tour desk. *In room:* No phone.

Old Faithful Snow Lodge and Cabins *★★*   If your last visit to Yellowstone included a stay at the Old Faithful Snow Lodge, put the memory out of your mind. The old dormitory-style lodge was torn down in 1998, and this new, award-winning structure could aptly be called the New Faithful Snow Lodge. Its contemporary big-beam construction and high ceiling in the lobby echo the Old Faithful Inn, and a copper-lined balcony curves above the common area, where guests can relax in wicker furniture. The folks behind the place paid attention to every last detail: The public areas have a contemporary

(but appropriate) style, some of the lodge's wood was recycled from the same mill that provided the lumber for the Old Faithful Inn in 1904, and wrought-iron bears abound on everything from lamps to fireplace grates. The modern rooms are spacious and comfortable, second only to the upper-end accommodations at the Lake Yellowstone Hotel. There's also a small collection of surrounding cabins with motel-style furnishings (many of which were built after the 1988 fires) and—a rarity in the park—in-room coffeemakers.

At Old Faithful, P.O. Box 165, Yellowstone National Park, WY 82190. (C) 866/439-7375 or 307/344-7311. Fax 307/344-7456. www.travelyellowstone.com. 134 units. $184 double; $91–$133 cabin. AE, DC, DISC, MC, V. Closed Oct to mid-Dec and early Mar to early May. **Amenities:** Restaurant; lounge; tour desk. *In room:* Coffeemaker; no phone (cabins).

2 Where to Camp in Yellowstone

Camping at Yellowstone's 12 developed campgrounds can be a happy affair, with the stars overhead, the scent of pine, and friendly neighbors from all over the world. The campgrounds are spaced throughout the park.

For those who carry their tents on their backs and want no neighbors other than their hiking buddies, there's plenty of room out there. Some areas in the Yellowstone backcountry are delicate habitat—the southeast arm of Yellowstone Lake is an example—and visitors must camp in designated areas for a limited time only. This in no way diminishes the sense of being in a true wilderness. Check with the **Yellowstone Backcountry Office** ((C) **307/344-2160**) for rules, reservations, and advice.

GETTING A CAMPSITE   The National Park Service has shifted management of five major campgrounds to Xanterra Parks & Resorts, which means, predictably, higher fees, but, thankfully, it also means you can make reservations. The other seven campgrounds still managed by the park are available only on a first-come, first-served basis. These **lower-cost campgrounds** are at Indian Creek, Lewis Lake, Mammoth, Norris, Pebble Creek, Slough Creek, and Tower Fall. I happen to like the Norris and Lewis Lake sites, which tend to be available when others are full. Check with rangers about campsite availability when you enter the park; generally, you need to arrive early to get a site—some campgrounds fill up as early as 8am.

Xanterra Parks & Resorts operates the large campgrounds at Bridge Bay, Canyon, Grant Village, Madison, and Fishing Bridge. Some are rather barren of trees unless you get a site on the fringes.

You can make reservations by calling © **866/439-7375** or 307/344-7311, or by writing Xanterra Parks & Resorts, P.O. Box 165, Yellowstone National Park, WY 82190.

REGULATIONS   You can set up your tent only in designated areas, and stays are limited to 14 days between June 15 and September 15, and to 30 days the rest of the year, except at Fishing Bridge, where there is no limit. Checkout time at all campgrounds is 10am. Quiet hours are enforced between the hours of 8pm and 8am (10pm–7am at Fishing Bridge). No generators or loud music is allowed during these hours.

THE CAMPGROUNDS   For exact information on prices, opening dates, and amenities, refer to the chart "Amenities for Each Campground: Yellowstone National Park," below.

These are campgrounds, not motels, so the amenities are sparse; but some have laundry facilities, showers, bathrooms, and potable water, which are luxuries to campers who've experienced the world's more primitive campgrounds.

In the northeast area of the park, the **Tower Fall campground** is near a convenience store, restaurant, and gas station at Tower Lodge, 19 miles north of Canyon Village and 18 miles east of Mammoth. **Slough Creek campground** ⊛ is in a remote section of the Lamar Valley near the northeast entrance; the good news is that there are fewer people, good fishing, and the possibility of wolf sightings; the bad news is that restroom facilities are pit toilets.

Canyon campground is the busiest in the park. Sites are in a heavily wooded area; the store, restaurants, visitor center, and laundry at Canyon Center are all nearby.

Because it's in an area of spring bear activity, attempts have been made over the years to close the **Fishing Bridge RV Park.** It's still open, but only hard-sided camping vehicles are allowed here.

Bridge Bay is located near the shores of Yellowstone Lake, so you get tremendous views, especially at sunrise and sunset. Unfortunately, though surrounded by the forest, much of the area is wide open, so there's not a whole lot of privacy. It's close to the marina (where fishing charters originate) and the boat-rental operation.

Madison ⊛ is in a wooded area just south of the river, a popular spot with good access to fishing and hiking. **Norris** ⊛ is one of the park's better camping areas, with attractive, wooded locations in the heart of the park, close to wildlife activity and the Gibbon River. These camp areas seem less like outdoor motels than the big campgrounds on the park's east side.

Amenities for Each Campground: Yellowstone National Park

CAMPGROUND	TOTAL SITES	RV HOOKUPS	DUMP STATION	TOILETS	DRINKING WATER	SHOWERS	FIRE PITS/ GRILLS	PUBLIC LAUNDRY	PHONE	RESERVE	FEES	OPEN
INSIDE THE PARK												
Bridge Bay *	425	No	Yes	Yes	Yes	No	Yes	No	Yes	Yes	$17	Late May to mid-Sept
Canyon *	250	No	No	Yes	Yes	Yes	Yes	Yes	Yes	Yes	$17	June to mid-Sept
Fishing Bridge RV Park *	346	Yes	Yes	Yes	Yes	Yes	Yes	Yes	Yes	Yes	$35	Mid-May to mid-Sept
Grant Village *	400	No	Yes	Yes	Yes	Yes	Yes	Yes	Yes	Yes	$17	Mid-June to Sept
Indian Creek	75	No	No	Yes	Yes	No	Yes	No	No	Yes	$12	June–Sept
Lewis Lake	85	No	No	Yes	Yes	No	Yes	No	No	No	$12	Mid-June to Nov
Madison *	277	No	Yes	Yes	Yes	No	Yes	No	Yes	Yes	$17	Early May to mid-Oct
Mammoth	85	No	No	Yes	Yes	No	Yes	No	Yes	No	$14	Year-round
Norris	100	No	No	Yes	Yes	No	Yes	No	Yes	No	$14	Mid-May to Sept
Pebble Creek	30	No	No	Yes	Yes	No	Yes	No	No	No	$12	Mid-June to Sept
Slough Creek	29	No	No	Yes	Yes	No	Yes	No	No	No	$12	Late May–Oct
Tower Fall	32	No	No	Yes	Yes	No	Yes	No	No	No	$12	Mid-May to late Sept
NEAR THE PARK												
Bakers Hole	73	Yes	No	Yes	Yes	No	Yes	No	Yes	Yes	$14	Late May to mid-Sept
Lonesomehurst	27	No	No	Yes	Yes	No	Yes	No	No	Yes	$14	Late May to mid-Sept
Rainbow Point	86	No	No	Yes	Yes	No	Yes	No	Yes	Yes	$14	Late May to mid-Sept

* Reserve through Xanterra Parks & Resorts; Fishing Bridge RV Park accepts only hard-sided vehicles.

3 Where to Camp near Yellowstone

There are three National Forest Service campgrounds in the **West Yellowstone** area, all located in the Gallatin National Forest (see "Amenities for Each Campground: Yellowstone National Park," above, for amenities, prices, and opening dates). They accommodate both RVs and tents, but during some periods in late summer they accept hard-sided vehicles only. All three are first-come, first-served, so it's best to stake out a spot early. The heavily forested **Bakers Hole,** just 3 miles north of West Yellowstone on U.S. Hwy. 191, is popular because of its fishing access. Both tents and RVs are accepted, and 30 sites have electric hookups. **Lonesomehurst,** 8 miles west of the park on U.S. Hwy. 20, and then 4 miles north on Hebgen Lake Road, is only a third of the size of Bakers Hole and fills up quickly in summer. It has tent and RV sites, some of them right on the shore of Hebgen Lake. You can reach **Rainbow Point** by driving 5 miles north of West Yellowstone on U.S. Hwy. 191, then 3 miles west on Forest Service Road 610, and then north for 2 miles on Forest Service Road 6954. Tucked away in the forest near Hebgen Lake, it accommodates both tents and RVs (no hookups) and has boating and fishing access. For further information on these campgrounds, call the **Hebgen Lake Ranger District** (© **406/823-6961**). You can find a wealth of information on the Forest Service website at www. fs.fed.us/r1/gallatin.

In addition, there are a few RV parks in or near West Yellowstone. While these parks have full utility hookups and are generally designed for hard-sided vehicles, if there's space left over and you're willing to pay the price for a utility hookup that you won't be able to fully utilize, an owner of an RV park might allow you to pitch your tent. The shady **Hide-Away RV Campground,** 320 Electric St. (© **406/646-9049;** www.hideawayrv.com), has cable TV hookups, wireless Internet, and showers. Rates are $28 to $30 for sites with hookups, and $19 for tents. The **Madison Arm Resort** on the south shore of Hebgen Lake (© **406/646-9328;** www.madisonarmresort. com) has both RV and tent sites ($30–$32 and $23 per night, respectively), cabins ($120 a night), a marina, and a peaceful setting. Both are open from mid-May to early October.

4 Where to Dine in Yellowstone

While they're not world-class establishments, Yellowstone's restaurants are well suited to their location and the appetites of their patrons: The portions definitely won't leave anyone going hungry.

Most of the menus include a selection of unadventurous, all-American meat-and-potatoes grub alongside a few more creative entrees. Consistency can be a problem because the volume is high and the kitchen staffs are seasonal.

If you're not up for restaurant dining but you don't want to cook over your camp stove the whole time, there is counter-style fast-food service at the **Yellowstone Park General Stores,** as well as snack shops and cafeterias at Canyon, Mammoth, Grant Village, Lake Lodge, and Old Faithful.

MAMMOTH HOT SPRINGS

You'll find the **Terrace Grill** at the opposite end of the building in which the **Mammoth Hotel Dining Room** is located. Here fast-food fare is served in a less formal and less pricey dining room; reservations are not accepted.

Mammoth Hotel Dining Room ✿ STEAKS/SEAFOOD   At Mammoth, there's a good balance between casual and formal because the dining room is reminiscent of an above-average neighborhood restaurant: comfortable and pleasant without too much of the hotel's Victorian past. The view of the Old Fort Yellowstone buildings and surrounding slopes is also quite enjoyable. The breakfast buffet is essentially identical to what you'll find here at other locations, featuring eggs, French toast, and the like. The lunch menu focuses on an array of sandwiches, including smoked turkey on Parmesan-crusted sourdough, a grilled vegetarian philly, and grilled bison bratwurst. The dinner menu includes prime rib, salmon, and other upper-end standbys, and the vegetarian entrees are surprisingly good.

At Mammoth Hot Springs. ℭ 307/344-7311. Reservations recommended in winter. Breakfast $4–$11; lunch $7–$12; dinner $9–$20. AE, DC, DISC, MC, V. Closed Oct to late Dec and early Mar to early May. Daily 6:30–10am, 11am–2pm, and 5–10pm.

CANYON VILLAGE AREA

Like restaurants in the other park centers, the eating options at Canyon Village consist of three choices: a casual soda fountain, a fast-food cafeteria, and a conventional dining room.

The **Canyon Glacier Pit Snack Bar,** which is operated by Yellowstone Park General Stores, is in the same building as the grocery store and souvenir shop. Seating is on stools in the fashion of a 1950s soda fountain. Breakfast consists of egg dishes, lunch is soup and sandwiches, and dinner is traditional Western food.

The **Canyon Lodge Cafeteria** is a fast-food alternative managed by Xanterra Parks & Resorts and is across the parking lot in the Canyon Lodge area. Hours are the same as at the snack bar, and the menu bears some striking similarities—but you might get through the cafeteria line faster than you would get a stool at the soda fountain. Next door is an inexpensive deli, **The Picnic Stop,** with sandwiches, salads, and other light fare.

Canyon Lodge Dining Room *Kids* STEAKS/SEAFOOD   This is a spacious dining area, a tad sterile perhaps, and when it fills up, it's noisy. The salad bar is long and loaded, but otherwise the dinner fare is largely geared toward the carnivore, with a wide selection of steaks alongside some seafood and pasta selections. The breakfast buffet is a good way to start your day, with all the standard American fixings. The crowds can be large at Canyon Village, but there is a relaxed and unhurried feel to this place that you don't find at some of the park's other busy points. Families, in particular, might appreciate the ability to take their time with their meals.

At Canyon Lodge. ℭ **307/344-7901.** Reservations are not accepted. Breakfast $5–$10; lunch $7–$12; dinner $9–$20. AE, DC, DISC, MC, V. June to mid-Sept daily 7–10:30am, 11:30am–2:30pm, and 5–10pm.

TOWER-ROOSEVELT AREA

Roosevelt Lodge Dining Room STEAKS/SEAFOOD   This is supposed to be the cowboy alternative to the fancier cuisine served at the bigger Yellowstone hotels, but the unadventurous menu will win over only the most naive city slickers. For breakfast, it's eggs and flapjacks; lunch is burgers and sandwiches. Come suppertime, the menu is dominated by middle-of-the-road American specialties, namely barbecue and steaks. A better idea: Join Roosevelt's Old West Dinner Cookout, and ride by horse or wagon through the Pleasant Valley to a chuckwagon dinner that includes cornbread, steak, watermelon, those famous beans, and apple crisp. It's a daily summer event (reservations required) that costs $63 to $75 for an adult, depending on the route of your horseback ride, or $53 if you go by wagon. Children pay $10 less.

At Tower Junction. ℭ **307/344-7901.** Reservations are not accepted, except for Old West cookouts. Breakfast $5–$8; lunch $6–$9; dinner $9–$25. AE, DC, DISC, MC, V. Summer daily 7–10:30am, 11:30am–4pm, and 5–9pm.

YELLOWSTONE LAKE

For the eat-on-the-run traveler, a **deli** in the Lake Yellowstone Hotel serves lighter fare in an area that is slightly larger than a broom closet. Just down the road, the **Yellowstone Park General Store** offers three meals in a section of the store that is shared with tourist items; the best bet here is breakfast or a burger. There is also a **cafeteria** serving three meals a day at Lake Lodge.

Lake Yellowstone Hotel 👪👪 CONTINENTAL This represents the finest dining Yellowstone has to offer, with a view of the lake stretching south from a vast dining room that doesn't feel crowded even when it's full. One of the best ways to start your day is with a generous breakfast buffet, but the stuffed French toast is also quite good. Lunch entrees are gourmet sandwiches and burgers. The dinner menu is the most adventurous in the park. Appetizers include chilled cucumber soup and lobster ravioli, while entrees include elk medallions and lobster tail, bison prime rib, and Idaho trout stuffed with mushrooms and tomatoes.

On the north side of the lake. 📞 **866/439-7375.** Dinner reservations required. Breakfast $5–$11; lunch $7–$12; dinner $17–$37. AE, DC, DISC, MC, V. Mid-May to early Oct daily 6:30–10:30am, 11:30am–2:30pm, and 5–10pm.

GRANT VILLAGE

The casual choice here is the **Lake House,** footsteps away from the Grant Village restaurant. It specializes in inexpensive fish entrees, as well as burgers and beer. No reservations are accepted. The **Village Grill** in the Yellowstone General Store here also serves three meals daily.

Grant Village Dining Room 👪 AMERICAN Breakfast and lunch at the Grant Village restaurant are much like those at the other restaurants in the park, although the chef often surprises diners with interesting dinner items that stray from the norm. Lunch might include pan-fried trout covered with toasted pecans and lemon butter, huge burgers, and ham and brie on a pretzel roll. The dinner menu ranges from pistachio-crusted chicken to portabella mushroom cannelloni to prime rib, but the specialty is trout, pan-fried with pecans. Quality and ambience here are comparable to those of the better dining rooms at the major park hotels.

At Grant Village. 📞 **866/439-7375.** Dinner reservations recommended. Breakfast $5–$10; lunch $7–$10; dinner $9–$20. AE, DC, DISC, MC, V. June–Sept daily 6:30–10am, 11:30am–2:30pm, and 5:30–10pm.

OLD FAITHFUL AREA

Choices abound here. For quick and inexpensive, the **Geyser Grill** at the **Old Faithful Snow Lodge** and the cafeterias at the **Old Faithful Lodge Cafeteria** serve lunch and dinner in a fast-food environment that fits the mood of a crowd on the move; the **Bear Paw Snack Shop,** an ice-cream stand in the lobby of the **Old Faithful Inn,** is your best choice for dessert. The **Yellowstone General Store** also has a lunch counter.

Obsidian Dining Room ✿ STEAKS/SEAFOOD   In the snazzy new Snow Lodge, a spacious restaurant provides a comparatively contemporary alternative to the dining room at the Old Faithful Inn. It's a little quieter, a little less expensive, and a little less formal. It still has some flash on the menu—braised bison short ribs shank and linguine with Tuscan chicken, for instance—and there is a breakfast gem, the veggie breakfast burrito. All things considered, it's a huge improvement over the cramped restaurant of the old Snow Lodge.

At the Old Faithful Snow Lodge. ℂ 307/344-7311. Reservations not accepted in summer. Breakfast and lunch $5–$12; dinner $14–$24. AE, DC, DISC, MC, V. Early May to mid-Oct and mid-Dec to mid-Mar daily 6:30am–10am, 11:30am–3pm, and 5–9:30pm.

Old Faithful Inn Dining Room ✿ STEAKS/SEAFOOD   The food notwithstanding, the true highlight is the gnarled log architecture of this distinguished historic inn. Breakfast is buffet or a la carte, and there's a lot to choose from. There's another buffet at lunchtime (headlined by barbecue beef and chicken), as well as a generous assortment of salads and sandwiches. The dinner menu is extensive, with rib-eye steaks, several fish dishes, and some vegetarian dishes. The fare has gotten more distinguished in recent years, with such creative options as pork *osso buco* and pan-seared elk medallions making regular appearances on the menu. However, quality and service remain inconsistent.

At the Old Faithful Inn. ℂ 866/439-7375. Dinner reservations required. Breakfast and lunch $5–$10; dinner $15–$31. AE, DC, DISC, MC, V. Mid-May to mid-Oct daily 6:30–10:30am, 11:30am–2:30pm, and 5–10pm. Closed in winter.

5 Where to Stay in Grand Teton National Park

The three concessionaires that operate lodgings within Grand Teton provide a range of accommodations that can suit any wallet or taste, but not every schedule. I say fairly often in this guide that fall and spring are the best times to have the parks to yourself, but these are not the easiest times to find a room. If you come in early May, you'll find padlocks on the doors everywhere but at Flagg Ranch, which technically isn't in Grand Teton but on the John D. Rockefeller Jr. Memorial Parkway. Likewise, by mid-October, you'll be bunking in Jackson.

You can get information about or make reservations for Jackson Lake Lodge, Jenny Lake Lodge, and Colter Bay Village through the **Grand Teton Lodge Company,** P.O. Box 250, Moran, WY 83013 (ℂ **800/628-9988** or 307/543-2811; www.gtlc.com). For **Signal**

Mountain Lodge, contact P.O. Box 50, Moran, WY 83013 (© **307/ 543-2831;** www.signalmountainlodge.com). Reservations at **Flagg Ranch** can be made by contacting P.O. Box 187, Moran, WY 83013 (© **800/443-2311;** www.flaggranch.com).

Rooms in Grand Teton National Park properties have telephones but no televisions or air-conditioning. You'll find televisions in the lounge areas at the Jackson Lodge, Signal Mountain Resort, and Flagg Ranch.

FLAGG RANCH VILLAGE AREA

2 miles from the south entrance to Yellowstone; 5 miles from the northern boundary of Grand Teton

Like Grant Village in Yellowstone, Flagg Ranch offers travelers the full gamut of services: cabins, tent and RV sites, an above-average restaurant, and a gas station. It has been a popular jumping-off spot for snowmobilers during winter months, but the cabins now close for the snowy season; snow-machine rental is the only service available December to March (© **800/224-1384**). Also, because it's situated in a stand of pines in the middle of nowhere, there's not much to do in the immediate vicinity except watch the Snake River roll by.

Flagg Ranch Resort ⋐   A few years ago, this resort just outside Yellowstone National Park was showing its age—the sort of place where a hunter would rent a drafty room in which to collapse after a few days in the woods. Not anymore: It's all fixed up, transformed into an all-season resort on the Snake River with log-and-luxury ambience. The newest accommodations are duplex and fourplex log cabins, constructed in the 1990s, featuring king-size beds, spacious sitting areas with writing desks and chests of drawers, wall-to-wall carpeting, and bathrooms with tub/shower combinations and separate vanities.

There's no livestock on the ranch these days, but herds of snowmobilers used to gather here in the winter to warm up before entering Yellowstone; however, the cabins are now closed during winter. In the summer, there are float trips, horseback rides, and excellent fishing in Polecat Creek or the Snake River. The lodge is a locus of activity, with its double-sided fireplace, fancy dining room, gift shop, espresso bar and pub with large-screen television, convenience store, and gas station. A campground and RV facility are situated on the grounds amid a stand of pine trees.

P.O. Box 187, Moran, WY 83013. © **800/443-2311** or 307/543-2861. www.flagg ranch.com. 92 cabins, 171 campsites. $165–$175 cabin double; $45 RV site; $20 tent site. AE, DISC, MC, V. Closed mid-Oct to mid-May. **Amenities:** Restaurant; lounge; tour desk; self-serve laundry.

COLTER BAY VILLAGE AREA

11 miles from the park's northern boundary; 10 miles from the Moran (east) entrance

The village provides an excellent base of operations for visitors who want to hike or enjoy the lake. It encompasses two restaurants, a visitor center, an amphitheater, a museum, a general store, a post office, a sporting-goods shop, and laundry facilities. Scenic cruises, fishing charters, and boat rentals of all kinds can be arranged at the marina. The village operates from mid-May to late September.

Colter Bay Village 🅰️ *Kids*   You might call this the people's resort of Grand Teton, with simpler lodgings, lower prices, and a lively, friendlier atmosphere that seems particularly suited to families. Situated on the eastern shore of Jackson Lake, Colter Bay Village is a full-fledged recreation center. Guest accommodations are in rough log cabins perched on a wooded hillside; they are clean and simply furnished with area rugs on tile floors and reproductions of pioneer furnishings—chests, oval mirrors, and extra-long bedsteads with painted headboards.

If you want to take a trip back to the early days of American auto travel, when car camping involved unwieldy canvas tents on slabs by the roadside, you can spend an inexpensive night in "tent cabins." (Sleeping bags, pillows, and blankets are available to rent.) The shower and bathroom are communal. Overall, the village provides an excellent base of operations for visitors because it has the most facilities of any area in the park.

P.O. Box 250, Moran, WY 83013. ℂ 800/628-9988 or 307/543-2811. www.gtlc. com. 166 units. $41–$165 log cabin; $41 tent cabin. MC, V. Closed late Sept to late May. **Amenities:** 2 restaurants; tour desk; self-serve laundry. *In room:* No phone.

Jackson Lake Lodge 🅰️🅰️   Much the way that Old Faithful Inn or the Lake Yellowstone Hotel captures historic eras of Yellowstone tourism, Jackson Lake Lodge epitomizes the architectural milieu of the period when Grand Teton became a park. That era was the 1950s, an age of right angles, flat roofs, and big windows. While not as distinctive as Yellowstone's standouts, the lodge is more functional and comfortable than its northern counterparts. The setting is sublime, overlooking Willow Flats with the lake in the distance, and, towering over it without so much as a stick in the way, the Tetons and Mount Moran. You don't even have to go outside to see this impressive view—the lobby has 60-foot-wide windows showcasing the panorama. A few guest rooms are in the three-story main lodge, but most are in cottages scattered about the property, some of which have large balconies and mountain views. Lodge rooms are spacious and cheery, and most offer double beds, electric heat, and newly tiled bathrooms. Both the lodge and cottage rooms are comparable to an upper-tier chain hotel, with an American Indian motif. For a premium, the view rooms provide guests with a private picture window facing the Tetons.

P.O. Box 250, Moran, WY 83013. © **800/628-9988** or 307/543-2811. www.gtlc. com. 385 units. $189–$269 double; $450–$625 suite. MC, V. Closed mid-Oct to mid-May. **Amenities:** 2 restaurants; lounge; heated outdoor pool; airport shuttle; activity desk; wireless Internet. *In room:* Dataport, coffeemaker, hair dryer, iron.

SIGNAL MOUNTAIN AREA
15 miles from the north entrance; 9 miles from the Moran (east) entrance

Signal Mountain Lodge *(★)* *(Finds)*   Signal Mountain has a different feel—and different owners—from the other lodgings in Grand Teton, adding to the sense that any place you choose to stay in this park is going to give you a fairly unique atmosphere. What they all have in common is the Teton view, and this lodge, located right on the banks of Jackson Lake, might have the best. To top it off, it's got lakefront retreats, which you can really inhabit, with stoves and refrigerators and foldout sofa beds for the kids. Other accommodations, mostly rustic log cabins, come in a variety of flavors, from motel-style rooms in four-unit buildings set amid the trees to family bungalows with decks, some enjoying beach frontage. These carpeted units are nicely maintained, featuring handmade pine furniture, electric heat, covered porches, and tiled bathrooms; some have fireplaces, and all are nonsmoking. Recreational options include rafting and fishing, and sailboat tours on the lake. A convenience store and gas station are on the property.

P.O. Box 50, Moran, WY 83013. © **307/543-2831.** www.signalmountainlodge.com. 80 units. $151 double; $120–$240 cabin units. AE, DISC, MC, V. Closed late Oct to early May. **Amenities:** 2 restaurants; tour desk. *In room:* Kitchenette.

JENNY LAKE AREA
28 miles from the northern boundary; 17 miles from the Moran (east) entrance; 16 miles from the south entrance

Jenny Lake Lodge *(★★★)*   My favorite property in any national park, this lodge justifiably prides itself on seclusion, award-winning food, and the individual attention that comes with a cabin resort kept intentionally small. The property is a hybrid of mountain-lake resort and dude ranch, with various extras included in its prices, such as horseback rides, meals, walking sticks, umbrellas, and cool cruiser bicycles. The cabins, each named for a resident flower, are rustic on the outside and luxurious within—decorated with bright braided rugs, dark wood floors, beamed ceilings, cushy plaid armchairs, and tiled bathrooms. Rooms have one queen-size, one king-size, or two queen beds. Some were old dude-ranch cabins from the 1920s, and some were built on the property in 1992; the latter have larger baths and more modernity, but not as much character.

Catering to an older, affluent, and exceedingly loyal clientele, the style here is a throwback: a blend of peaceful rusticity and occasional reminders of class and formality (jackets are "appreciated"). Generally, though, if you aren't sweating the prices, Jenny Lake Lodge offers a wonderful chance to unwind in a fairly isolated, feet-up-on-the-rail atmosphere with scenery and service that can't be matched.

P.O. Box 250, Moran, WY 83013. ℂ **800/628-9988** or 307/543-2811. www.gtlc. com. 37 units. $525 double; $695–$750 suite. Extra person $140 a night. Rates include MAP (modified American plan), horseback riding, and use of bicycles. AE, MC, V. Closed mid-Oct to May. **Amenities:** Restaurant; lounge; tour desk; wireless Internet. *In room:* Dataport, fridge, coffeemaker.

MOOSE AREA
36 miles south of the northern boundary; 18 miles from the Moran (east) entrance; 8 miles south of Jenny Lake.

Moulton Ranch Cabins *(Value* A century-old homestead now offers an off-the-beaten-track alternative to the bustling developments on Jackson and Jenny lakes. The small but comfortable cabins here are a few miles west of Moose Junction, scattered around a verdant, private acre entirely surrounded by the park. The cabins, built in stages from the 1930s to 2004, range from dinky to family-sized, and packages are available to those who require numerous cabins. The Granary and Bunkhouse are larger, with kitchenettes and space for six to sleep.

Mormon Row, Kelly, WY 83011. ℂ **307/733-3749.** www.moultonranchcabins.com. 5 units. $75–$190 for up to 6 people. MC, V. Closed Oct–Apr. No pets. No smoking. *In room:* Kitchenette, no phone.

Spur Ranch Cabins *☆* An outfitter's camp since the 1940s, Dornan's is now a collection of year-round cabins built in the 1990s. Located at a family-owned operation in Moose that also includes a market, a wine shop, an outdoors store, guide services, and dining, the dozen cabins here are a good option for families and larger groups. All the units have tub/shower combinations, fitting lodgepole-pine furnishings, and fully equipped kitchens. Two of the cabins are right on the Snake River, but they're often booked a year in advance during peak season.

P.O. Box 39, Moose, WY 83012. ℂ 307/733-2522. www.dornans.com. 12 units. $175–$250 for up to 6 people. AE, DISC, MC, V. **Amenities:** 2 restaurants; lounge. *In room:* Kitchen.

6 Where to Camp in Grand Teton

Because Grand Teton is so much smaller than its counterpart to the north, distances between campgrounds are reduced substantially. As a consequence, selecting a site in one of the five National Park Service campgrounds within the park becomes a matter of preference (rather than geography) and availability. There are five campgrounds in Grand Teton: the Grand Teton Lodge Company operates Gros Ventre, Jenny Lake, and Colter Bay; Signal Mountain Lodge runs Signal Mountain and Lizard Creek. Two other campgrounds, the Colter Bay Trailer Village and the Flagg Ranch campground, are operated by park concessionaires and are the only campgrounds with RV hookups (Flagg Ranch has sites suitable for RVs as well as tents, while the Colter Bay Trailer Village is for RVs only). The only sites in the park where RVs are not allowed are those at Jenny Lake, which has a tent-only campground.

GETTING A CAMPSITE   Campgrounds operate on a first-come, first-served basis, but reservations are available to groups of 10 or more from the **Grand Teton Lodge Company,** P.O. Box 250, Moran, WY 83013 (ℂ **800/628-9988** or 307/543-2811; www.gtlc. com). You can get recorded information on site availability by calling ℂ **307/739-3603.** You may also make reservations for **trailer sites** at Colter Bay campground by contacting the Grand Teton Lodge Co. Additionally, **Grand Teton Campground** is a concessionaire-operated campground located in the Flagg Ranch complex on the John D. Rockefeller Jr. Memorial Parkway. The area has 97 sites with utility hookups, 74 tent sites, showers, and a launderette. For reservations, contact **Flagg Ranch,** P.O. Box 187, Moran, WY 83013 (ℂ **800/443-2311;** www.flaggranch.com).

THE CAMPGROUNDS   For exact information on prices, opening dates, and amenities, refer to the chart "Amenities for Each Campground: Grand Teton National Park," below. Note that where campgrounds accommodate RVs, they are not given a separate section away from tent campers.

All the park-run campgrounds but Jenny Lake can accommodate tents, RVs, and trailers, but there are no utility hookups at any of them. **Jenny Lake Campground** 🐾🐾, a tents-only area, is situated

Amenities for Each Campground: Grand Teton National Park

CAMPGROUND	TOTAL SITES	RV HOOKUPS	DUMP STATION	TOILETS	DRINKING WATER	SHOWERS	FIRE PITS/ GRILLS	LAUNDRY	PUBLIC PHONE	RESERVE	FEES	OPEN
INSIDE THE PARK												
Colter Bay	350	No	Yes	Yes	Yes	Yes	Yes	Yes	Yes	No	$17	Late May to late Sept
Colter Bay Trailer Village	112	Yes	Yes	Yes	Yes	No	Yes	Yes	Yes	Yes	$32–$49	Late May to late Sept
Gros Ventre	365	No	Yes	Yes	Yes	No	Yes	No	Yes	No	$17	Early May to mid-Oct
Jenny Lake *	51	No	No	Yes	Yes	No	Yes	No	Yes	No	$19	Mid-May to late Sept
Lizard Creek	60	No	No	Yes	Yes	No	Yes	No	Yes	No	$17	Early June to early Sept
Signal Mountain	81	No	Yes	Yes	Yes	No	Yes	No	Yes	No	$17	Mid-May to Oct
NEAR THE PARK												
Flagg Ranch	171	Yes	Yes	Yes	Yes	Yes	Yes	Yes	Yes	Yes	$20–$45	Mid-May to late Sept
Snake River Park KOA	90	Yes	Yes	Yes	Yes	Yes	Yes	Yes	Yes	Yes	$27–$33/ $38–$49	Mid-Apr to early Oct

* Tents only are allowed here.

in a quiet, wooded area near the lake. You have to be here first thing in the morning to get a site.

The largest campground, **Gros Ventre,** is the last to fill, if it fills at all—probably because it's located on the east side of the park, a few miles from Kelly on the Gros Ventre River Road. If you arrive late in the day and you have no place to stay, go here first.

Signal Mountain Campground ⚔, with views of the lake and access to the beach, is another popular spot that fills first thing in the morning. It overlooks Jackson Lake and Mount Moran, as well as a pleasant picnic area and boat launch. There are a store and a service station nearby.

Colter Bay Campground and Trailer Village has access to the lake but is far enough from the hubbub of the village to offer a modicum of solitude; spaces are usually gone by noon.

Lizard Creek Campground, at the north end of Grand Teton National Park near Jackson Lake, offers an aesthetically pleasing wooded area near the lake with views of the Tetons, bird-watching, and fishing (and mosquitoes—bring your repellent). It's only 8 miles from facilities at Colter Bay, and its sites fill by 2pm.

7 Where to Camp near Grand Teton

There are several places to park the RV or pitch a tent around Jackson Hole, and a few of them are reasonably priced and not too far away from the park. Most charge around $40 per night, although prices seem to change at the drop of a hat, just like local motel prices. Your best bets are outside of the city limits, away from the crowds and the constant buzz of traffic. See the chart "Amenities for Each Campground: Grand Teton National Park," above, for amenities, prices, and opening dates.

8 Where to Dine in Grand Teton

Just as in Yellowstone, there are not enough places at the table to serve all the travelers in Grand Teton during the busiest mealtimes of July and August, but the higher-end options are the best restaurants in any of the national parks. Because there is more than one concessionaire operating the full-service dining rooms, there is no central number for making reservations.

NEAR THE NORTHERN BOUNDARY

In addition to Flagg Ranch, tasty gourmet pizzas are available at **Leeks Marina** (© 307/543-2494), which is located inside the park, a few miles north of Colter Bay.

The Bear's Den *Kids* AMERICAN   Served at the main lodge at Flagg Ranch, the food at this oasis is better than what's typically found in what most refer to as a "family restaurant," and servings are generous. The dinner menu includes fish, chicken, and beef dishes, as well as home-style entrees such as ranch beef stew and chicken potpie; lunch and dinner are unadventurous but hearty. The ambience is also pleasant during both winter and summer months; wooden chairs and tables with colorful upholstery liven up this newly constructed log building.

At Flagg Ranch, John D. Rockefeller Jr. Pkwy. © 800/443-2311. Reservations accepted. Breakfast $5–$11; lunch $8–$11; dinner $11–$24. AE, DISC, MC, V. Summer 7–10:30am, 11:30am–1pm, and 5–9:30pm.

COLTER BAY

John Colter Cafe Court DELI/FAST FOOD   Here you'll find the two sit-down restaurants in the village (although there's also a snack shop in the grocery store). Three meals are served daily during the summer months. The **cafe** serves sandwiches, burgers, and pretty good Mexican fare. Breakfasts at the **Chuckwagon** are hearty; lunch is a soup-and-salad bar and hot sandwiches; dinner is casual and family-friendly. Among the dinner entrees are trout, lasagna, pork chops, beef stew, and New York strip steaks. The ambience is very casual and straightforward because these restaurants cater mostly to families.

Across from the visitor center and marina in Colter Bay Village. © 307/543-2811. Reservations not accepted. Breakfast $3–$6; lunch $5–$10; dinner $8–$18. MC, V. Daily 6:30am–10pm. Closed Oct–Apr.

JACKSON LAKE JUNCTION

The **Blue Heron** cocktail lounge at the Jackson Lake Lodge is one of the nicest spots in either park to enjoy a drink. The lounge here offers the same views as at The Mural Room (see below), as well as live entertainment.

The Mural Room *★★* BEEF/WILD GAME   Jackson Lake's main dining room is quiet and fairly formal, catering to a more sedate crowd as well as corporate groups; it's also more expensive than other park restaurants. The floor-to-ceiling windows provide stellar views across a meadow that is moose habitat and to the lake and the Cathedral

Group. (The staff applauds sunset every night.) Walls inside are adorned with hand-painted Western murals created by Carl Roeters.

The food is the perfect complement to the view, and markedly superior to most of what you'll find in Yellowstone. Three meals are served daily in summer. Breakfast items include a continental breakfast, Belgian waffles, and vegetarian eggs Benedict. Dinner might be a grand five-course event that includes a shrimp cocktail, French onion soup, and Caesar salad, followed by an entree of Idaho trout, buffalo prime rib, vegetable lasagna, or rack of lamb. Aside from the dining room at Jenny Lake Lodge and Lake Yellowstone Hotel, this is the most romantic and upscale eatery in either park.

At Jackson Lake Lodge. © 800/628-9988 or 307/543-2811, ext. 3463. Reservations not accepted. Breakfast buffet $13, lunch $7–$14; dinner $17–$35. MC, V. Summer daily 7–9:30am, 11:30am–1:30pm, and 5:30–9pm.

Pioneer Grill *Kids* AMERICAN   Bedecked with regional homesteading antiques and photos, this 1950s-style luncheonette, with its curling counter and old-fashioned soda fountain, offers hearty meals and a casual, friendly atmosphere. Breakfasts are basic but ideal for hiking appetites—bagels, eggs, flapjacks, and the like. For lunch, try one of the Grill's ever-popular buffalo burgers, or a plump turkey sandwich. Dinner is similarly laid-back and traditional—you can't miss with the pan-fried local rainbow trout. When a tour bus stops at the lodge, the restaurant is often overrun with business, so you might want to head next door to The Mural Room if you're looking for peace or romance. If you're looking for convenience, good service, and a relatively quick meal, though, this is the spot. It's the only restaurant in the area to offer a kids' menu.

At Jackson Lake Lodge. © 800/628-9988 or 307/543-2811. Reservations not accepted. Breakfast $4–$10; lunch and dinner $6 $18. MC, V. Summer daily 6am–10pm.

Signal Mountain Lodge *Value* SANDWICHES/MEXICAN/ CONTINENTAL   There are actually two restaurants here, serving delicious food in the friendliest style in the park. The fine dining room and lounge are called **Peaks** and **Deadman's Bar,** respectively, and the **Trapper Grill** supplements the continental fare with Mexican entrees, pizzas, and plump sandwiches. You eat up the scenery, too, with a view of Jackson Lake and Mount Moran.

Bargain hunters flock to the bar for the decadent nachos supreme: a foot-tall mountain of chips, cheese, chicken, beef, beans, and peppers that runs a mere $14. You'll easily fill four people for that price, leaving you plenty of change for the bar's signature blackberry margaritas. Because the bar has one of three televisions in the park and is equipped with cable for sports nuts, the crowd tends to be young and noisy. Full meals are served in the proper dining room, with an emphasis on sustainable cuisine. Entrees include free-range chicken with organic black beans and rice, vegetarian lasagna, and filet mignon served on a potato cake with sautéed spinach, the most expensive entree.

At Signal Mountain Resort. © **307/543-2831.** Reservations required for breakfast and dinner. Breakfast $6–$8; lunch $7–$10; dinner $10–$35. AE, DISC, MC, V. Summer daily 7–10am and 11:30am–10pm.

JENNY LAKE

Jenny Lake Lodge Dining Room ✸✸✸ CONTINENTAL   The finest meals in either park (or, for that matter, in *any* park) are served here, where a talented chef creates culinary delights for guests and, occasionally, a president of the United States. Breakfast, lunch, and dinner are served here, and all are spectacular. (Nonguests should have lunch here if they can.) The five-course dinner is the bell-ringer, though. Guests choose from appetizers that might include elk carpaccio; salads with organic greens, pecans, and dried cherries; and entrees such as pan-roasted squab, herb-rubbed rabbit leg, or a venison strip loin. Desserts are equally creative and tantalizing. Price is no object, at least for guests, because meals are included in the room charge; nonguests should expect a hefty bill. Casual dress is discouraged, with jackets requested for dinner.

At Jenny Lake Lodge. © **307/733-4647.** Reservations required. Prix-fixe breakfast $19; lunch main courses $9–$17; prix-fixe dinner $67, not including alcoholic beverages. AE, MC, V. Summer daily 7:30–9am, noon–1:30pm, and 6–8:45pm.

MOOSE

Chuckwagon fare (three meals a day) and pasta dishes and pizzas (lunch and dinner) are available at two separate facilities at **Dornan's** (© **307/733-2415**). The outdoor **Spur Bar** is a great place to watch the sun set and enjoy a cocktail.

8

Gateways to Yellowstone & Grand Teton National Parks

Yellowstone and Grand Teton national parks are accessible from all four points of the compass. One of the biggest decisions facing you will be where to commence your journey and base yourself while you're in the area, if you choose not to stay in one of the parks themselves.

1 West Yellowstone, Montana

At the west entrance of Yellowstone National Park

Yellowstone's west entrance is a bastion for tourism, chock-full of accommodations, restaurants, souvenir shops, and outfitters. The personality of the town has changed since the popularity of snowmobile excursions increased winter traffic on Yellowstone's roads; it now offers more, and better, year-round facilities.

Originally called Riverside, and then Yellowstone, the name was officially changed to West Yellowstone in 1920 when Gardiner residents grudgingly complained that people would assume that the town was the park. Regardless of its name, this place is about shopping, not nature, and its biggest attraction is a zoolike look at regional wildlife in the Grizzly and Wolf Discovery Center.

ESSENTIALS

GETTING THERE   For information on air service and car rentals, see "Getting There," in chapter 2. To drive to West Yellowstone from Bozeman (91 miles), take U.S. Hwy. 191 south to its junction with U.S. Hwy. 287 and head straight into town. From Idaho Falls, take I-15 north about 50 miles to U.S. Hwy. 20, which takes you directly into West Yellowstone, a 53-mile drive.

VISITOR INFORMATION   Contact the **West Yellowstone Chamber of Commerce,** 30 Yellowstone Ave., P.O. Box 458, West Yellowstone, MT 59758 (© **406/646-7701;** www.westyellowstone chamber.com).

GETTING OUTSIDE

Yellowstone is obviously the big draw here, but there is plenty of wilderness west of the park in the Targhee and Gallatin national forests. The area around West Yellowstone ranks among the best **fishing** locales in the country. There are also numerous **hiking** and **kayaking** opportunities near the town. Come winter, **snowcoach tours** and **snowmobiling tours** are huge draws for West Yellowstone, and Yellowstone rangers come into town and lead **snowshoe walks.** The town also has a gem of a network of groomed cross-country ski trails that interconnect with trails on public lands. Every major hotel and motel in town offers snowmobile packages that include a room and a sled rental; just be sure to book well in advance. For more information on all of these activities, see chapter 4.

SEEING THE SIGHTS

Grizzly and Wolf Discovery Center   Those who haven't the patience to search out and observe the free-ranging wildlife of Yellowstone might want to try this not-for-profit educational center. The interpretive center gives a detailed explanation of these animals' history in this country, along with the difficult and controversial efforts to revive them in the wild. This is a closer look than you'll likely get with animals in the wild, but did you really come to Yellowstone to look at grizzlies imported from Alaska in an enclosure?

201 S. Canyon St. in Grizzly Park. ℂ **800/257-2570** or 406/646-7001. www.grizzly discoveryctr.org. $9.75 adults, $9 seniors, $5 children 5–12, free for children under 5. Daily 8am–dusk; shorter hours in winter.

Yellowstone Historic Center ⍟   Located in the historic 1909 Union Pacific depot, this is the only museum that focuses on Yellowstone's cultural history, providing an interesting snapshot into the ways of the park's first tourists, with scads of memorabilia, postcards, and concessionaire ephemera. There are also displays on the historic Yellowstone railroad and other transportation, covering epochal events such as the 1959 earthquake that created Quake Lake and the 1988 fires, along with a mounted grizzly bear known in his animate days as "Old Snaggletooth."

At Yellowstone Ave. and Canyon St. ℂ 406/646-1100. www.yellowstonehistoric center.org. $5 adults, $4 seniors, $3 children and students, free for children under 3. Families receive 20% discount. Mid-May to mid-Oct daily 9am–9pm. Closed rest of year.

Yellowstone IMAX Theater   This theater is next door to the Grizzly and Wolf Discovery Center, and together they form the centerpieces of a real-estate development on the edge of the park, which includes several new hotels. Regardless, the IMAX concept works pretty well here—there are things an airborne camera can show you on a six-story-tall screen that you'll never see on your own two feet. A film called *Yellowstone* plays fairly often, with swooping views of the canyon, falls, and other sights.

101 S. Canyon St. ℂ **406/646-4100.** www.yellowstoneimax.com. $9 adults, $8.50 seniors, $6.50 children 3–12, free for children under 3. Summer 8:30am–9pm, shorter hours in winter. Call for exact show times.

WHERE TO STAY

Make your reservations early if you want to visit in July or August, or if you're going to spend Christmas to New Year's here. If you're smart, you'll come in the fall, when there are plenty of empty rooms and better rates, and spend your days fishing the Henry's Fork or one of the other great streams in the vicinity. Rates for rooms often reflect the seasonal traffic, and prices fluctuate. Unless noted, all these establishments are open year-round.

West Yellowstone Central Reservations handles booking for many of the hotels (ℂ **888/646-7077;** www.yellowstonereservation. com). You'll find chains like **ClubHouse Inn** (ℂ **406/646-4892;** www.clubhouseinn.com) at 105 S. Electric St., with summertime doubles for $119 to $169; and **Days Inn** (ℂ **800/548-9551** or 406/ 646-7656; www.daysinn.com), at 301 Madison Ave., with rates of $115 to $165 for a double. There are three **Best Western** affiliates, ranging from about $100 to $150 a night for a double during the summer. Call ℂ **800/528-1234,** or go online to **www.bestwestern. com** for information and reservations. The **One Horse Motel,** at 216 N. Dunraven St. (ℂ **800/488-2750** or 406/646-7677; www. onehorsemotel.com), is a top-notch independent across the street from City Park, with doubles for $82 to $92 a night. Another good inexpensive option (with more character than the chains, to boot), the 1912 **Madison Hotel,** 139 Yellowstone Ave. (ℂ **800/838-7745** or 406/646-7745; www.madisonhotelmotel.com), has historic rooms for $41 to $75 for a double and newer motel doubles for $70 to $130. Another option with historic cachet—and a one-time favorite of broadcasting legend Charles Kuralt—is the **Parade Rest Guest Ranch,** 10 miles north of West Yellowstone at 1279 Grayling Rd. (ℂ **800/753-5934** or 406/646-7217; www.paraderestranch.com), in a serene setting near Hebgen Lake. Rates are about $180 per day for adults and $100 to $140 for kids, all meals and horseback riding included.

Bar N Ranch ⟨⟨⟨ One of the oldest brands in Montana, the Bar N is an excellent new lodging option in West Yellowstone, operating a spiffed-up lodge and cabin complex since 2004. Located on 200 acres of unsullied ranchland with 2 miles of the Madison River and a fishing pond, the lodge is an image of the New West, with a great river-rock fireplace and a knotty pine banister leading up to the rooms upstairs. The lodge rooms mix equal parts Ralph Lauren and Old West, exuding a simple but rich style with antler lamps, hardwood floors, stark white or warm walls, and jetted tubs. The cabins are one- and two-bedroom units arranged in a half-circle around the lodge, with decor that echoes that of the lodge; all of them have fireplaces and private outdoor hot tubs. The staff can arrange for guides to take guests fishing, rafting, or horseback riding for an extra fee. The lodge has Wi-Fi Internet access.

890 Buttermilk Creek Rd. (P.O. Box 250), West Yellowstone, MT 59758. ℂ **406/646-0300.** Fax 406/646-0301. www.bar-n-ranch.com. 14 units, including 7 cabins. Lodge rooms $213–$227 double; cabins $260–$330 double; lower rates Oct–June. AE, DC, DISC, MC, V. **Amenities:** Restaurant; small outdoor pool; Jacuzzi; tour desk; wireless Internet. *In room:* TV/DVD player, fridge, coffeemaker, no phone.

Holiday Inn SunSpree Resort ⟨ This big resort is the town's best hotel. The rooms are sizable and comfortable, well maintained, and freshly updated. At the tour desk, you can arrange fishing and rafting trips, bike and ATV rentals, and chuckwagon cookouts. The Iron Horse Saloon serves regional microbrews, and the Oregon Short Line Restaurant serves Western cuisine including game and seafood dishes. At the center of the restaurant sits the restored railroad club car that brought Victorian gents to Yellowstone a century ago.

315 Yellowstone Ave. (P.O. Box 470), West Yellowstone, MT 59758. ℂ **800/646-7365** or 406/646-7365. www.doyellowstone.com. 123 units. $99–$175 double; $119–$225 suite. AE, DISC, MC, V. **Amenities:** Restaurant; lounge; large indoor pool; health club; Jacuzzi; sauna; bike rental; children's program; tour desk; self-serve laundry. *In room:* A/C, TV, dataport, microwave, fridge, coffeemaker, hair dryer, iron.

Moose Creek Cabins ⟨ *Finds* A 1950s motel complex that got a slick revamp in 2004, Moose Creek Cabins offers comfortable and stylish rooms and cabins in the heart of West Yellowstone. The one-time Ranger Motel—which spent 2 decades as employee housing before becoming Moose Creek—is a good value and one of the better maintained properties in town. There are stand-alone kitchenette cabins (good for families) and cabin-style motel rooms with queen beds; both are laden with pine and charming individual themes.

220 Firehole Ave., West Yellowstone, MT 59758. ℂ 406/646-9546. www.moose creekcabin.com. 13 units and cabins. $79–$92 double; $105–$145 cabin. MC, V. *In room:* Cable TV, wireless Internet, kitchenette, coffeemaker, no phone.

Three Bear Lodge *(Kids* The cozy, pine-furnished rooms of this family-style inn are located less than 3 blocks from the park entrance. The motel-style rooms are of above-average quality, reliable, and clean, and there are some in-room hot tubs and a few large family rooms for those traveling with kids. Like just about every other lodging in West Yellowstone, the Three Bear offers snowmobile and snowcoach tours in the winter, as well as van tours in the summer.

217 Yellowstone Ave. (P.O. Box 1590), West Yellowstone, MT 59758. ℂ 800/646-7353 or 406/646-7353. Fax 406/646-4567. www.threebearlodge.com. 74 units. $73–$108 double. AE, DISC, MC, V. **Amenities:** Restaurant; lounge; outdoor heated pool (seasonal); exercise room; 2 indoor Jacuzzis; sauna. *In room:* TV, coffeemaker, hair dryer, iron.

WHERE TO DINE

West Yellowstone is a good place to stop for a quick bite on your way into the park. Apart from the choices listed below, **Uncle Laurie's Riverside Café,** 237 U.S. Hwy. 20 (ℂ **406/646-7040**), is a small but excellent alternative to steak 'n' eggs breakfast joints. The menu migrates from breakfast calzones and huckleberry cinnamon rolls to lunches of cold sandwiches, wraps, and "stinky burgers," so named for their garlic content. For coffee and baked goods, visit the espresso bar at the excellent **Book Peddler** in Canyon Square (ℂ **406/646-9358**). **Morning Glory Coffee,** 129 Dunraven St. (ℂ **406/646-7061**), roasts its own beans on-site and offers a low-key atmosphere for getting going.

Beartooth Barbecue *☆* BARBECUE A bustling and funky space that plates up some mean Texas-style barbecue, this is my pick for a casual meal in West Yellowstone. At the bar or a table in the bric-a-brac-laden room (hanging from the walls are sleds, ristas, a traffic light, and sports memorabilia), order a plate of St. Louis–cut spareribs or beef brisket for lunch or dinner (or a sandwich with brisket, sausage, or chicken), and plenty of tangy sauce. The bar has beers from the local Wolf Pack Brewery on draft and serves wine by the glass, but no liquor is served. Breakfasts are pancakes, burritos, and egg dishes.

111 Canyon St. ℂ **406/646-0227**. Breakfast $6–$9; lunch and dinner $8–$24. MC, V. Daily 7am–10pm.

The Canyon Street Grill *(Value* AMERICAN   It's hard not to like an establishment whose slogan is "We are not a fast-food restaurant. We are a cafe reminiscent of a bygone era when the quality of the food meant more than how fast it could be served." With checkerboard floors and shiny red booths, this delightful 1950s-style spot serves hearty food for breakfast, lunch, and dinner. Hamburgers and chicken sandwiches are popular, accompanied by milkshakes made with hard ice cream or a crisp glass of huckleberry cream soda.

22 Canyon St. (C) **406/646-7548.** Main courses $4–$11. MC, V. May–Nov Mon–Sat 11am–11pm; Dec–Mar Mon–Sat 11am–3pm. Closed Apr.

Eino's Tavern (R) *(Finds* AMERICAN   Locals snowmobile out from West Yellowstone to Eino's (there's a trail that follows U.S. Hwy. 191) to become their own chefs at the grill here. It's a novel concept, and it keeps patrons coming back to this casual restaurant with a fine view of Hebgen Lake time and time again. There's usually a line out the door, but it's fun to peruse the walls, plastered with dollar bills and other currency as well as bras and funny photos, while you wait. After placing your order for a steak, teriyaki chicken, hamburger, or hot dog, keep a straight face when you're handed an uncooked piece of meat. Go to the grill, slap it on, and stand around, drink in hand, shooting the breeze with other patrons until your food is exactly the way you like it. Steaks and chicken come with your choice of a salad (or twice-baked potatoes in winter), and hamburgers come with chips.

155 Eino's Loop (9 miles north of West Yellowstone on U.S. Hwy. 191). (C) **406/646-9344.** Main courses $5.50–$26. No credit cards; ATM on premises. Winter daily 9am–9pm; rest of year daily noon–9pm. Closed Thanksgiving to mid-Dec.

The Outpost Restaurant *(Kids* AMERICAN   Tucked away in a downtown mall, this rustic restaurant laden with Western bric-a-brac serves old-fashioned home-style fare, such as its hearty beef stew, with fork-size chunks of carrots and potatoes. There's also salmon, steak, trout, liver, and an excellent salad bar. For breakfast, if you're really hungry, you can't beat the Campfire Omelette, smothered in homemade chili, cheese, and onions. The menu isn't all that adventurous, and there's none of the vices you'll find in the local taverns (no video poker, beer, wine, liquor, or smoking); but it offers solid fare in a quiet, family-friendly atmosphere. The homemade desserts include chocolate cream pie and a wild huckleberry sundae.

115 Yellowstone Ave. (in the Montana Outpost Mall). (C) **406/646-7303.** Breakfast $4.50–$10; lunch $5–$11; dinner $7–$20. AE, DISC, MC, V. Daily 6:30am–10:30pm. Closed mid-Oct to mid-Apr.

Sydney's Mountain Bistro ☆☆ CONTEMPORARY AMERI-
CAN   The most upscale option in a meat-and-potatoes town, Sydney's offers an intimate, white-tablecloth setting, an excellent wine
list, and a menu that balances seafood and vegetarian fare with beef,
poultry, and pork. With interesting preparations—such as flash-fried
calamari for starters and entrees including sweet-chile salmon and
orange Thai curry chicken—and a breezy patio complementing the
upscale atmosphere inside, this is my pick for a special meal in West
Yellowstone. Lunches are fairly traditional, mainly sandwiches and
burgers, as well as a quiche of the day and a savory walnut pesto salad.

38 Canyon St. ℭ **406/646-7660.** Brunch and lunch $5–$9.50; dinner $10–$26.
MC, V. Mon–Fri 11am–3pm; Sat–Sun 10am–3pm; Tues–Sat 5–9:30pm.

2 Gardiner, Montana ☆

At the north entrance to Yellowstone National Park

At the other end of the spectrum from West Yellowstone is Gardiner,
which provides the only year-round access to Yellowstone on the north
side. Although this tiny town (pop. 1,000) booms and busts with the
tourist season, full-time residents manage to lead regular lives that
include soccer practice, a day on the river, and a night on the town.
For these folks, deer, elk, and bison meandering through the streets are
no big deal. If you need additional information, contact the **Gardiner
Chamber of Commerce,** 222 Park St., P.O. Box 81, Gardiner, MT
59030 (ℭ **406/848-7971;** www.gardinerchamber.com).

GETTING OUTSIDE

Gardiner is the spot to go for white-water rafting on the Yellowstone
River. Several outfitters take guests on half- and full-day trips on
routes skirting the park's northern boundary; the best of the bunch
is the **Yellowstone Raft Company,** U.S. Hwy. 89 (ℭ **800/858-
7781** or 406/848-7777; www.yellowstoneraft.com), with half-day
trips for $35 and full days for $78; children get on the boat for $25
half-day or $58 full day. While this is not a **snowmobiling** hub on
the magnitude of West Yellowstone, a few motels here rent snow
machines or offer snowcoach tours. And **hiking** and **fishing** opportunities are bountiful in every direction from town.

WHERE TO STAY

Dinky, personable, and a bit eccentric, Gardiner has long had ultra-
friendly lodging—thin-walled motels where, if you show up late,
they've gone to bed and left a key in the door. These days it also has
some newer, chain-affiliated properties, built to accommodate the

ever-increasing traffic to the park. As with all the gateway towns, make your reservations early if you're coming during the peak season. The steep off-season decline in traffic results in discounts that can be considerably less expensive than the high-season rates quoted below, so be sure to ask.

Inexpensive motels are moving in and filling up during the summer months: the **Yellowstone Park Travelodge,** 109 Hellroaring Rd. (© **406/848-7520**), and **Super 8,** 702 U.S. Hwy. 89 (© **800/800-8000** or 406/848-7401; www.super8.com), are open year-round with rates during the high season between $90 and $105 for a double. The **Best Western by Mammoth Hot Springs,** on U.S. Hwy. 89 (© **800/828-9080** or 406/848-7311; www.bestwestern.com), is another option, with doubles for $119 to $129.

Absaroka Lodge ☆☆

Every room in this lodge has its own furnished balcony with jaw-dropping views of the Yellowstone River and the mountain scenery beyond it. The lodge's riverbank location—with a nice slope of lawn overlooking the river gorge—is just a few blocks from the village center, and the rooms are well appointed with queen-size beds. Suites with kitchenettes cost a little more; there is also a pair of cabins without balconies. Like most other properties in town, the lodge has staff ready and able to assist in arrangements with outfitters for fly-fishing, rafting, and, in the fall, hunting.

U.S. Hwy. 89 at the Yellowstone River Bridge (P.O. Box 10), Gardiner, MT 59030. © **800/755-7414** or 406/848-7414. Fax 406/848-7560. www.yellowstonemotel. com. 41 units. Summer $95–$105 double; winter $45–$55 double. AE, DC, DISC, MC, V. *In room:* A/C, TV, wireless Internet, kitchenette.

Comfort Inn

This log cabin–style hotel looks like it belongs here, unlike a lot of chain operations. The centerpiece is a 3,000-square-foot rustic lobby decorated with wild-game trophies, and a large second-floor balcony that offers views of Yellowstone scenery and passing wildlife. Family rooms that sleep six and luxurious suites with hot tubs are also available.

107 Hellroaring Dr. (P.O. Box 268), Gardiner, MT 59030. © **800/424-6423** or 406/848-7536. Fax 406/848-7062. www.yellowstonecomfortinn.com. 77 units. Summer $100–$175 double; winter $50–$100 double. AE, DISC, MC, V. **Amenities:** Restaurant; bar/casino; 3 indoor Jacuzzis; self-serve laundry. *In room:* A/C, TV, coffeemaker, hair dryer, iron.

Yellowstone Suites Bed and Breakfast ☆ *Finds*

This quiet B&B on the south bank of the Yellowstone River is a good alternative to the motels that line U.S. Hwy. 89. Originally built in 1904, legend has it that the second story's quarried-stone exterior is actually a leftover from the Roosevelt Arch. The rooms are frilly and cozy, with a teddy-bear motif in the Roosevelt Room and a Victorian theme in the Jackson Room; the Yellowstone Suite has satellite television and a kitchenette. The real perks here are the impeccably gardened backyard and the breakfasts, which might feature cinnamon rolls or cheese blintzes.

506 Fourth St. (P.O. Box 277), Gardiner, MT 59030. © 800/948-7937 or 406/848-7937. www.yellowstonesuites.com. 4 units. Summer $105–$150 double; winter $75–$98 double. Rates include complimentary full breakfast. MC, V. **Amenities:** Outdoor Jacuzzi. *In room:* A/C, wireless Internet, kitchenette, no phone.

WHERE TO DINE

An indication that Gardiner has kept in touch with its mining-town roots is the relative dearth of fancy restaurants—you'll find mostly steakhouse fare, hearty breakfasts, and travelers' food. A few upscale eateries have come and gone in recent years, but the dish-clattering local color of the parkside coffee shops is hard to beat.

The Chico Inn ✸✸ CONTINENTAL   It's 35 miles north of Gardiner, but if you're in the area, stop here for some of the best food in the Rockies and a soak in this resort's hot springs. The carnivorous traveler will enjoy the selection of top-drawer beef, the pine nut–crusted Alaskan halibut is a seafood aficionado's dream, and wine lovers won't be disappointed one bit by the award-winning list. Many of the incredibly fresh veggies originate in the resort's garden and greenhouse, and the menu always includes a vegetarian selection. You'll want to linger over the food, so consider a night's stay.

Old Chico Rd., Pray, MT. © 800/468-9232 or 406/333-4933. Reservations recommended. Main courses $20–$30. AE, DISC, MC, V. Summer daily 5:30–10pm; winter Sun–Thurs 5:30–9pm, Fri–Sat 5:30–10pm; Sun brunch 8:30–11:30am. Located 35 miles north of Gardiner.

Helen's Corral Drive-In BURGERS   Okay, so it's not much to look at, and the menu's most adventurous item is a basket of fried shrimp. But proprietor Helen Gould has, since 1960, built the place's reputation on hamburgers and buffalo burgers that are nothing short of colossal. With a half pound of meat, several slices of American cheese, bacon, and all the usual veggies, these burgers have been known to measure a full 7 inches from bun to bun. The monstrous things garnered the nickname "Helen's Hateful Hamburgers" after a dissatisfied customer wrote a letter to the local paper dubbing them just that. Gould ran with it, using the intended insult as a sarcastic slogan in promotions and on T-shirts. "She put us on the map, that lady did," says Gould.

U.S. Hwy. 89 at Yellowstone St. (C) **406/848-7627.** Reservations not accepted. Menu items $2.25–$10. No credit cards. Memorial Day to Labor Day daily 11am–11pm; Sept–Oct 11am–9pm.

Sawtooth Deli (★ DELI/AMERICAN   This stalwart eatery on Park Street is a reliable spot for any meal, from the hearty American breakfasts to the plump subs at lunch to the seafood and pasta available come dinnertime. We especially like the Philly cheese steaks and veggie subs for lunch and the pesto pasta for dinner. With a basic main room and a breezy patio, the casual counter service at lunch migrates to table service for dinner. There is a full bar.

222 W. Park St. (C) **406/848-7600.** Main courses $5–$8 breakfast and lunch; $11–$21 dinner. MC, V. Tues–Sat 8am–4pm; summer Tues–Sat 8am–4pm and 5–9:30pm.

3 Cooke City, Montana (★

Near the northeast entrance to Yellowstone National Park

Mining gold and platinum and other precious metals pumped intermittent life into Cooke City for 100 years, but now there is only park tourism. Fewer than 100 residents live year-round in the town today, and Silver Gate, right next to the park entrance, is even smaller.

Contact the **Colter Pass/Cooke City/Silver Gate Chamber of Commerce** at P.O. Box 1071, Cooke City, MT 59020 ((C) **406/838-2495;** www.cookecitychamber.org), for information. The chamber operates a visitor center at 205 Main St. that is open daily from 11am to 6pm in summer.

A room for the night will be less expensive than in other gateway towns, typically from $60 to $120 a night. The **Soda Butte Lodge,** 209 Main St. ((C) **800/527-6462** or 406/838-2251; www.cookecity. com), is the biggest motel in Cooke City, and it includes the **Prospector Restaurant** and a small casino; or, you can go to the cheaper, bare-bones **Alpine Motel,** 105 Main St. ((C) **888/838-1190** or 406/838-2262; www.cookecityalpine.com). Opening in 2005, the newest property is a woodsy **Super 8,** 303 Main St. ((C) **877/339-2070** or 406/838-2070). For a bite to eat and a great selection of beers, try the funky **Beartooth Cafe** ((C) **406/838-2475**), also on Main Street.

In Silver Gate, the **Grizzly Lodge,** U.S. Hwy. 212 ((C) **406/838-2219;** www.yellowstonelodges.com), offers respectable, albeit dated, motel rooms on Soda Butte Creek for $50 to $75 June through

October. The **Log Cabin Café** (© **406/838-2367**) is a rustic-meets-refined eatery specializing in trout dinners.

4 Jackson, Wyoming ✶✶

Near the south entrance of Grand Teton National Park

More so than any of the other gateway towns to Yellowstone and Grand Teton, Jackson has managed to reap the fruits of tourism and diversify beyond it, thanks in no small part to a white-hot real-estate market. Sure, the heart of Jackson is thick with shops and motels and tourists, and, yes, urban sprawl is a serious issue in the surrounding valley; it's admirable, though, that the town has used some of its prosperity to preserve open space and enhance the cultural agenda of the community.

Jackson has a wealth of outdoor recreation to occupy the hordes of visitors. In summer, you can play golf at world-class courses, chase trout in pristine streams or lakes, drift down a river in a raft or kayak, or ride horses at one of the area's dude ranches. Come winter, you can carom down the mountain slopes, cross-country ski on the seemingly endless trails, or ride a snowmobile into the forest.

And if you're tired of the great outdoors, well, you can go shopping. Jackson has national brand-name fashion outlets, tourist curio shops, excellent art galleries, clothing stores, antiques shops, and outdoor-equipment suppliers. The retail frenzy concentrates around the town's delightful central square, a grassy park with entryways arched by tangles of elk antlers.

Oh, yeah, and there are a couple of nice parks up the road, too.

ESSENTIALS

Air service to Jackson and rental-car agencies are discussed in chapter 2.

GETTING THERE   If you're driving, come north from I-80 at Rock Springs on U.S. Hwy. 189/191, or east from I-15 at Idaho Falls on U.S. Hwy. 26, and either travel via Snake River Canyon on that highway or veer north over Teton Pass on Wyo. 32. If you are driving south from Yellowstone National Park, stay on U.S. Hwy. 89, which runs north-south through both parks and into town. Likewise, from I-80, take U.S. Hwy. 189 or 191 north to the park, or U.S. Hwy. 89 from I-15 in Ogden, Utah. For up-to-date weather information and road conditions, contact the Chamber of Commerce (see below) or call © **888/WYO-ROAD** (in-state) or 307/772-0824.

VISITOR INFORMATION The **Jackson Hole Chamber of Commerce** is a source of information concerning just about everything in and around Jackson. Along with the Bridger-Teton, Yellowstone, and Grand Teton rangers, chamber representatives can be found at the **Greater Yellowstone Visitor Center** (no phone), 532 N. Cache St., open daily from 8am to 7pm in summer and 9am to 5pm in winter. For information on lodging, events, and activities, contact the chamber at P.O. Box 550, Jackson, WY 83001 (© 307/733-3316; www.jacksonholechamber.com). For lodging information and reservations, call **Jackson Hole Central Reservations** (© 888/838-6606; www.jacksonholewy.com).

GETTING AROUND Taxi service is available from **Buckboard Cab** (© 307/733-1112) and **Teton Taxi** (© 307/733-1506). **All-trans** (© 800/443-6133 or 307/733-3135; www.jacksonholealltrans. com) offers shuttle service from the airport and national park tours. Before you call a cab, remember that many of the hotels and car-rental agencies in the Jackson area offer free shuttle service to and from the airport.

The **Southern Teton Area Rapid Transit (START)** offers bus transport from Teton Village to Jackson daily for $3 (half-price for seniors, students, and kids 9–13; children 8 and under ride free). Service includes about 70 trips a day between downtown and Teton Village in the winter, and 15 in the summer; it shuts down around 12:30am year-round. For specific schedule information, contact START at © 307/733-4521 or browse **www.startbus.com**.

GETTING OUTSIDE

Whether you're a raw beginner, a seasoned pro, or an adrenaline addict, Jackson can make you feel at home. There's mountain biking, hiking, fishing, kayaking, and river running in the summer, and skiing, snowmobiling, and snowboarding in the winter.

SPORTING GOODS & EQUIPMENT RENTALS Serious climbers with serious wallets will appreciate the gear at **Teton Mountaineering**, at 170 N. Cache St. (© 800/850-3595 or 307/733-3595; www.tetonmtn.com), a block from the square, where you can get killer Nordic skis and high-grade fleece jackets. **Adventure Sports,** at Dornan's in the town of Moose (© 307/733-3307), has a small selection of mountain bike, kayak, and canoe rentals, and advice on where to go with the gear. When snowboards are put away for the summer, the **Boardroom** switches to BMX bikes and skateboards, at 225 W. Broadway (© 307/733-8327). **Hoback Sports,**

520 W. Broadway (© **307/733-5335;** www.hobacksports.com), has a large selection of skis, boards, and summer mountain bikes for rent and sale. **Skinny Skis,** at 65 W. Deloney Ave. off Town Square (© **888/733-7205** or 307/733-6094; www.skinnyskis.com), is a year-round specialty sports shop and has an excellent selection of equipment and clothing. For serviceable factory seconds at steeply discounted prices, head north to the little town of Moose near the entrance to Grand Teton National Park and shop **Moosely Seconds** ✂ (© **307/739-1801**).

SUMMER SPORTS & ACTIVITIES

FISHING   Yellowstone and Grand Teton national parks have incredible fishing in their lakes and streams; see the park sections for details.

The Snake River emerges from Jackson Lake Dam as a broad, strong river, with decent fishing from its banks in certain spots—such as right below the dam—and better fishing if you float the river. Fly-fishers should ask advice at local stores on recent insect hatches and good stretches of river, or hire a guide to keep them company. Outdoor gear stores will provide all the tackle you need and more information on fishing conditions in the area than you can likely process. **High Country Flies** ✂, 185 N. Center St. (© **866/733-7210** or 307/733-7210; www.highcountryflies.com), has a vast selection of high-quality fishing gear, flies, and fly-tying supplies, along with lessons and guided trips, as well as free advice if you just want to gab about where to cast. The **Jack Dennis Outdoor Shop,** on the Town Square at 50 E. Broadway (© **307/733-3270;** www.jack dennis.com), is a much bigger store with room to display some big boats, and it also offers lessons and guides. The going rate for guided fishing is about $450 for a full day for two people.

GOLF   The semiprivate Robert Trent Jones, Jr.–designed **Jackson Hole Golf and Tennis Club** (© **866/915-4482** or 307/733-3111; www.jhgtc.com), north of Jackson off U.S. Hwy. 89, has an 18-hole course that's one of the best in the country—and it underwent a major renovation and saw a new clubhouse open in 2007. Seasonal greens fees range from $65 to $195 for 18 holes, cart included. The **Teton Pines Resort,** 3450 N. Clubhouse Dr. (© **800/238-2223** or 307/733-1005; www.tetonpines.com), designed by Arnold Palmer and Ed Seay, is a challenging course; greens fees range from $85 to $160, cart included, depending on the season. Both courses are open to the public.

HIKING   In addition to the myriad trails in Grand Teton National Park (see chapter 6), there are trails in the surrounding forest—they might be less maintained, but they also get less use, which means more solitude for hikers. Adjacent to Grand Teton on the east and south is **Bridger-Teton National Forest;** go east and over the Continental Divide, and you're in **Shoshone National Forest.** Together, these forests encompass a huge piece of mountain real estate, including glaciers, 13,000-foot peaks, and some of the best alpine fishing lakes in the world. Among the mountain ranges included in these forests are the **Absarokas,** the **Gros Ventre,** the **Wyoming,** and the **Wind River Range.** The **visitor center,** located in the sod-roofed A-frame at 532 N. Cache St., provides all the hiking and access information you'll need for Bridger-Teton, including the Gros Ventre and Teton wilderness areas. If you want detailed information in advance, call the Forest Service's district office (© **307/739-5500;** www.fs. fed.us/r4/btnf).

For those who would like a hiking/backpacking (or snowshoeing/cross-country skiing) guide—for about $150 a day—contact **The Hole Hiking Experience** (© **866/733-4453** or 307/690-4453; www.holehike.com).

HORSEBACK RIDING   Trail rides are a staple of the Western-vacation experience, and there are several companies in the area that will put you in the saddle. Some hotels, including those in Grand Teton National Park, have stables and operate trail rides for their guests. For details, contact **Jackson Hole Outfitters** (© **307/654-7008;** www.jacksonholetrailrides.com), **Spring Creek Ranch Riding Stables** (© **800/443-6139** or 307/733-8833; www.springcreek ranch.com), or the **Mill Iron Ranch** (© **888/808-6390** or 307/733-6390; www.millironranch.net). Rides typically cost around $50 for 2 hours or $125 for a day.

KAYAKING, CANOEING & SAILING   Several operators in Jackson run schools and guide paddlers of all skill levels. The two major outfits are the **Snake River Kayak and Canoe School,** 225 N. Cache St. (© **800/529-2501** or 307/733-9999; www.snakeriver kayak.com), and **Rendezvous River Sports,** 945 W. Broadway (© **307/733-2471;** www. jacksonholekayak.com).

RAFTING   There are two parts to the Snake River—the smooth water, much of it running through Grand Teton National Park north of Jackson, and the white water of the canyon, to the south and west. A rafting trip down the upper Snake, usually from Jackson Lake Dam or Pacific Creek to Moose, is not about wild water but about wildlife: Moose, bald eagles, osprey, and other creatures come to the water just like we do. Several operators provide scenic float trips in the park; see chapter 6 for a list.

The most popular way to experience the Snake River is whitewater rafting; these are wet, wild, white-knuckle tours. Several companies offer adrenaline-pumping day trips down the Snake, but don't plan on being just a passenger—this is a participatory sport. Contact **Barker-Ewing** (© 800/448-4202; www.barker-ewing.com), **Charlie Sands Wildwater** (© 800/358-8184 or 307/733-4410; www. sandswhitewater.com), **Dave Hansen Whitewater** (© 800/732-6295 or 307/733-6295; www.davehansenwhitewater.com), **Jackson Hole Whitewater** (© 800/700-7238; www.jhwhitewater.com), or **Mad River Boat Trips** (© 800/458-7238; www.mad-river.com). Generally, a full-day trip runs around $70 to $90, lunch included, and a half-day trip costs about $40 to $60.

WINTER SPORTS & ACTIVITIES

CROSS-COUNTRY SKIING   With five Nordic centers and a couple of national parks at your feet, plus the 3.5-million-acre Bridger-Teton National Forest, cross-country skiers have plenty of choices. If you're new to cross-country skiing on any level, you might choose to start on the groomed, level trails at one of the Nordic centers. If, however, you have experience in the steep, deep powder of untracked wilderness, visit or call the National Park Service in **Grand Teton National Park** (© 307/739-3300; www.nps.gov/grte) or the **Bridger-Teton National Forest** in downtown Jackson at 340 N. Cache St. (© 307/739-5500; www.fs.fed.us/r4/btnf), and check in before you go.

The local ski shops are excellent sources of unofficial advice about the area's backcountry. Keep in mind that many of the trails used by cross-country skiers are also used by snowmobiles. For those seeking instruction, lessons are available at the Nordic centers, or you can check the schedule of **Teton Parks and Recreation** (© 307/733-5056; www.tetonwyo.org/parks), which takes visitors on various cross-country ski outings from mid-December to mid-March.

The **Jackson Hole Nordic Center,** 7658 Teewinot St., Teton Village (© 307/733-2292; www.jacksonhole.com), on the flats just east of Teton Village, is a small part of the giant facility that includes some of the best downhill skiing around (see below). Trail passes ($12) allow access to 17km (11 miles) of groomed trails.

Teton Pines Cross Country Skiing Center (© 800/238-2223 or 307/733-1005; www.tetonpines.com) has 12km (7.5 miles) of groomed trails that wind over the resort's golf course. **Spring Creek Ranch Nordic Center,** 1800 N. Spirit Dance Rd., Jackson (© **800/443-6139** or 307/733-8833; www.springcreekranch.com), maintains about 15km (9.3 miles) of groomed trails, and you don't have to be a guest to enjoy them. For more information, see "Where to Stay," below.

At **Grand Targhee** (© **800/827-4433** or 307/353-2300; www.grandtarghee.com), you can rent or buy anything you need in the way of equipment and take off on the resort's 15km (9.3 miles) of groomed trails.

DOG SLEDDING   If your idea of mushing is not oatmeal but a pack of yipping dogs, you might want to try your hand at dog sledding, an enjoyable open-air way to tour the high country during the winter. **Jackson Hole Iditarod** (© **800/554-7388** or 307/733-7388; www.jhsleddog.com), associated with Iditarod racer Frank Teasley, offers both half- and full-day trips in five-person sleds (the fifth companion is your guide), and you can take a turn in the driver's stand. The half-day ride costs around $190 per person, gives the dogs an 11-mile workout, and includes a light lunch before you head back to the kennels. For about $265 a head, you can take the full-day excursion out to Granite Hot Springs, a 22-mile trip total. You get a hot lunch, with your choice of trout or steak. Another outfitter, **Washakie Outfitting** (© **800/249-0662;** www.dogsledwashakie.com), leads trips out of Teton Village and in the national forests around Togwotee Pass. These trips book up quickly, so call several days in advance to reserve a spot.

DOWNHILL SKIING   This is one of the premier destinations for skiers in the entire country. Despite a relatively remote location, chilly temperatures, and a high percentage of black-diamond trails (although still plenty of intermediate trails), skiers flock here in droves. The two largest ski resorts in the area have been putting in faster chairs in recent years, eliminating long waits in lift lines.

Jackson Hole Mountain Resort ★★, 3395 W. Village Dr. (P.O. Box 290), Teton Village, WY 83025 (© **888/333-7766** or 307/733-2292; www.jacksonhole.com), is making improvements to move into the elite international ranks; incidentally, prices are moving up, too. Head to the top of **Rendezvous Mountain** and plunge down Tensleep Bowl if you want to get a taste of skiing on the edge, or try the gentler, intermediate runs down the sides of **Apres Vous Mountain.** (*Note:* The resort's tram was shut down in 2006; a new $25-million,

100-passenger tram was under construction at press time and slated to open in Dec 2008.)

Grand Targhee Resort ⟨ℱℱ⟩, Ski Hill Road, P.O. Box SKI, Alta, WY 83422 (𝒞 **800/827-4433** or 307/353-2300; www.grandtarghee. com), has the best snow in the universe: deep, forgiving powder from November to spring (an average of over 500 in. annually), and a more peaceful, less crowded village that provides a worthy alternative to Teton Village.

Snow King Resort, 400 E. Snow King Ave., P.O. Box SKI, Jackson, WY 83001 (𝒞 **800/522-5464** or 307/733-5200; www.snow king.com), lights up its hill above Jackson at night; it's the smallest of the valley's resorts, with fairly steep and unvaried terrain, but it's within walking distance of downtown Jackson.

SNOWMOBILING   Although West Yellowstone is the most popular base for snowmobiling in the Yellowstone area, Jackson has a growing contingent of snowmobile aficionados and outfitters.

The operators who rent snowmobiles (including the necessary clothing and helmets) also have guides to take you on 1-day and multiday tours of Jackson Hole and the surrounding area. **High Country Snowmobile Tours, Wyoming Adventures,** and **Rocky Mountain Snowmobile Tours** share a website and reservation service (𝒞 **800/647-2561;** www.snowmobiletours.net), offering guided trips in Jackson Hole, Yellowstone, and the surrounding wildlands. **Jackson Hole Snowmobile Tours,** 515 N. Cache St. (𝒞 **800/ 633-1733** or 307/733-6850; www.jacksonholesnowmobile.com), offers 1-day trips in Yellowstone and multiday trips along the Continental Divide. A typical guided, full-day outing costs from $200 to $300, with pickup and drop-off service, equipment, fuel, a continental breakfast, and lunch at Old Faithful included. Also in Jackson, snowmobiles can be rented at **Leisure Sports,** 1075 S. U.S. Hwy. 89 (𝒞 **307/733-3040;** www.leisuresportsadventure.com).

A BIRD'S-EYE VIEW

AERIAL TOURING   For a much quicker climb to the mountaintops, call **Soaring Eagle Glider Flights** (𝒞 **307/732-2359**), at the Jackson Hole Airport, or **Teton Aviation** (𝒞 **800/472-6382** or 208/ 354-3100; www.tetonaviation.com), in Driggs, Idaho. You'll actually be looking down at the summits that climbers strain to top, and you'll get a new perspective on the immensity of the Grand Teton (although you won't get too close—the park has some air-space restrictions). Take your pick: Soaring Eagle offers motorized glider trips for $199 to $299 (one passenger) on the east side of the peaks, and Teton has 1-hour flights in planes and gliders ($185–$225) that take you to 11,800 feet on the west side of the Grand.

BALLOONING   The folks at the **Wyoming Balloon Company** ⟨ (𝄢 **307/739-0900;** www.wyomingballoon.com) like to fire up early, in the still air that cloaks the Teton Valley around 6am. Their "float trips" stay aloft for a little more than an hour, cruising over a 3,000-acre ranch with a full-frontal view of the Tetons. The journey concludes with a champagne toast at the landing site. Prices are $275 adults and $225 for children ages 6 to 12 (no kids under 6 allowed).

WILDLIFE-WATCHING

National Elk Refuge ⟨   It's not exactly nature's way, but the U.S. Fish and Wildlife Service makes sure that the elk in this area eat well during the winter by feeding them alfalfa pellets. It keeps them out of the haystacks of area ranchers and creates a beautiful tableau on the peaceful flats along the Gros Ventre River: thousands of elk, some with huge antler racks, dotting the snow for miles. Drivers along U.S. Hwy. 89 might also see trumpeter swans, coyotes, moose, bighorn sheep, and, lately, wolves. As autumn begins to chill the air in September, you'll hear the shrill whistles of the bull elk in the mountains; as snow begins to stick on the ground, about 5,000 animals make their way down to the refuge—the world's largest winter concentration of elk. Although the cultivated meadows and pellets help the elk survive the winter, some biologists say this approach results in overpopulation and the spread of diseases such as brucellosis.

Regardless, this is a great opportunity to see these magnificent wapiti up close. Each winter from mid-December to March, the Fish and Wildlife Service offers **horse-drawn sleigh rides** that weave among the refuge elk. Riders early in the winter will find young, energetic bulls playing and banging heads, while late-winter visitors (when the Fish and Wildlife Service begins feeding the animals) wander through a more placid scene. Rides embark from the Greater Yellowstone Visitor Center (532 N. Cache St.) daily between 10am and 4pm on a first-come, first-served basis. Tickets for the 45-minute rides cost $16 for adults and $12 for children 5 to 12, and can be purchased at the visitor center. Ask about a combination pass for the sleigh ride and the Wildlife Art Museum.

Located 3 miles north of Jackson on U.S. Hwy. 26/89. 𝄢 **307/733-9212.** http://national elkrefuge.fws.gov. Free admission. Visitor center: summer daily 8am–7pm; winter daily 9am–5pm.

AREA ATTRACTIONS

Beyond its role as a staging area for explorations of Grand Teton and Yellowstone national parks, Jackson is a place to relax, shop, play some golf, or kick up your heels at an authentic Western saloon. There are also a number of attractions, running the gamut from history and art to pure entertainment. From Memorial Day to Labor Day at **Town Square,** actors reenact an Old West gunfight at 6:15pm every day except Sunday. **Stagecoach rides** are also available from Town Square all summer long, $5 for adults and $3 for kids.

Jackson Hole Aerial Tram and Gondola Rides

Here you can see the Tetons from an elevation above 10,000 feet—or 9,000 for the Bridger Gondola—but don't expect a private tour. During busy summer days, the tram carries 45 passengers, packed in like the skiers that take the lift in the winter. The top of Rendezvous Mountain offers an incredible view; but it can get pretty chilly, even in the middle of summer, so bring a light coat. Atop the Bridger Gondola at 9,095 feet, two restaurants—upscale **Couloir** and the **Headwall Deli**—offer a place to eat before you head back down. (*Note:* The resort's tram was shut down in 2006; a new $25-million, 100-passenger tram was under construction at press time and slated to open in Dec 2008.)

At Jackson Hole Ski Resort, 7658 Teewinot St., Teton Village. © 307/739-2753. www.jacksonhole.com. Tickets $10–$22 adults and seniors, $6–$10 children 6–14, free for children under 6. Sept and late May to mid-June daily 9am–5pm; mid-June to Aug daily 9am–6pm. Tram runs approximately every half-hour. Call for current information when the tram reopens in 2008.

Jackson Hole Museum

Dedicated local volunteers maintain this repository of early photographs, artifacts, and other items of historical significance, and they'll carefully guide you through the collections. You can browse the exhibits or go down the street to the Historical Society at Glenwood Street and Mercill Avenue to do some research. At the museum, you'll find collections of trade beads, antique pole furniture, pistols, and Indian artifacts, spread out in 3,000 square feet of floor space.

105 N. Glenwood St. (at the corner of Deloney St.). © 307/733-2414. Year-round research facility © 307/733-9605. www.jacksonholehistory.org. Admission $6 families, $3 adults, $2 seniors, $1 students and children. Mon–Sat 9:30am–6pm; Sun 10am–5pm. Closed Oct–May.

National Museum of Wildlife Art

If you don't spot this museum on your way into Jackson from the north, consider that a triumph of design: Its jagged, red-sandstone facade is meant to blend into the steep hillside facing the elk refuge. Within this 50,000-square-foot castle is some of the best wildlife art in the country. There are 12 exhibit galleries that display traveling shows and collections dating from 2000 B.C. to the present, including a gallery devoted to the American bison as well as a showcase for local great Carl Rungius. Younger visitors will be entertained by the many interactive exhibits and a "Kid's Kit" loaner to tote around the museum. The facility also houses a repository of internationally acclaimed wildlife films, and in the winter, it's a popular preamble to sled tours of the elk refuge (you can also view the wildlife through spotting scopes on the balcony, and combination passes are available). There's a good little cafe, too.

2820 Rungius Rd. (3 miles north of town on U.S. Hwy. 89, across from the National Elk Refuge). © 800/313-9553 or 307/733-5771. www.wildlifeart.org. Admission $10 adults, $9 students and seniors, free for children under 18 when accompanied by adult. Daily 9am–5pm (fall–spring Sun 1–5pm).

ART GALLERIES

Collectors, tired of bighorn sheep on the crags and weather-beaten cowboys on their horses, often dismiss Western art. But while Jackson has plenty of that genre in stock, some of its two dozen galleries are more adventurous and sophisticated.

Cayuse Western Americana, 255 N. Glenwood St. (© 800/405-4096 or 307/739-1940; www.cayusewa.com), focuses on antiques of all kinds, from beadwork to spurs to belt buckles to paintings. The **Center Street Gallery,** 30 N. Center St. (© 800/733-1115; www.centerstreetgallery.com), focuses on contemporary Western art. **Lyndsay McCandless Contemporary,** 130 S. Jackson (© 307/734-0649; www.lmcontemporary.com), showcases abstract wildlife and other edgy work. A mile north of town, at 1975 U.S. Hwy. 89 (toward the park), is the **Wilcox Gallery** (© 307/733-6450; www.wilcoxgallery.com), which showcases more than 20 painters and sculptors from across the nation. The **Wilcox Gallery II** is in town at 165 N. Center St. (© 307/733-3950).

WHERE TO STAY

The thin-walled, dimly lit motels of the past are just memories now—Jackson lodgings these days come with palatial trappings and, in some cases, prices that start at $500 a night. Prices are generally discounted in the off season (spring/fall), but not during ski season.

Clustered together near the junction west of downtown where Wyo. 22 leaves U.S. Hwy. 26/89 and heads north to Teton Village is

Jackson

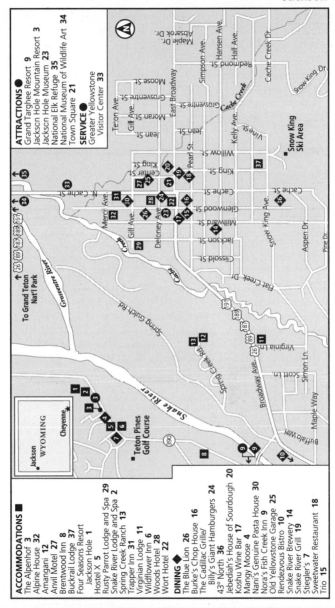

ATTRACTIONS ●
Grand Targhee Resort **9**
Jackson Hole Mountain Resort **3**
Jackson Hole Museum **23**
National Elk Refuge **35**
National Museum of Wildlife Art **34**
Town Square **21**

SERVICE ●
Greater Yellowstone
Visitor Center **33**

ACCOMMODATIONS ■
The Alpenhof **3**
Alpine House **32**
Amangani **12**
Anvil Motel **27**
Brentwood Inn **8**
Buckrail Lodge **37**
Four Seasons Resort
Jackson Hole **1**
Hostel X **5**
Rusty Parrot Lodge and Spa **29**
Snake River Lodge and Spa **2**
Spring Creek Ranch **13**
Trapper Inn **31**
Virginian Lodge **11**
Wildflower Inn **6**
Woods Hotel **28**
Wort Hotel **22**

DINING ◆
The Blue Lion **26**
Burke's Chop House **16**
The Cadillac Grille/
Billy's Giant Hamburgers **24**
43° North **36**
Jedediah's House of Sourdough **20**
Koshu Wine Bar **17**
Mangy Moose **4**
Nani's Genuine Pasta House **30**
Nora's Fish Creek Inn **9**
Old Yellowstone Garage **25**
Rendezvous Bistro **10**
Snake River Brewery **14**
Snake River Grill **19**
Stiegler's **7**
Sweetwater Restaurant **18**
Trio **15**

187

a colony of chain franchises: **Motel 6,** 600 S. U.S. Hwy. 89 (© 307/733-1620); **Super 8,** 750 S. U.S. Hwy. 89 (© 307/733-6833; www.super8.com); and the more upscale and expensive **Days Inn,** 350 S. U.S. Hwy. 89 (© 307/733-0033; www.daysinn.com), with private hot tubs and fireplaces in suites. High-season prices for the motels range from $100 to $200.

On the inexpensive end of the scale, the **Anvil Motel,** 215 N. Cache St. (© **800/234-4507** or 307/733-3668; www.anvilmotel. com) offers hostel beds in the well-kept "Bunkhouse" for $25 a night, with ski lockers, a communal kitchen, and a hot tub. Motel rooms run $128 to $148. I also like the summer-only **Buckrail Lodge,** at the base of Snow King Mountain at 110 E. Karns Ave. (© **307/733-2079;** www.buckraillodge.com), a comfortable independent that's been nicely maintained by the two families that have owned it since it opened in the 1960s. Doubles are $95 to $117.

IN JACKSON

Alpine House 🌲🌲   Stylish, environmentally conscious, and melding the best of the B&B and hotel worlds, Alpine House began as a six-room operation in 1996 and expanded nearly fourfold in 2000 when it also opened a spa. Modeled after Scandinavian lodging, the rooms are woodsy and Western but modern and functional, with one king, one queen, or two queens and nice views. Some have lofts with additional beds; all have a shared or private balcony, a fireplace, and a soaking tub. The public areas, indoors and out, are quiet and serene. Owners Hans and Nancy Johnstone are former Olympians and great resources for planning outdoor adventures in Jackson Hole.

285 N. Glenwood St. (P.O. Box 1126), Jackson, WY 83001. © **800/753-1421** or 307/739-1570. Fax 307/734-2850. www.alpinehouse.com. 22 units, including 1 suite and 1 apt. $145–$230 double; $170–$275 suite or apt condo. Rates include full breakfast. AE, MC, V. **Amenities:** Lounge; outdoor Jacuzzi; sauna; spa. *In room:* A/C and cable TV (except original 6 rooms), kitchenette.

Rusty Parrot Lodge and Spa 🌲🌲   The name sounds like an out-of-tune jungle bird, but the Rusty Parrot demonstrates excellent pitch, cultivating a country lodge and spa right in the heart of busy Jackson. Located across from Miller Park, the Parrot is decorated in the nouveau Western style of peeled log, with an interior appointed with elegant furnishings and river-rock fireplaces. One very attractive lure is the Body Sage Spa, where you can get yourself treated to all sorts of scrubs, wraps, massages, and facials. Another is the excellent restaurant, the Wild Sage. The breakfast that comes with your room includes omelets, fresh pastries, fruits, cereals, and freshly ground coffee; food also appears later in the day, but the lodge likes to make that a surprise (sorry). Rooms are gigantic, and several have private balconies.

175 N. Jackson St. (P.O. Box 1657), Jackson, WY 83001. ℂ **800/458-2004** or 307/733-2000. www.rustyparrot.com. 31 units, including 1 suite. $290–$425 double; $625–$750 suite. Rates include full breakfast. AE, DC, DISC, MC, V. **Amenities:** Restaurant; lounge; outdoor Jacuzzi; spa. *In room:* A/C, cable TV, wireless Internet.

Trapper Inn ☆   Just 2 short blocks from Town Square, the Trapper Inn was reborn as a slick hotel when it opened 36 new rooms in a pair of attractive "mountain contemporary" buildings in 2006. The rooms are stylish and spacious—the newest are all suites that adjoin, with a kitchen in every other unit—and the employees here are some of the most helpful you'll find in Jackson.

285 N. Cache St. (P.O. Box 1712), Jackson, WY 83001. ℂ **888/771-2648** or 307/733-2648 for reservations. www.trapperinn.com. 90 units, including 36 suites. $170–$189 double; $239–$249 suite. Rates include expanded continental breakfast. AE, MC, V. **Amenities:** Indoor pool; indoor Jacuzzi; self-serve laundry. *In room:* A/C, cable TV, wireless Internet, kitchen, fridge, coffeemaker.

Virginian Lodge *Value*   It's not brand-new. It's not a resort, it doesn't have a golf course, and the highway is right outside the door. Since its overhaul in 1995, however, the Virginian is one of the better motels in Jackson: The prices remain reasonable, the interior courtyard (with a large grassy play area and central pool) is a world away from the Broadway-facing exterior, and it's a busy, cheerful place to stay. You can get a room with a private Jacuzzi or a kitchenette, and many have "dry" bars and sofa sleepers.

750 W. Broadway, Jackson, WY 83001. ℂ **800/262-4999** or 307/733-2792. Fax 307/733-4063. www.virginianlodge.com. 170 units. $108 double; $138–$218 suite. AE, DC, DISC, MC, V. **Amenities:** Restaurant; lounge; outdoor pool; Jacuzzi; game room; wireless Internet in lobby; self-serve laundry. *In room:* A/C, TV, kitchenette.

Woods Hotel ☆ *Finds*   Originally opening in 1950, the Woods Hotel was collecting cobwebs from 1998 to 2006 until new ownership reinvented the place as a boutique lodging in 2007. The brick exterior (and vintage sign) belies the innlike rooms, featuring spare Western-chic style: leather headboards, warm earth tones, and a few rugged touches. The standard rooms are small and lack air-conditioning, but the brick structure stays surprisingly cool and the suites and one family room (with bunk beds) give guests more space to stretch out, plus microwaves and minifridges.

120 N. Glenwood St. (P.O. Box 266), Jackson, WY 83001. ℂ **800/963-2200** or 307/733-2200. www.thewoodshotel.com. 11 units, including 4 suites. $149 double; $179–$189 suite. AE, MC, V. *In room:* Cable TV, wireless Internet, no phone.

Wort Hotel 🌟🌟 Located on Broadway just off the Town Square, the Wort stands like an old tree. Opened in the early 1940s by the sons of Charles Wort, an early-20th-century homesteader, the Tudor-style two-story building was largely rebuilt after a 1980 fire. Nowadays, it has an old-fashioned style, both in the relaxed **Silver Dollar Bar** (distinctively graced with 2,032 silver dollars) and in the quiet, formal dining room. In the manner of an old cattle-baron hotel, the lobby is graced by a warm, romantic fireplace; another fireplace and a huge, hand-carved mural accents a mezzanine sitting area, providing a second hideaway. The rooms aren't Tudor at all—the Wort labels them "New West." Brass number plates and door-knobs welcome you into comfortable, air-conditioned guest rooms with modern decor, thick carpeting, and armoires. The Silver Dollar Suite features a wet bar inlaid with silver dollars as in the bar below.

50 N. Glenwood St., Jackson, WY 83001. © **800/322-2727** or 307/733-2190. www. worthotel.com. 59 units, including 5 suites. $165–$289 double; $399–$699 suite. Valet parking $10 daily. AE, DISC, MC, V. **Amenities:** Restaurant; lounge; health club; Jacuzzi. *In room:* A/C, cable TV, wireless Internet, coffeemaker, iron.

NEAR JACKSON

Amangani 🌟🌟🌟 Cut into the side of East Gros Ventre Butte, Amangani's rough rock exterior blends incredibly well so that the lights from its windows and pool appear at night to glow from within the mountain. Understated and rustic, all details are done with high contemporary style. From the high-ceilinged corridors to the idyllic outdoor pool, this place is all about class and privacy, not to mention superlative views. Hotelier Adrian Zecha has resorts like this around the world, from Bali to Bora Bora, and while the designs are tailored to the landscape, the approach is the same: personal service, luxury, and all the little touches. To name a few of the latter, there are iPod cradles in every bedroom, cashmere throws on the daybeds, and stunning slate and redwood interiors.

1535 NE Butte Rd., Jackson, WY 83002 (on top of East Gros Ventre Butte). © **877/ 734-7333** or 307/734-7333. www.amanresorts.com. 40 units. $565–$1,400 double. AE, DC, DISC, MC, V. **Amenities:** Restaurant; lounge; year-round outdoor pool; health club; spa; Jacuzzi. *In room:* A/C, TV/VCR, wireless Internet, minibar, hair dryer, iron, safe.

Bentwood Inn 🌟🌟 *(Finds* This B&B is an architectural marvel. Built from 200-year-old timber cleared from Yellowstone to make room for a rest area, the inn is a 6,000-square-foot log mansion with 43 corners. The parlor, centered about a three-story river-rock fire-place, is an ideal place to while away a thunderstorm, but the real beauty here is outside, situated just west of the Snake River and south of Teton Village on 3 acres of cottonwood and pine forest with a breezy deck and back lawn. The rooms themselves, all with remote-controlled gas fireplaces, private balconies, and Jacuzzi tubs, are extensions of the innovative design, with touches equally urban and rural, from ornate tile work to longhorn skulls above the bed. The breakfasts are simultaneously hearty and gourmet, and the fridge is always stocked with a wide range of soft drinks and libations. One room is pet-friendly.

4250 Raven Haven Rd. (P.O. Box 561), Jackson Hole, WY 83001. ℂ 307/739-1411. Fax 307/739-2453. www.bentwoodinn.com. 5 units, including 1 suite. $195–$295 double; $245–$325 suite. Rates include complimentary full breakfast and evening wine and cheese. AE, DISC, MC, V. 4 miles west of Jackson (on Teton Village Rd.). **Amenities:** Game room. *In room:* Cable TV/VCR, hair dryer, iron.

Spring Creek Ranch ☆☆   Perched atop East Gros Ventre Butte, 1,000 feet above the Snake River and minutes from both the airport and downtown Jackson, this resort commands a panoramic view of the Grand Tetons and 1,000 acres of land populated by deer, moose, and the horses at its riding facility in the valley below. It seems a little less exclusive now that Amangani has opened next door. But Spring Creek still has much going for it: The rooms, divided among nine buildings with cabin-like exteriors, all have wood-burning fireplaces, Native American floor and wall coverings, and balconies with views of the Tetons. Most rooms have a king- or two queen-size beds, and the studio units boast kitchenettes. In addition to its own rooms, the resort arranges accommodations in the privately owned condominiums and vacation homes that dot the butte—large, lavishly furnished, and featuring completely equipped kitchens. The resort also has an "Adventure Spa," offering a combination of guide service and post-outing treatments, and in-house naturalists who lead guests on "Wildlife Safaris" into the parks.

1800 Spirit Dance Rd. (on top of the East Gros Ventre Butte; P.O. Box 4780), Jackson, WY 83001. ℂ 800/443-6139 or 307/733-8833. www.springcreekranch.com. 126 units. $300–$500 double; $375–$2,200 condo or home. Lower rates in spring and fall. AE, MC, V. **Amenities:** Restaurant; outdoor pool; tennis court; spa; Jacuzzi; concierge; tour desk; complimentary shuttle; room service. *In room:* A/C, cable TV/VCR, dataport, kitchenette, fridge, coffeemaker.

Wildflower Inn ☆☆   A terrific B&B on 3 lush and secluded acres near Teton Village, the Wildflower Inn is the brainchild of jack-of-all-trades Ken Jern, a log-home builder and climbing guide, and his wife, Sherrie, a former ski instructor who now runs the inn full-time. Besides being founts of local information, the Herns are remarkable hosts who pride themselves on both the big picture and the little details. Rooms, named after local wildflowers, are comfortable and luxurious, with private decks, exposed logs, and a remarkable sense of privacy for an inn. Guests also get access to house bikes, rain gear, and trekking poles—not to mention hammocks. Breakfasts are excellent, including veggie frittatas, sour cream coffeecake, and yeast-raised waffles.

3725 Teton Village Rd. (P.O. Box 11000), Jackson, WY 83002. © 307/733-4710. Fax 307/739-0914. www.jacksonholewildflower.com. 5 units, including 1 suite. $320–$350 double; $400 suite. MC, V. **Amenities:** Indoor Jacuzzi; complimentary bikes. *In room:* TV, wireless Internet, hair dryer, no phone.

IN TETON VILLAGE

You can take advantage of the attractions of Jackson, to the south, and Grand Teton, to the north, without suffering the crowds by journeying to Teton Village, which is approximately equidistant from both. Located at the foot of the ski hill, the village and surrounding area offer several fine eating and dining establishments, and activities nearby include skiing, ballooning, and hiking in Grand Teton National Park. During winter months, this is the center of activity in the valley. While lodging in the town of Jackson tends to be a little cheaper in the winter than the summer, at Teton Village the ratio is reversed—rooms by the ski hill get more expensive after the snow falls. For a wide range of basic condos and deluxe vacation homes, contact **Jackson Hole Resort Lodging** (© **800/443-8613** or 307/733-3990; www.jhresortlodging.com). All establishments are open year-round unless otherwise indicated.

The Alpenhof ☆☆   No other spot in the village has quite the Swiss-chalet flavor of this long-standing hostelry, which has a prize location only 50 yards from the ski-resort tram. Four stories tall, with a pitched roof and flower boxes on the balconies, it offers a little old-world atmosphere, as well as excellent comforts and service. The rooms feature brightly colored alpine fabrics, handcrafted Bavarian furnishings, and tiled bathrooms with big, soft towels. You can choose from two junior suites with wet bars and five rooms with fireplaces, and many rooms have balconies or decks. Economy rooms offer two doubles or one queen-size bed, while deluxe units are larger. The resident **Alpenrose** restaurant specializes in fondue.

3255 W. Village Dr. (P.O. Box 288), Teton Village, WY 83025. © 800/732-3244 or 307/733-3242. Fax 307/739-1516. www.alpenhoflodge.com. 42 units, including 1 suite. $189–$489 double; $499 suite. Lower rates in spring and fall. AE, DC, DISC, MC, V. Closed Nov. **Amenities:** 2 restaurants; lounge; outdoor pool; Jacuzzi; sauna. *In room:* A/C, TV, wireless Internet, hair dryer, iron.

Four Seasons Resort Jackson Hole ⭑⭑⭑ The newest—and most deluxe—lodging option in Teton Village, the ultrastylish Four Seasons opened in December 2003 and immediately set a new standard for ski-in, ski-out luxury. From a year-round pool landscaped to resemble a mountain creek to the cowboy-hatted doorman to the rooms—stately, luxurious, and definitively Western—this is one of the top slopeside properties in the country. The range of rooms starts at the high end and goes up from there, but even the standard kings are large and plush, and most units have a balcony or a fireplace. One especially notable perk: the hotel's "Base Camp," a full-service outdoor-activity concierge who can arrange mountain biking, hiking, fishing, and ballooning excursions, and who will outfit you in style. In winter, the service transforms into a first-rate ski concierge, and s'mores and hot chocolate are served outside, where heated towels are distributed at the pool. The eating and drinking facilities are also a cut above, and range from casually hip to extraordinarily extravagant.

7680 Granite Loop (P.O. Box 544), Teton Village, WY 83025. (C) **307/732-5000.** Fax 307/732-5001. www.fourseasons.com/jacksonhole. 156 units, including 16 suites and 24 condos. $400–$750 double; $700–$4,000 condo or suite. Lower rates spring and fall. Valet parking $20 daily. AE, DC, DISC, MC, V. **Amenities:** 2 restaurants; lounge; year-round outdoor pool; health club; spa; 3 Jacuzzis; sauna; extensive equipment rental; game room; concierge; tour desk; business center; salon; 24-hr. room service; dry cleaning. *In room:* A/C, TV/DVD player w/pay movies, dataport, high-speed Internet ($10 per day), kitchen, fridge, coffeemaker, hair dryer, iron, safe.

Hostel X ⭑ *Value* If you came to Wyoming to ski, not to lie in the lap of luxury, get yourself a room at Hostel X and hit the slopes. Owned and operated by the Wilson family since 1967 and called "the soul of Jackson Hole," it's a great bargain for those who don't need the trimmings. And it's not a dormitory, either—comfortable but simple private rooms (about the caliber of a roadside motel) hold up to four people; they have either one king bed or four twins. There's also a good place to prep your skis, a library, a kids' playroom stocked with toys, and a common room with chessboards, a ping-pong table, a fireplace, Internet access, and a TV. You can walk to the Mangy Moose and other fun spots, and nobody will be able to tell you apart from the skiers staying at the Four Seasons.

3315 W. Village Dr. (P.O. Box 546), Teton Village, WY 83025. (C) **307/733-3415.** Fax 307/739-1142. www.hostelx.com. $60 double. MC, V. Closed early Apr to late May and Oct to early Dec. **Amenities:** Game room; self-serve laundry. *In room:* No phone.

Snake River Lodge and Spa ⭑⭑ This perpetually changing establishment has gained some stability under the management of

RockResorts. Lodgepole beams, wooden floors, and stone fireplaces accent the main reception area. The main lodge provides accommodations where classy overshadows rustic, with exposed wooden-beam ceilings, down comforters, and luxurious furnishings. There are three levels of suites, from oversize versions of the standard rooms to three-bedroom versions with top-of-the-line kitchens, good sound systems, and Jacuzzi tubs. The 17,000-square-foot spa is the state's largest, featuring everything from microdermabrasion to hydrotherapy to free weights. Winter visitors can ski directly to a ski valet and drop their skis off for an overnight tune-up.

7710 Granite Loop Rd. (P.O. Box 348), Teton Village, WY 83025. (© **866/975-7625** or 307/732-6000. Fax 307/732-6009. www.rockresorts.com. 130 units. $249–$439 double; $590–$1,775 suite. Lower rates in spring and fall. AE, MC, V. **Amenities:** Restaurant; lounge; indoor/outdoor pool; health club; spa; Jacuzzi; children's programs; concierge; room service; dry cleaning. *In room:* TV, kitchenette, coffeemaker, hair dryer, safe.

WHERE TO DINE

Jackson has more dining options than all the other towns in this book combined, running the gamut of cuisine and price. You'll find the predictable steak/seafood/pasta menus—usually injected with a few de rigueur wild-game dishes, too—but you'll also find more-unusual options. In addition to the choices reviewed below, you can get a quick bite at **Shades Cafe,** 82 S. King St. (© **307/733-2015**), which serves good coffee, sandwiches, and other breakfast and lunch entrees. Another a.m. stalwart, the **Betty Rock Cafe,** 325 W. Pearl Ave. (© **307/733-0747**), serves creative breakfasts and plenty of espresso. For an old-fashioned chuckwagon dinner, mosey out with the **Bar-T-5 Covered Wagon Cookout and Wild West Show** (© **800/772-5386** or 307/733-5386).

EXPENSIVE

The Blue Lion ✶✶✶ ECLECTIC   In the fast-moving, high-rent world of Jackson dining, the Blue Lion stays in the forefront by staying the same. Owned and operated by Ned Brown since 1978, the restaurant is located in a two-story blue clapboard building across from a park that looks like a comfy family home. Inside, in intimate rooms accented with soft lighting, or outside on a picture-perfect patio, diners enjoy slow-paced and elegant meals. The menu features rack of lamb and wild-game specialties, such as grilled elk loin in a peppercorn sauce. Fresh fish is flown in daily for dishes such as the nori-crusted ahi.

160 N. Millward St. ℭ **307/733-3912.** www.bluelionrestaurant.com. Reservations recommended. Main courses $15–$33. AE, DC, DISC, MC, V. Summer daily 5:30–10pm; winter daily 6–10pm.

Burke's Chop House ⭐⭐ STEAKS/GAME/SEAFOOD

Formerly the chef at the steakhouse under the Million Dollar Cowboy Bar, Michael Burke struck out on his own and opened this ambitious eatery in downtown Jackson in February 2004. The sleek dining room—punctuated by plenty of dark wood, a sweeping bar, and a few antique car parts and scenic photographs—provides an understated setting for the unpretentious but excellent fare. The menu includes smoked baby back pork ribs with homemade bourbon barbecue sauce, cornmeal-crusted trout, and a nice selection of steaks and chops. The buffalo tenderloin and filets are particularly satisfying.

72 S. Glenwood St. ℭ **307/733-8575.** Reservations recommended. Main courses $16–$36. AE, DC, DISC, MC, V. Daily 6pm–close (usually 9–10pm).

The Cadillac Grille ⭐ CALIFORNIA ECLECTIC

The nostalgic neon and hip American cuisine give this restaurant a trendy air that attracts see-and-be-seen visitors as well as locals. The chefs work hard on presentation, but they also know how to prepare a wide-ranging variety of dishes, from fire-roasted elk tenderloins to pancetta-crusted Alaskan halibut. A *Wine Spectator* favorite, the wine list is equally long and varied. The Grille's upscale dining room is one of three options at this address; you can also eat at the posh bar, or the '50s-themed confines of **Billy's Giant Hamburgers,** where a great burger runs about $5. For the best of both worlds, order a burger at the bar.

55 N. Cache St. ℭ **307/733-3279.** Reservations recommended. Lunch $5–$18; dinner $12–$35. AE, MC, V. Daily 11:30am–3pm and 5:30–9:30pm.

43° North ⭐ STEAK/SEAFOOD/GAME

A former radio station at the foot of Snow King Mountain is now a top-notch eatery and nightspot, capped with a popular rooftop deck. The lunch menu includes Angus buffalo, veggie, and beef burgers alongside fish tacos and barbecue pork. (I especially enjoyed the sweet-potato frites.) Dinners are more upscale: Think pan-seared elk chops, pecan-crusted salmon, and an excellent Wyoming rib-eye. After the kitchen closes, the throngs arrive in force for live music (Wed–Sat) and drinks from the 180-year-old restored Irish bar.

645 S. Cache St. ℭ **307/733-0043.** Reservations accepted for dinner. Main courses $9–$13 lunch; $20–$36 dinner. AE, DISC, MC, V. Daily 11:30am–9:30pm (Sun from 10:30am). Bar open till 2am.

Old Yellowstone Garage ✦ ITALIAN   Since relocating west from Dubois in 2000, the Old Yellowstone Garage has continued its long-standing tradition of serving up delectable Italian in a casual Western atmosphere. The self-dubbed "slow food" served here includes starters such as *cozze mie* (mussels in a garlic–white wine sauce), calamari, and antipasti plates. The dinner menu includes risotto (prepared differently every day), San Remo (deep-fried zucchini stuffed with mascarpone), and slow-cooked lamb shank, a wintertime favorite. Wood-oven pizzas round out the menu (and *are* the menu on Sun and Mon), the specialty being the *pizze bianca,* with homemade cheeses and fresh herbs. All of this is served up in a room with hardwood floors, big windows, and spare modern style, marked simply on the outside with the letters OYG.

175 Center St. ✆ **307/734-6161**. www.oyg.com. Reservations accepted. Pizzas $13–$20; main courses $18–$48. AE, DISC, MC, V. Daily 6–10pm.

Snake River Grill ✦✦✦ CONTEMPORARY AMERICAN This is a popular drop-in spot for locals, including some of the glitterati who sojourn in the area—Harrison Ford and Calista Flockhart, to name two. The front-room dining area overlooks the busy Town Square, but there's a more private, romantic room in the back. It's an award-winning restaurant for both its wine list and its menu, which features regular fresh-fish dishes (ahi tuna is a favorite), crispy pork shank, and some game-meat entrees such as venison chops and Idaho trout. The pizzas—cooked in a wood-burning oven—are topped with exotic ingredients such as duck sausage or eggplant with portobello mushrooms.

84 E. Broadway, on the Town Square. ✆ **307/733-0557**. www.snakerivergrill.com. Reservations recommended. Main courses $20–$40. AE, MC, V. Summer daily 5:30–10pm; winter daily 6–10pm. Closed Nov and Apr.

Stiegler's ✦ *Finds* AUSTRIAN/CONTINENTAL   Austrian cuisine isn't exactly lurking beyond every street corner, waiting to be summoned with a Julie Andrews yodel, but the discerning Austrian will certainly appreciate Stiegler's. Since 1983, Stiegler's has been confusing, astonishing, and delighting customers with such favorites as elk Försterin, bratwurst, and schnitzel, as well as less recognizable (and not as heavy as Austrian food's reputation might suggest) delicacies. Each plate is served with at least three veggies for a terrific presentation and variety of tastes. The desserts are more familiar: apple strudel and crepes. Peter Stiegler, the Austrian chef, invites you to "find a little *Gemütlichkeit*"—the feeling you get when you're surrounded by good friends, good food, and, of course, good beer. The inviting copper bar has its own menu ($10–$19, with great burgers) and there are intimate tables and booths inside and a poolside patio outside.

Teton Village Rd. at the Aspens. © 307/733-1071. Reservations recommended. Main courses $16–$37. AE, MC, V. Tues–Sun 5:30–9:30pm. Closed Mon.

MODERATE

Koshu Wine Bar ★★ (Finds) ECLECTIC   Housed in the back half of the Jackson Hole Wine Company, this small, sleek dining room serves ingenious, addictive, Asian-inspired creations. The Far East is just a starting point, with offerings that meld dozens of influences into dishes such as ahi tartare and pork ribs; the menu changes on a near-daily basis. Thanks to its location in a wine store, patrons can choose from 800 varieties of wine at retail price (plus a nominal corking fee).

200 W. Broadway in the back of the Jackson Hole Wine Company. © 307/733-5283. Reservations recommended. Main courses $15–$30. AE, MC, V. Daily 6–10:30pm. Bar open till 2am, depending on crowd.

Mangy Moose (Kids) AMERICAN   Coming off the slopes at the end of a hard day of skiing or snowboarding, you can slide right to the porch of this Teton Village institution. Good luck getting a seat inside, but if you like a lot of noise and laughter, a beer or a glass of wine, and tasty food, you'll be patient—it beats getting into your car and driving into town. The decor matches the pandemonium: It looks like an upscale junk shop, with bicycles, old signs, and, naturally, a moose head or two hanging from the walls and rafters. The food is customary Wyoming fare (steak, seafood, and pasta)—I'm a big fan of the buffalo meatloaf and the fresh Idaho trout. There is often live music in the saloon, which serves both lunch and dinner, and an affiliated cafe, the RMO Cafe, serves coffee, breakfast, and lunch in a separate room from 7am to 5pm.

1 W. Village Dr., Teton Village. © 307/733-4913. Reservations recommended for larger parties. Main courses $14–$35 in the dining room; $4–$7 in the bar and cafe. AE, MC, V. Daily 5:30–10pm (dining room), 7am–5pm (cafe), and 11:30am–10pm (bar).

Nani's Genuine Pasta House ★★★ (Finds) ITALIAN   In a warmly appointed dining room with red-and-white checkered tablecloths and a slick wine bar, the food is extraordinary at Nani's. You are handed two menus when you are seated: a "Carta Classico" featuring pasta favorites such as *amitriciana* (tomato, onion, guanciale, and freshly ground black pepper) and fresh mussels in wine broth, and a list of specialties from a different featured region of Italy. Depending on when you visit, it might be Sicily, where Head Chef

Camille Parker's family has its roots, or Emilia-Romagna, where pro-
sciutto, parmesan, and balsamic vinegar are culinary staples. Parker
ventures to Italy annually for research, and you can literally taste her
passion. Your only problem with her restaurant might be finding
it—it's tucked away behind a little relic of a motel, but it is definitely
worth seeking out.

242 N. Glenwood St. (✆) **307/733-3888.** www.nanis.com. Reservations recommended. Main courses $13–$33. MC, V. Daily 5–10pm. Bar open most nights till 11pm.

Nora's Fish Creek Inn ⊀ (Finds) AMERICAN   If you like to eat
among locals, and if you like to eat a lot, Nora's is the place to hang
out in Wilson, 6 miles northwest of Jackson—just look for the 15-
foot trout on the roof. Rough, but pleasant to look at, it's an institution, and if you come here often, you'll start to recognize the
regulars, who grumble over their coffee and gossip about doings in
the valley. Breakfast is especially good, when there are pancakes and
huevos rancheros that barely fit on the huge plates. Prices are inexpensive compared to those at any of the other restaurants in town.
Dinner is fish, fish, and more fish, namely fresh Idaho trout.

5600 W. Wyo. 22, Wilson. (✆) **307/733-8288.** Reservations accepted for dinner.
Breakfast and lunch $5–$10; dinner $15–$25. AE, DISC, MC, V. Mon–Fri
6:30am–2pm; Sat–Sun 6:30am–1:30pm; daily 5–9pm. Call for winter hours.

Rendezvous Bistro ⊀⊀ AMERICAN/SEAFOOD   The Rendezvous opened in 2001 and garnered a fast local following. It's easy
to see why: The place is contemporary yet casual, the food is affordable but very good, and the service is excellent. Climb into one of the
intimate booths and order a dozen oysters on the half shell and slurp
away, but save some room for a main course, ranging from steak frites
to tuna tartare to a grilled chile-rubbed pork chop. It might sound
formal, but it's really not—the beauty is that the food is the best
upscale value in town, while the atmosphere is very laid-back.

380 S. Broadway. (✆) **307/739-1100.** Reservations recommended. Main courses
$15–$25. AE, DISC, MC, V. Sun–Thurs 5:30–10pm; Fri–Sat 5:30–11pm. Closed Sun in
winter; closed mid-Apr to mid-May.

Sweetwater Restaurant ⊀⊀ AMERICAN   Although this little
log restaurant serves American fare, it does so in a decidedly offbeat
way. The eclectic menu includes, for example, a Greek salad, a Baja
chicken salad, and a cowboy-grilled, roast-beef sandwich. During the
summer, there's outside dining. The dinner menu is just as quirky
and livened by nightly specials; try the unique chile-lime crab cakes
before diving into a giant grilled salmon filet glazed with tequila,

lemon, and honey or buffalo pot roast with jack-cheese grits. Vegetarians will want to sample the spinach and feta casserole. The lunch slate is full of creative salads and sandwiches.

85 King St. ① **307/733-3553.** www.sweetwaterrest.com. Reservations recommended. Lunch $8–$11; dinner $16–$25. AE, DISC, MC, V. Summer daily 11:30am–3pm and 5:30–9:30pm; winter daily 11:30am–2:30pm and 5:30–9pm.

Trio ⨳⨳ CONTEMPORARY AMERICAN   Opened in 2005 by a trio (thus the name) of owner/chefs who formerly worked at the Snake River Grill, this instant local favorite offers a winning combination of inviting atmosphere and remarkable food. Served in a dimly lit, social room with a fossil-rock bar and semi-open kitchen, the seasonal menu might include appetizers such as sautéed shrimp with Szechuan peppercorns and wonton crisps, and entrees like buffalo-sausage rigatoni and a killer Idaho rainbow trout on a bed of blackened corn and avocado. Everything is uniformly mouthwatering, and the portions are perfectly sized and impeccably presented and served. Lunch is mostly gourmet salads, pizzas, and sandwiches. Both lunch and dinner brings killer fries—made of either sweet potatoes with black pepper aioli or russets with addictive blue cheese fondue.

45 S. Glenwood Dr. ① **307/734-8038.** www.bistrotrio.com. Reservations recommended. Main courses $8–$15 lunch; $14–$30 dinner. AE, MC, V. Mon–Fri 11am–2pm; daily 5:30pm–close (usually 9–10pm).

INEXPENSIVE

Jedediah's House of Sourdough *Kids* AMERICAN   You feel like you've walked into the kitchen of some sodbuster's log cabin home when you enter Jedediah's—the structure was built in 1910 and now resides on the National Register of Historic Places. Bring a big appetite for breakfast and a little patience—you might have to wait for a table, and then you might have to wait for food while you stare at the interesting old photos on the wall. But it's worth it, especially for the rich flavor of the sourjacks (sourdough pancakes) served with blueberries. Lunches include soups, salads, and burgers and sandwiches—on sourdough, of course. The sourdough starter here is also historic: It dates back to the 1870s.

135 E. Broadway. ① **307/733-5671.** Breakfast $6–$12; lunch $7–$11. AE, DC, DISC, MC, V. Daily 7am–2pm.

Snake River Brewery ⨳ *Value* MICROBREWERY   One of the West's best (and busiest) microbreweries, the industrial-meets-contemporary-looking establishment offers a menu of pasta, applewood-fired pizzas and panini, and salads, plus a few entrees like "Slash and Burn Trout," served with fennel relish. The real standouts are the beers, especially Custer's Last Ale and Zonker Stout, regular winners at the Great American Beer Fest. This place is a local favorite and a great lunch spot, with daily $7 specials like turkey-and-brie wraps and chipotle BBQ sandwiches.

265 S. Millward St. ℂ 307/739-2337. www.snakeriverbrewing.com. Most dishes $8–$14. AE, DISC, MC, V. Daily 11:30am–11pm. Bar open till midnight.

JACKSON AFTER DARK

Talented musicians from well-known orchestras participate in the **Grand Teton Music Festival** ℛ (ℂ 307/733-3050; www.gtmf.org) held in summer in the amphitheater next to the tram lift. Tickets are usually available on short notice, especially for the weeknight chamber music performances, which are often terrific.

Wyoming's only year-round professional theatrical group, the **Off Square Theatre Company,** performs classic and contemporary comedies and dramas at the Center for the Arts, 265 S. Cache St. (ℂ 307/733-3021; www.offsquare.org). Tickets (typically $20–$30) for all shows should be reserved.

Those less impressed with dramaturgy should head down to the **Silver Dollar Bar,** at 50 N. Glenwood St. in the Wort Hotel (ℂ 307/733-2190), for a drink with one of the real or wannabe cowpokes at the bar. And, yes, those 2,032 silver dollars are authentic. At the very famous **Million Dollar Cowboy Bar** on the Town Square, at 25 N. Cache St. (ℂ 307/733-2207; www.milliondollar cowboybar.com), you can dance the two-step to live bands. If you want some high-octane dancing fun led by some talented local hoofers, head west to Wilson and the **Stagecoach Bar** (ℂ 307/733-4407) on Wyo. 22 on a Sunday night. It's the only night there's live music in this classic Western joint, and the place is jammed wall to wall.

5 Cody, Wyoming ℛℛ

53 miles from the east entrance to Yellowstone

Almost from the moment trappers first reported the unworldly marvels of Yellowstone, would-be entrepreneurs were setting up shop. However, none could match the vision of William F. "Buffalo Bill" Cody, the famed scout and showman who in 1887 set about building a hunting resort, an irrigation project, and a city on the eastern edge of the park. Today, Cody is one of the most beautifully situated communities in Wyoming, near the juncture of rivers that pour from the rugged Absaroka Range. The drive from the east entrance of Yellowstone to Cody cuts through the magnificent East Yellowstone

(Wapiti) Valley, a drive Theodore Roosevelt once called the most scenic 50 miles in the world.

The town oozes Western charm year-round, but it's at its best during the summer: The daytime skies are cloudless, and the longest-running rodeo in the country provides nightly entertainment under the stars. Museums, a re-created Western town, and retail shops supply plenty of diversions. Cody's friendly residents preserve and promote their particular brand of Western heritage to visitors the world over. And it's not too hard of a sell: Jackson might be the state's most renowned mountain paradise, but Cody's Western charm feels much more authentic.

ESSENTIALS

Information on air service to Cody and rental-car agencies is discussed in "Getting There," in chapter 2.

GETTING THERE   If you're driving from Cheyenne, travel north on I-25 to Casper and then west on U.S. Hwy. 20/26 to Shoshone, where U.S. Hwy. 20 turns north to Thermopolis. From there, it's another 84 miles to Cody on Wyo. 120. From Jackson, take U.S. Hwy. 191 to the West Thumb Junction in Yellowstone, drive east along the northern boundary of Yellowstone Lake, and continue on U.S. Hwy. 14/16/20 to Cody. If you enter Wyoming from the west on I-80, drive north from Rock Springs on U.S. Hwy. 191 to Farson, Wyo. 28 to Lander, Wyo. 789 to Thermopolis, and Wyo. 120 to Cody. Call ✆ **888/WYO-ROAD** (in-state) or 307/772-0824 for **road and travel information.**

VISITOR INFORMATION   For printed information on this area of Wyoming, contact **Buffalo Bill's Cody/Yellowstone Country,** 836 Sheridan Ave., P.O. Box 2454, Cody, WY 82414 (✆ **800/393-2639** or 307/587-2297; www.yellowstonecountry.org), or the **Wyoming Business Council Travel and Tourism Division,** I-25 at College Drive, Cheyenne, WY 82002 (✆ **800/225-5996** or 307/777-7777; www.wyomingtourism.org).

GETTING OUTSIDE

Because of its proximity to Yellowstone, the best place to get outdoors near Cody is the park itself, but be aware that the town's only access to Yellowstone during the winter months is by snowmobile over dizzying Sylvan Pass. Once you're outside the park, Cody doesn't have the plethora of activities that Jackson Hole does, but it's still a bustling community. **Buffalo Bill State Park,** located along the canyon and reservoir 6 miles west of Cody, is a hot spot for lovers of the outdoors, with opportunities for hiking, fishing, and a variety of watersports. Its **Buffalo Bill Reservoir** is regarded as one of the premier spots for windsurfing in the United States. The park also has facilities for camping and picnicking. In the winter, cross-country and downhill skiing, ice climbing, and snowmobiling are popular in the Cody area. Drop by **Core Mountain Sports,** 1019 15th St. (℮ **307/527-7354;** www.coremountainsports.com), for a menu of activities, including rafting, fishing, and climbing.

If you'd rather not be a driver in the park's heavy summer traffic, guided Yellowstone National Park tours are available locally through **Grub Steak Expeditions,** P.O. Box 1013, Cody, WY 82414 (℮ **800/527-6316** or 307/527-6316; www.grubsteaktours.com). Bob Richard, Grub Steak's proprietor (and one of the most knowledgeable guides you'll find), is a third-generation Cody resident and former Yellowstone ranger.

BIKING   If you want to explore the area on two wheels, bike rentals are available from **Absaroka Bikes,** 2201 17th St. (℮ **307/ 527-5566**). Although there isn't a marked network of bike paths in the Cody area, you can ride on the Forest Service trails west of town off U.S. Hwy. 14/16/20 in the Shoshone National Forest. For specific trail information, call the **Forest Service** (℮ **307/527-6241;** www.fs.fed.us/r2/shoshone).

CROSS-COUNTRY SKIING   If you favor a groomed course for cross-country skiing, try the **North Fork Nordic Trails** in Shoshone National Forest, near the east entrance to the park off U.S. Hwy. 14/16/20. You can circuit 25km (16 miles) of trails adjacent to the Pahaska Tepee Resort.

FISHING   Yellowstone's legendary fly-fishing waters are a short drive away, though you should try the smaller but excellent angling streams west of Cody: **Clark's Fork of the Yellowstone,** the **North and South Forks of the Shoshone,** and **Sunlight Creek.** To the east, the warmer and slower **Big Horn River** and **Big Horn Lake** nurture catfish, walleye, and ling for boat fishers. For advice on the trout streams near Cody, ask at **Tim Wade's North Fork Anglers,** 1107 Sheridan Ave. (℮ **307/527-7274;** www.northforkanglers.com), which stocks gear and clothing and also guides day trips for $325 to $400 for two people. If you like to troll or cast from a boat, try **Buffalo Bill Reservoir,** which has produced some big mackinaw, as well as rainbow, brown, and cutthroat trout.

FLOAT TRIPS   In summer, one of the most popular things to do in Cody is to float along the Shoshone River, the major eastern drainage of the Yellowstone River. The mild Class I and II rapids make it an enjoyable trip for almost anyone. Contact **Wyoming River Trips,** 1701 Sheridan Ave. (© **800/586-6661** or 307/587-6661; www.wyomingrivertrips.com), along with **Core Mountain Sports,** 1019 15th St. (© **307/527-7354;** www.coremountainsports.com). Prices run from about $25 to $70, depending on the length and difficulty of the trip.

GOLF   Greens fees at the 18-hole **Olive Glenn Golf and Country Club,** 802 Meadow Lane (© **307/587-5551;** www.oliveglenngolf.com), are $35 for 9 holes, and $55 for 18, cart included.

SNOWMOBILING   The most popular Cody snowmobiling trails originate from nearby **Pahaska Tepee Resort,** located 51 miles from Cody on U.S. Hwy. 14/16/20 (see "Where to Stay," later in this chapter). Don't take the Pahaska Tepee Trail over 8,541-foot Sylvan Pass if you're afraid of heights; but if you're not, go for it: You'll connect with the Yellowstone National Park trails and the lengthy Continental Divide Snowmobile Trail, and have some breathtaking views, including of Avalanche Peak (10,566 ft.) and Cody Peak (10,267 ft.). The **Sunlight trail system** is located 36 miles north of Cody and winds through the wilds to a stunning view of the Beartooth Mountains. Sledders start from a parking area at the junction of Wyo. 296 and U.S. Hwy. 212 and follow the Beartooth Scenic Byway east for 16 miles to a warming hut. To the east, there are 70 miles of snowmobile routes in the Bighorn Mountains. Snowmobiles can usually be rented in Cody at **Mountain Valley Engine Service,** 422 W. Yellowstone Ave. (© **307/587-6218;** www.mountainvalleyengine.com).

WINDSURFING   The 8-mile-long, 4-mile-wide **Buffalo Bill Reservoir,** which receives wind from three mountain gorges, is one of the top windsurfing destinations in the continental United States. It's best experienced in the warmer months of June to September. There is a boat ramp near the campground on the north side of the reservoir, just off U.S. Hwy. 14/16/20. There are no places to rent a windsurf board in the vicinity.

SPECIAL EVENTS

The Buffalo Bill Historical Center is a tremendous resource for unique events in Cody. The April festival of **Cowboy Songs and Range Ballads** features storytelling, poetry, and some fine yodeling and balladry. In mid-June, the **Plains Indian Powwow** features traditional dance competitions, crafts shows, and Native American food. Call the **Buffalo Bill Historical Center** (*©* **307/587-4771;** www.bbhc.org) for exact dates of these and other events and special exhibits. Every July 1 to July 4, during the **Cody Stampede,** the streets are filled with parades, rodeos, fireworks, street dances, barbecues, and entertainment, capped by a top-notch rodeo. Call *©* **800/ 207-0744** or 307/587-5155 for tickets (also see www.codystampede rodeo.org).

SEEING THE SIGHTS

Buffalo Bill Historical Center ✸✸✸   Nicknamed the "Smithsonian of the West," this vast museum is top-drawer, casting a scholarly eye on the relics of the West's young history while offering some flash and entertainment for the easily distracted. From its beginnings in a rustic log building, it's grown into a thoroughly impressive modern edifice that now houses five different museums in all.

The **Buffalo Bill Museum** is a monument to one of the earliest manifestations of America's celebrity culture, displaying the wares that turned a frontier scout and buffalo hunter into a renowned showman. Posters trumpet his world-famous Wild West shows featuring "Custer's Last Rally" and "Cossack of the Caucasus," and there are some grainy film clips of the show itself. The **Whitney Gallery of Western Art** showcases work by the adventurous artists who carried their palettes to the frontier to record firsthand the wilderness beauty, the proud Indian cultures, and the lives of trappers and cowboys in the 19th century. Bygone Western artists such as Frederic Remington, Charlie Russell, Albert Bierstadt, and Gutzon Borglum share exhibition space with contemporary practitioners. The **Plains Indian Museum** is devoted to the history of Plains tribes, including the Blackfeet, Cheyenne, Crow, Gros Ventre, Shoshone, and Sioux. Interactive exhibits explain the migrations and customs of the tribes and display art and artifacts, including cradleboards, ceremonial dresses and robes, pipes, and beadwork. Situated in an eye-catching rotunda populated by dozens of engaging exhibits, the **Draper Museum of Natural History** focuses on man's investigation of nature over time, with specific attention on the Greater Yellowstone Ecosystem (there's a map composed of 27,000 tiles) and many interactive displays. The **Cody Firearms Museum** displays weaponry dating back to 16th-century Europe in its collection of more than 5,000 pieces.

The center also features rotating special exhibitions, and its research library is an unparalleled resource for all things Western. Additionally, numerous educational programs are held throughout the year. Expect to spend anywhere from 2 hours to 2 days exploring the center, depending on your level of interest.

720 Sheridan Ave. (C) 307/587-4771. www.bbhc.org. Admission $15 adults, $13 seniors, $10 students 13–17, $6 children 6–12, free for children under 5; maximum $40 per family. Admission is good for 2 consecutive days. Group tour rates available by request. Nov–Mar Tues–Sun 10am–3pm; Apr daily 10am–5pm; May to mid-Sept daily 8am–8pm; mid-Sept to Oct daily 8am–5pm.

Buffalo Bill Reservoir   The **Buffalo Bill Dam** drops like a slim concrete knife 325 feet into the gorge carved by the Shoshone River west of Cody, and you can walk out atop the dam and look down the steep canyon or back across the deep blue water of the reservoir. Several workers died building it, and when it was completed in 1910, it was the tallest dam in the world. The lake behind it serves anglers, boaters, and windsurfers, while providing irrigation water to farmers downstream. An octagonal visitor center perched next to the dam provides exhibits on the reservoir, wildlife, and area recreation. There is a boat launch along the north lakeshore off U.S. Hwy. 14/16/20 and a clean, spacious campground that lacks shade.

6 miles west of Cody on U.S. Hwy. 14/16/20 at the top of Shoshone Canyon. (C) 307/527-6076 for visitor center. www.bbdvc.org. Free admission. May–Sept Mon–Sat 8am–6pm, Sun 10am–6pm.

Cody Nite Rodeo ★★ *Kids*   If you want to see an authentic Wyoming rodeo, Cody (aka "The Rodeo Capital of the World") offers a sure thing: a nightly tussle between bulls, broncos, and cowboys, as well as roping, cutting, and kids' events such as the "calf scramble"—about 100 young patrons chasing a bewildered young calf. Pay an extra $2, and you get a seat just above the chutes in the Buzzard's Roost. The 6,000-seat stadium sits out on an open terrace above the Shoshone River west of town—not a bad place to be on a cool Wyoming evening beneath the stars. Once a year, some of the nation's top rodeo competitors show up for the Fourth of July Cody Stampede (see "Special Events," above). Before the rodeo, there's a kiddie area with rides, games, and rodeo activities.

Stampede Park (on U.S. Hwy. 14/16/20 west of town toward the Wapiti Valley). (C) 800/207-0744 or 307/587-5155. www.codystampederodeo.com. Admission $17 adults, $8 children 7–12, free for children under 7. June–Aug nightly at 8pm; gates open at 7pm.

Cody Trolley Tours ★   An informative, witty look back at Cody's colorful past with a focus on the town's founding father himself, Buffalo Bill, this hour-long tour in a restored trolley takes visitors on a loop that includes historic homes, public art, and the Buffalo Bill

Reservoir. The owner/operators, Mike and Margie Johnson, deliver a running commentary augmented by visual aids and recorded snippets that will keep the kids interested. While the couple's narration occasionally comes off as an economic-development pitch for Cody, it also packs a dense serving of fun facts and trivia into the 60-minute drive.

1192 Sheridan Ave. (tours begin and end on the front porch of the Irma Hotel). *©* 307/527-7043. www.codytrolleytours.com. Admission $20 adults, $18 seniors, $8 children 5–17, free for children under 5. Ask about a combination ticket for the Buffalo Bill Historical Center. Tours offered early June to late Sept Mon–Sat at 11am, 3pm, and 6:30pm; Sun 11am and 3pm.

Museum of the Old West at Old Trail Town (Kids)
Walking the authentically creaky boardwalks here, you'll pass by gray storefronts and clapboard cabins gathered from ghost towns around the region and assembled on the original town site of Cody City, a short jog from the rodeo grounds. Soft-spoken archaeologist Bob Edgar hasn't wasted any paint on these relics, which include an 1883 cabin from Kaycee where Butch Cassidy and the Sundance Kid once conspired, a saloon decorated with bullet holes, and what must be the largest collection of worn-out buckboard carriages in the U.S. Also on-site: the relocated graves of a number of Western notables, including John "Liver-eatin'" Johnston, the model for Robert Redford's *Jeremiah Johnson.*

1831 Demaris Dr. *©* 307/587-5302. www.museumoftheoldwest.org. Admission $7 adults, $6 seniors, $3 children 6–12, free for children under 6. Mid-May to Sept daily 8am–8pm.

Tecumseh's Old West Miniature Village and Museum (Kids)
You have to pass through a trading post of Western tourist plunder and hand-crafted beadwork to get to this finely detailed miniature diorama of Wyoming and Montana history. Described by proprietor Jerry Fick as his "lifetime work," the room-size landscape depicts everything from fur trappers floating the rivers to Custer's last moments at Little Big Horn. There is also a sizable collection of Indian and pioneer artifacts and taxidermy.

142 W. Yellowstone Ave. *©* 307/587-5362. www.tecumsehs.com. Free admission. June–Aug daily 8am–8pm; May and Sept 9am–6pm. Call for hours in winter.

WHERE TO STAY

If you want to book lodging before you arrive, a good accommodations resource is **Cody Lodging Company Houses,** 1302 Beck Ave. (*©* **800/587-6560** or 307/587-6000; www.codyguesthouses.com), which manages numerous properties, from Victorian B&Bs to three-bedroom houses. Rates range from $100 to $500 a night. If you're on a budget, try **Bison Willy's Base Camp,** 1625 Alger St. (© 877/587-0629 or 307/587-0629; www.bisonwillys.com), a home converted into a hostel of sorts with dormitory-style bunks going for $20 a night and private double rooms for $79. There are a communal kitchen, a "beer deck," and a dog kennel on-site.

Buffalo Bill Village Resort: Comfort Inn, Holiday Inn, and Buffalo Bill Village Historic Cabins ☆

Consisting of three distinct lodging options at the same convenient location, Buffalo Bill Village has something for everybody. The Holiday and Comfort inns are similar to their chain brethren elsewhere, while the village of historic cabins offers a rustic exterior and a more Western feel, with modern conveniences inside. The former two are priced nearly identically and have similar amenities. The one- and two-bedroom cabins at Buffalo Bill Village are simply equipped—with a bed, phone, and TV—and surrounded by plenty of room for the kids to roam. The cabins themselves first housed the contractors who built the city circa 1920, and became the centerpiece of this family-owned resort in the 1950s. The Holiday Inn followed in the '70s, the Comfort Inn in the '90s. Also on-site: an Old West-style boardwalk where you can shop for curios or sign up for tours and river trips, an outdoor heated pool, and several restaurants.

17th St. and Sheridan Ave., Cody, WY 82414. © 800/527-5544. Fax 307/587-2795. www.blairhotels.com. Comfort Inn: 75 units. $69–$169 double. Holiday Inn: 189 units. $69–$169 double. Buffalo Bill Village Historic Cabins: 83 units. $59–$159 double. AE, DC, DISC, MC, V. Historic Cabins closed Oct–Apr. **Amenities:** Restaurant; lounge; outdoor pool; health club; tour desk; courtesy car; shopping arcade; self-serve laundry; dry cleaning. *In room:* A/C, TV, high-speed Internet, coffeemaker, hair dryer, iron.

The Chamberlin Inn ☆☆

A boardinghouse opened here in 1903, and the property evolved and devolved over the course of the next century until Ev and Susan Diehl took over the property in 2005 and completely restored it—and then some. Centered on a serene and green courtyard, the new-and-improved Chamberlin Inn is now Cody's best lodging option, just a block from the center of town and featuring charming historic rooms and apartment units. Of special note are the Hemingway Suite—"Papa" stayed here in 1932—with an angling motif and a small Hemingway library; and the lavish Courthouse unit, the original town courthouse reimagined as a luxury apartment.

1032 12th St., Cody, WY 82414. ℂ 888/587-0202 or 307/587-0202. www.chamberlin inn.com. 24 units, including 10 suites and apartments. $145–$165 double; $235–$650 suite or apt. AE, DISC, MC, V. *In room:* A/C, cable TV, wireless Internet, kitchen, coffeemaker.

Cody Cowboy Village 𝔞

New in 2006, this property is a couples-oriented resort in a family-oriented town. The "village," consisting of a cluster of cabin units near the rodeo grounds, is a world away from the bustling boardwalks of downtown Cody. The log cabins meld contemporary and cowboy in their decor. All have a deck in front; suites feature microwaves and fridges. Most units have one king bed, but six have two queens.

203 W. Yellowstone Ave., Cody, WY 82414. ℂ 307/587-7555. www.codycowboy village.com. 50 units, including 10 suites. $79–$139 double; $99–$189 suite. Rates include continental breakfast. AE, MC, V. **Amenities:** Small outdoor pool. *In room:* Cable TV, wireless Internet.

The Irma Hotel *(Overrated*

Buffalo Bill's entrepreneurial gusto ultimately left him penniless, but it also left us this century-old hotel (named for his daughter) in the heart of town. Cody hoped to corral visitors who got off the train on their way to Yellowstone, and one of his lures was an elaborate cherrywood bar, a gift from straight-laced Queen Victoria. You can still hoist a jar on Her Royal Majesty's slab in the Silver Saddle Saloon, or spend the night in a renovated room that might have once housed a president or prince.

Suites are named after local characters from the town's early days: The Irma Suite, on the corner of the building, has a queen-size bed, a writing table, a vanity in the bedroom area, a small sitting area, and an old-fashioned bathroom with a tub/shower combination. While the Irma's aura will surely please history buffs, those acclimated to ultramodern convenience will probably want to look elsewhere. But the hotel's location in the middle of town and the regular schedule of reenacted gunfights out front help compensate.

1192 Sheridan Ave., Cody, WY 82414. ℂ 800/745-4762 or 307/587-4221. Fax 307/ 587-1775. www.irmahotel.com. 73 units, including 15 restored suites. $52–$110 double; $55–$145 suite. AE, DC, DISC, MC, V. **Amenities:** Restaurant; lounge. *In room:* A/C, cable TV, wireless Internet, hair dryer.

The Mayor's Inn 𝔞𝔞

This two-story A-frame, built in 1905 for Mayor Frank Houx, found itself in the path of a wrecking ball in 1997. However, before it was demolished, it was sold and moved on a truck to its current location, just a few blocks away. It's now one of Cody's best B&Bs, with rooms such as the Yellowstone, featuring a lodgepole-pine bed frame and black-and-white photos of the park's early years, and the Hart Mountain Suite, with romance and floral decor in spades. There's also a carriage house (breakfast not included) with a well-equipped kitchen. The breakfasts here are a hearty treat, featuring sourdough flapjacks and buffalo sausage.

1413 Rumsey Ave., Cody, WY 82414. ℂ **888/217-3001** or 307/587-0887. Fax 307/587-0890. www.mayorsinn.com. 5 units, including 1 suite. $120–$160 double; $210 suite. Rates include full breakfast. AE, DISC, MC, V. *In room:* A/C, cable TV, wireless Internet, hair dryer, hot tub, no phone.

Pahaska Tepee Resort ℛ Buffalo Bill's hunting lodge, only 2 miles from the east entrance to Yellowstone, was dubbed with his Lakota name, *Pahaska* (longhair), when he opened the lodge to park visitors in 1905. Near the top of the beautiful Wapiti Valley along U.S. Hwy. 14/16/20, Pahaska is a popular stop for people visiting the Yellowstone area. The cabins are scattered on the hill behind the historic (and colorfully decorated) lodge. Accommodations have limited amenities and might best be described as "mini-motels" with two to five rooms, each with a private entrance. Some bathrooms have only showers, some have tubs—it's best to ask in advance. The resort also has a gift shop, restaurant, and trail-ride stables.

183 Yellowstone Hwy., Cody, WY 82414. ℂ **800/628-7791** or 307/527-7701. Fax 307/527-4019. www.pahaska.com. 47 units. Mid-June to Aug $100–$150 double, $595 condo, $1,095 lodge; off-season $72–$140 double, $495 condo, $995 lodge. DISC, MC, V. Closed mid-Oct to Apr. **Amenities:** Restaurant; lounge. *In room:* Kitchen.

WHERE TO DINE

For its size, Cody may have more good restaurants than you'd expect. If you need something less than a formal meal, such as a plateful of fuel food or a jolt of caffeine for a busy day, Cody has a good supply of familiar fast-food joints and a few informal, inexpensive places. **Peter's Cafe Bakery,** at 1219 Sheridan Ave. (ℂ **307/527-5040;** www.peters-cafe.com), across the street from the Irma, serves breakfast (freshly baked bagels, pastries, and espresso), plus subs and burgers for lunch and dinner. One of the best places day or night to get a steak or a beer and a burger (or Rocky Mountain oysters!) is the thoroughly Western **Proud Cut Saloon,** 1227 Sheridan Ave. (ℂ **307/527-6905**), where lots of rodeo riders keep a running tab.

Cassie's Supper Club ℛℛℛ WESTERN   Cassie's is the sort of classic roadhouse you might expect and look for in the West: big platters of beef, four bars serving drinks, and ornery roadhouse decor with taxidermy, antelope skulls, and assorted cowboy ephemera. This place has the routine down, having been in business since 1922.

Located along the highway west of town in what was once a "house of ill fame," Cassie's is now very respectable and quite good. Besides the requisite steaks—grilled to perfection—there's seafood (including a great walleye dinner), pasta, and chicken, plus a full menu of specialty drinks. In the Buffalo Bar, a 20-foot mural depicts horses, cowboys, and shootouts. The near-mythical dance floor bustles to the twang of live country music every night in summer.

214 Yellowstone Ave. © 307/527-5500. www.cassies.com. Reservations recommended. Lunch $7–$20; dinner $18–$48. AE, DISC, MC, V. Daily 11am–11pm; Jan–Mar Tues–Sun 11am–9pm.

Maxwell's Restaurant (Kids ECLECTIC AMERICAN A family restaurant in which "family" does not translate to "bland," Maxwell's has some spicy chicken and pasta dishes to go with its salads, seafood, and beef. The gourmet pizzas aren't a bad choice; neither is the pork tenderloin Marsala, sautéed in a light wine sauce with portobello mushrooms. You can even order a Philly cheese steak for lunch, uncommon in Wyoming. The low-backed booths and varnished wood tables are sometimes packed with boisterous families, raising the noise level and waitress stress, but it's a friendly crowd. The bread and dessert are homemade daily.

937 Sheridan Ave. © 307/527-7749. Reservations accepted. Lunch $6.50–$9; dinner $12–$28. AE, DISC, MC, V. Mon–Sat 11am–9pm.

Shiki (FF SUSHI An anomalous standout in meat-and-potatoes Cody, Shiki is a superlative sushi bar. With spare Asian decor—consisting primarily of artfully hung cloth and an attractive water feature—and booth, table, and bar seating, the setting matches the top-notch sushi rolls and tempura, teriyaki, and curry entrée. The sushi includes traditional rolls like spicy tuna and eel, as well as a few regional variations—like the Heart Mountain, with crab, cucumber, avocado, and crunchy tempura flakes. Don't be alarmed by the lack of an ocean nearby: Fresh fish is flown in two to three times a week from both coasts.

1420 Sheridan Ave. © 307/527-7116. Reservations not accepted. Sushi rolls $4–$14; main courses $11–$24. AE, MC, V. Mon–Fri 11am–2pm; Mon–Sat 4–9pm; Sun 11am–9pm. Closed Sun in winter.

Wyoming's Rib & Chop House (FF STEAKS One of an upscale regional chain with locations in Billings and Livingston, Montana, and Sheridan, Wyoming, this is the place to head for terrific ribs, chops, and steaks, but vegetarians will have difficulty finding a meatless main course. Chicken and seafood round out the menu, and desserts like "Pecan Meltaway"—a chocolate crust filled with ice cream, pecans, and more chocolate—provide decadent finales.

1367 Sheridan Ave. ⓒ **307/587-4917**. www.ribandchophouse.com. Main courses $6–$28. AE, DISC, MC, V. Mon–Fri 11am–10pm; Sat–Sun 4–10pm.

CODY AFTER DARK

The **Cody Stage,** 1110 Beck Ave. (ⓒ **307/587-7469**), is a local theater that stages several plays each year. **Dan Miller's Music Revue,** 1549 Sheridan Ave. (ⓒ **307/272-7855;** www.cowboymusicrevue. com), offers a cowboy-style musical variety show Monday through Saturday at 8pm.

For those with less cultured aims, Cody has a lively nightlife, headed by **Cassie's** (see above), with a dance floor laden with real and wannabe cowboys and cowgirls. Downtown, the historic **Silver Dollar Bar,** at 1313 Sheridan Ave. (ⓒ **307/527-7666**), has tasty burgers, live music, pool tables, and numerous TV screens. Housed in a converted brick garage, **Cooter Brown's,** in the alley behind 1134 13th St. (ⓒ **307/587-6261**), draws in hordes of hip, young Wyomans with DJs, bands, and regular drink specials.

9

A Yellowstone & Grand Teton Nature Guide

Although they are often linked in people's minds, Yellowstone and Grand Teton national parks couldn't be much more different. One is an immense wilderness plateau that sits atop a caldera seething with molten lava; the other is a striking set of peaks rising from a broad river plain. One encloses some of the most remote backcountry in the Lower 48 and provides crucial habitat for rare species such as grizzly bears and wolves; the other is only a quick drive away from a chic resort town and includes an airport and grazing cattle in its mixed-use approach.

What they *do* share is the affection of millions of visitors who come here annually to renew their ties to nature through the parks' shining mountains, alpine lakes, majestic elk, and astonishing geysers.

Unfortunately, mining, logging, and housing developments have impacted the area known as the **Greater Yellowstone Ecosystem** that surrounds the parks. The ecosystem is an interdependent system of watersheds, mountain ranges, wildlife habitat, and other components extending beyond the two parks into seven national forests, an Indian reservation, three national wildlife refuges, and nearly a million acres of private land. To put it into perspective, the ecosystem's 18 million acres span an area as big as Connecticut, Rhode Island, and Delaware combined. It is one of the largest intact temperate ecosystems on the planet.

It's also a massive and important source of water. West of the Continental Divide, snowmelt trickles into creeks, streams, and rivers through Yellowstone before draining into the Snake River, traveling through Grand Teton National Park and Idaho, and running into the Columbia River, which winds its way west through Oregon and into the Pacific Ocean.

Water on the eastern slopes of the divide passes through Yellowstone in the form of the Madison and Gallatin rivers, which meet the Jefferson River west of Bozeman, Montana, merging into the

Missouri. Then, as the song lyrics tell us, the Mighty Mo runs "down the Mississippi to the Gulf of Mexico."

As if that weren't enough, the headwaters of the Yellowstone River are in the remote Thorofare country south of Yellowstone Lake. After running north the length of the park, the Yellowstone meanders across Montana as the longest undammed river in America, until it converges with the Missouri in North Dakota.

1 The Parks Today

It has long been difficult for park managers to both provide the public with a good vacation and protect the natural wonders of the parks. One challenge is to make the parks accessible to three million annual visitors, many with different, even contradictory, expectations of a wilderness excursion. This brings about the construction of new facilities and ongoing road maintenance and repair. At the same time, the parks are wild preserves, and the National Park Service must cope with the impact of six million feet on the forests, meadows, and thermal areas, as well as on the day-to-day lives of the millions of animals that inhabit the area.

It's a tough balancing act. Some of the pivotal issues in the parks today include the impact of snowmobiles; the reintroduced wolves and the resulting livestock losses of ranchers in and around the parks; the inadequacy of the park's infrastructure to cope with three million annual human visitors; invasive non-native species, such as lake trout and zebra mussels; and the reduction of habitat surrounding the parks, coupled with a growing population of elk and bison seeking forage beyond park boundaries and possibly infecting domestic animals with a disease called brucellosis. And that's the short list.

Possible solutions are often "too little, too late," layering complex management strategies on an ecosystem that might do better if it were simply allowed to work things out naturally. The problem is, Grand Teton and Yellowstone have already been altered significantly by humans, so "natural" becomes a relative concept.

A good example is the reintroduction of a natural predator of the overpopulated elk: gray wolves, which were eliminated in the 1920s. These days, ranchland surrounds the parks, so the Defenders of Wildlife set up a trust to pay anyone who loses a calf to a wolf—and ranchers do because wolves haven't read the management plan. And wolves from Yellowstone have migrated south into Grand Teton and beyond; besides the packs that den in and around the Gros Ventre area, a lone wolf was spotted at the Wyoming-Colorado border, and another turned up dead on I-70 west of Denver in 2004.

Yellowstone's artificial boundaries also cause problems for bison. The state of Montana now allows hunters to shoot bison when they stray outside the park. Ranchers fear bison because of brucellosis, a disease that, when transmitted to cattle, causes cows to abort fetuses. Now there is talk of mass vaccinations of elk and bison, although, so far, there are almost no documented cases of either species infecting livestock.

As for the proliferation of snowmobiles and cars, most agree that there must be changes as visitation continues to grow. Currently, snowmobilers flock to the park as soon as the snow starts falling and remain until late February. While the popularity of the sport has had a positive effect on the tourism industry in the gateways of West Yellowstone, Jackson, and Gardiner, park officials are studying the long-term environmental impact of the machines. In their opinion, the snowmobiles create their own types of problems. The machines are noisy, and engine emissions create air pollution, which some say presents a health hazard. While better technology has reined in the noise and smog to a large degree, the snowmobiles still share narrow trails with wildlife during months when the animals' energy levels are depleted by bad weather and a lack of food. As a consequence, a 3-year phase-out of snowmobiles was agreed upon in 2000 but it was overturned before park policy could be changed.

Then there's the traffic issue. Park roads are narrow and twisty, so the intrusion of 30-foot-long motor homes and pickup trucks towing trailers creates congestion, especially during the peak summer months. There have been studies of transportation alternatives to unclog park roadways, even a costly monorail that would wind through Yellowstone, but no decisive action has been taken.

Recently, park scientists have battled to protect the native cut-throat trout in Yellowstone Lake from the impact of lake trout introduced by man. They have also recognized the enormous value of the microbes evolving in Yellowstone's super-hot thermal areas, and scientists are using them in new technologies ranging from nano-circuitry to industrial bleaching products. As the world awakens to the accelerating loss of vital species in shrinking wild habitat, it becomes ever more imperative to find ways in which to preserve the relatively unspoiled ecosystems, like that of Greater Yellowstone.

2 Landscape & Geology

The Yellowstone and Grand Teton region is one of the most dynamic seismic areas in the world—wracked by earthquakes, cracked by water boiling to the surface, and littered with the detritus of previous volcanic eruptions. Today, the bowels of the Yellowstone caldera are again filling with magma. Geologic studies show that, for the past 2 million years, the plateau has blown its top every 600,000 years or so—and the last explosion was about 600,000 years ago. That means that a titanic blow—bigger than anything seen in recorded history—could happen, well, any century now, give or take 10,000 years. The geological time frame is a long one, by human standards.

As you'll learn when you visit the exhibits on the park's geology at Moose, Mammoth, and the various geothermal areas, what you see on the surface—great layers of ash and the core of volcanic vents, such as Mount Washburn and Bunsen Peak—is only a fraction of the story of Yellowstone and Grand Teton.

Situated on 2.2 million acres, Yellowstone is significantly larger than its sister to the south. Encompassing 3,472 square miles, Yellowstone boasts 310 miles of paved roads and 1,000 miles of backcountry trails, and it is home to more geysers and hot springs than the combined total in the rest of the world.

Although it can't match Yellowstone's size, Grand Teton National Park is nothing to sneeze at. It has towering mountain spires, which have been compared to cathedral towers, reaching almost 14,000 feet skyward; picturesque glacial lakes; and a great deal of interesting topography. The roughly 500 square miles of Grand Teton contain about 160 miles of paved roads and over 250 miles of hiking trails.

THE FACES OF YELLOWSTONE NATIONAL PARK

By the completion of the 1872 Hayden expedition, explorers had identified several distinct areas in the park, each with its own physical characteristics. Less spectacular than the craggy mountain scenery of Grand Teton, and less imposing than the vast expanses of the Grand Canyon of Arizona, Yellowstone's beauty is subtle, reflecting the changes it has undergone during its explosive past.

Although Yellowstone has its share of mountains, much of the park is a high mountain plateau. The environment changes dramatically as you ascend the mountain slopes from the foothill zones in the valleys—the elevation at the entrance at West Yellowstone is 6,666 feet, for example, compared to 5,314 at the Gardiner entrance.

Because the park lies about halfway between the equator and the North Pole, its summers consist of long, warm days that stimulate plant growth at the lower elevations.

As you walk the park trails, you'll find that plant distribution changes with the elevation. At the lowest elevations, down around 5,300 feet above sea level, you'll find **grassy flats** and sagebrush growing on dry, porous soils, with creeks and rivers cutting through to form wildlife-rich **riparian zones.** Next up: the **foothills,** sloping upward toward peaks, sometimes dotted by deposits of glacial moraine. Douglas fir, pine, and other conifers, as well as stands of aspen, clad these slopes, and there are marshes and ponds fed by the spring snowmelt. Shrubs and flowers, such as huckleberry and columbine, favor these wet, shady spots.

Then comes the **mountain zone** (6,000–7,600 ft.), thickening forests dominated by lodgepole pine, broken by meadows where deer, elk, and moose often graze. The transition area between the highest forest and the bare surface above timberline is known as the **subalpine zone** (7,600–11,300 ft. of elevation). Finally, we come to the bare rock at the very top of the continental shelf, where small, hardy plants, such as glacier lilies and sky pilot, bloom briefly after the annual thaw.

Although the park is most famous for its geysers, visitors can choose among very different environments, reflections of the long-term effects of geologic activity and weather.

The limestone terraces at **Mammoth Hot Springs** give testimony to the region's subsurface volcanic activity. The park sits atop a rare geologic hot spot where molten rock still rises to within 2 miles of the Earth's surface, heating the water in a plumbing system that still mystifies scientists.

The **northern section of the park,** between Mammoth Hot Springs and the Tower-Roosevelt region, is a high-plains area that is primarily defined by mountains, forests, and broad expanses of river valleys that were created by ice movements.

The road between the Tower-Roosevelt junction and the northeast entrance winds through the **Lamar Valley,** an area that has been covered by glaciers three times, most recently during an ice age that began 25,000 years ago and continued for 10,000 years—in geologic terms, just yesterday. Because this area was a favorite of Theodore Roosevelt, it is often referred to as "Roosevelt Country." The beautiful valley where elk, bison, and wolves interact is dotted with glacial ponds and strewn with boulders deposited by moving ice.

Farther south are **Pelican** and **Hayden valleys,** the two largest ancient lake beds in the park. They feature large, open meadows with abundant plant life that provides food for a population of bison and elk.

In the warm months, you'll enjoy the contrast between the lush green valleys and **Canyon Country,** in the center of the park. Canyon Country is defined by the Grand Canyon of the Yellowstone, a colorful, 1,000-foot-deep, 24-mile-long gorge—in many opinions, just as dramatic as its cousin in Arizona. The Yellowstone River cuts through the valley, in some places moving 64,000 cubic feet of water per second, creating two waterfalls in the process, one of which is more than twice the height of Niagara Falls.

When you arrive at the **southern geyser basins,** you might feel that you've been transported through a geologic time warp. Here you will find the largest collections of thermal areas in the world—there are perhaps 600 geysers and 10,000 geothermal features in the park—and the largest geysers in Yellowstone. The result: boiling water that is catapulted skyward and barren patches of sterile dirt; hot, bubbling pools that are unimaginably colorful; and, of course, the star of this show, Old Faithful geyser. Plan on spending at least 80 minutes here because that's the typical period between eruptions that send thousands of gallons of boiling water through the sky at a speed exceeding 100 mph.

You'll see the park's volcanic activity on a 17-mile journey east to the **lake area,** the scene of three volcanic eruptions that took place more than 600,000 years ago. When the final eruption blasted more than 1,000 square miles of the Rocky Mountains into the stratosphere, it created the Yellowstone caldera, a massive depression measuring 28 by 47 miles, and Yellowstone Lake basin, some 20 miles long and 14 miles wide, reaching depths of 390 feet. You'll notice, as you travel the roads here, that the landscape consists of flat plateaus of lava that are hundreds of feet thick.

THE SPIRES OF GRAND TETON NATIONAL PARK

Your first sight of the towering spires of the **Cathedral Group**—the *trois tetons* (three breasts), as lonesome French trappers called them—will create an indelible impression. A bit of history makes them even more interesting.

Their formation began more than 2.5 billion years ago when sand and volcanic debris settled in an ancient ocean that covered this entire area. Scientists estimate that roughly 40 million to 80 million years ago, a compression of the Earth's surface caused an uplift of the entire Rocky Mountain chain from Mexico to Canada. This was just the first step in an ongoing series of events that included several periods during which a miles-thick crust of ice covered the area. Then, 6 million to 9 million years ago, the shifting of the earth's plates caused movement along the north-south Teton fault that produced a tremendous uplift. The valley floor also dropped precipitously, and these simultaneous forces pushed the rock that is now the **Teton Range** to its present site from a position 20,000 to 30,000 feet *below* what is today the floor of Jackson Hole.

The west block of rock tipped upward to create the Teton Range, and the eastern block swung downward to form the valley that is now called **Jackson Hole**—kind of like a pair of horizontal swinging doors that moved the earth 5 miles.

At this conclusion of the upheaval, and after eons of erosion and glacier activity, the **Grand Teton peak,** centerpiece of this 40-mile-long fault area, towered 13,770 feet above sea level, more than a mile above the visitor center at Moose Junction. Eleven other peaks over 12,000 feet high are in the park today, with conditions that support mountain glaciers. As you gaze upward at this magnificent range, you will notice that many of the cliffs are more than half a mile in height.

During geologic explorations of **Mount Moran** (elevation 12,605 ft.), which gets less attention than it deserves, it was discovered that erosion has removed some 3,000 feet of material from its summit, so it once must have been more than 15,000 feet high. Equally remarkable is the fact that the thin layer of Flathead sandstone on top of this peak is found buried at least 24,000 feet below the valley's surface—further evidence of the skyward thrust of the mountains.

Although this is the youngest range in the Rockies—yet another geologic anomaly—the rocks here are some of the oldest in North America, consisting of granitic gneisses and schists, which are the hardest and least-porous rocks known to geologists.

The Teton area experienced a cooling trend about 150,000 years ago, during which time glaciers more than 2,000 feet thick flowed from higher elevations, and an ice sheet covered Jackson Hole. When it melted for the final time, some 60,000 to 80,000 years ago, it gouged the 386-foot-deep, 16-mile-long depression now known as **Jackson Lake.**

The receding layers of ice also left other calling cards. Several beautiful **glacial lakes** were created, including Phelps, Taggart, Bradley, Jenny, String, and Leigh. The sides of **Cascade Canyon** were polished by receding ice. Glacial lakes, called **cirque lakes,** were carved at the heads of canyons, and the peaks of the mountains were honed to their present jagged edges. Five glaciers have survived on Mount Moran. The best trail for glacial views is the Cascade Trail, which leads to the Schoolroom Glacier. But you shouldn't walk on the Mount Moran glaciers unless you are experienced; it's very dangerous.

3 Plant Life in the Parks

When it comes to the variety of plants in the two parks, the only limiting factor is the high altitude—otherwise, the diversity of terrain, weather, and soils permits a fairly wide range of vegetation. Estimates vary, but in the ecosystem known as Greater Yellowstone, there are more than 1,500 native plant varieties. In an area larger than many of our states on the eastern seaboard—more than 3,900 square miles between the two parks—there's plenty of room for them to stretch their roots and branches. Because of the diverse terrain, some species are found living on the dry valley beds in hostile soil, close to other species that predominate in lush meadows and riverbeds. Some thrive in thermal areas, while others do well in alpine areas, near mountain lakes, and in cirques near glaciers.

The history of the parks' plant life makes for interesting reading. Examination of plant fossils indicates that life began during the Eocene epoch, approximately 58 million years ago, and continued for 25 million years. The inspection of petrified tree stumps in Yellowstone's Lamar Valley led to the identification of 27 distinct layers of forests, one atop the other.

Climatic conditions during the Eocene period were similar to those in the southeastern and south-central United States. Difficult as it might be to imagine, the area was once a warm, temperate zone in which rainfall might have averaged 50 to 60 inches per year at what was then an elevation of 3,000 feet above sea level.

These days, the elevation ranges from 5,000 to 13,000 feet, the average low temperature is approximately 30° F (–1°C), and hundreds of inches of snow fall each year. Plants have adapted to a growing season that is merely 60 days in duration. As a consequence, forests once populated with hardwoods (such as maple, magnolia, and sycamore) are now filled with conifers, the most common of which are pine, spruce, and fir. A smattering of cottonwood and aspen also thrive in the cool park temperatures.

Some experts speculate that during the glacial periods, the tallest mountains in the Lamar Valley of Yellowstone were islands amid a sea of ice, thus providing refuge for some species of plant life.

The parks have several growing zones. Above 10,000 feet in the alpine zone, plants adapt to wind, snow, and lack of soil by growing close to the ground, flowering soon after the snows melt. You'll find such flora on trails near Dunraven Pass in Yellowstone and in Cascade Canyon in Grand Teton.

In Yellowstone, the canyon and subalpine regions, at 7,000 to 10,000 feet, are known for **conifer forests** and open meadows of **wildflowers.** As elevation increases, wildflowers are abundant and healthy, while trees are stunted and shrublike.

In the valley in Grand Teton, at 6,400 to 7,000 feet, the porous valley soil supports plants that tolerate hot and dry summertime conditions. **Sagebrush, wildflowers,** and **grasses** thrive and predominate. Plants bloom in a pageant of colors from early June to early July.

Identifying the plants described below does not require a degree in botany, but Richard J. Shaw's book *Plants of Yellowstone and Grand Teton National Park* (Wheelwright Press) will help.

TREES

Coniferous trees are most common in the parks because of the high altitude and short growing season, but there are some hardy deciduous trees as well, such as cottonwood and aspen. The most common cone-bearing trees in the parks are lodgepole pines, which cover as much as 80% of Yellowstone, and Douglas fir, subalpine fir, Engelmann spruce, blue spruce, and whitebark pine. The key to identification is the trees' basic shape, the shape of their needles, and their cones.

LODGEPOLE PINE   This familiar tree grows tall and slender, with bare trunk at the bottom and needles near the top resulting in dense stands that look like the spears of a closely ranked army. The needles of the lodgepole are clustered in pairs, typically around 3 inches long. You'll see logs from this tree supporting tepees and in the construction of cabins.

*Lodgepole
Pine*

*Douglas
Fir*

DOUGLAS FIR "Doug fir" is actually a member of the pine family, with prickly cones and dark, deeply etched bark. This tree has flat, flexible, single needles that grow around the branch, giving the tree the appearance of fullness. Another giveaway is that its cones hang downward and do not disintegrate aloft, but litter the forest floor. These trees like the north-facing side of the mountain.

SUBALPINE FIR You can distinguish firs by their needles, which sprout individually from branches instead of in clusters, like a pine; and by their cones, which grow upright on the branch until they dry up and blow away. Look for the slender, conical crown of this tree. When heavy snows weigh down the lower branches, they often become rooted, forming a circle of smaller trees called a snow mat. You'll find subalpine fir at high elevations near timberline.

Subalpine Fir

ENGELMANN SPRUCE This tree also likes the higher elevations, growing in shaded ravines and in the canyons of the Teton Range above 6,800 feet and sometimes much higher. Look for it near Kepler Cascades, Spring Creek, and the south entrance of Yellowstone National Park. It is distinguished by single needles that are square and sharp to the touch, and by cones with papery scales that are approximately 1½ inches long.

Engelmann Spruce

Blue Spruce

BLUE SPRUCE   The Engelmann spruce's cousin, this tree is most commonly found along the Snake River near Jackson. True to its name, it is characterized by its bluish appearance; rather stiff, sharp needles; and cones that are twice the size of the Engelmann's.

OTHER PLANTS
Here's a brief listing of some of the most common and interesting plants found in the ecosystem.

Glacier Lily

Indian Paintbrush

GLACIER LILY   A member of the lily family with a nodding bloom on a 6- to 12-inch stem, this bright yellow spring flower is found in abundance in both parks at elevations of more than 7,500 feet. Also known as the fawn lily, trout lily, and adder's-tongue, it is especially common near Sylvan Pass and on Dunraven Pass.

INDIAN PAINTBRUSH   This is the Wyoming state flower. It exhibits a distinctive narrow, bright scarlet bloom that is most commonly found from mid-June to early September in the Snake River bottomland. Other species are white, yellow, orange, and pink.

PLAINS PRICKLY PEAR   This member of the cactus family is only one of two such species found in the park, most frequently in the Mammoth area and near the Snake River. It is distinguished by thick, flat green stems armed with spines and, during midsummer, a conspicuous yellow flower with numerous petals. American Indians,

---

Tips **Photo Tip**
To successfully record your discovery of the parks' flora, consider adding a microlens to your arsenal of camera gear that will allow you to focus within 6 inches of blossoms. Film speeds of 200 ISO or faster will add to the chances of proper exposure, even on cloudy days.

who recognized prickly pear's medicinal qualities, treated warts by lacerating them and then applying juice from the plant.

Plains Prickly Pear

Fringed Gentian

FRINGED GENTIAN   This member of the gentian family is the official flower of Yellowstone Park, where it is common and blooms throughout the summer. The purple petals are fused into a 2-inch-long corolla and sit atop 1- to 3-foot-tall stems. It is also found below Jackson Lake Dam in Grand Teton.

Silky Phacelia

SILKY PHACELIA   Silky is one of the most photogenic and easily recognized species in the parks. Growing in purple clumps alongside the road at Dunraven Pass, the flower derives its name from the silvery pubescence that covers stems and leaves. It's best photographed in July and August.

SHOOTING STAR   The shooting star is characterized by pinkish ½- to 1-inch-long flowers that dangle earthward like meteorites from a 12-inch stem; they bloom in June. It is commonly found near thermal areas, streambeds, and Yellowstone Lake.

YELLOW MONKEY FLOWER   The monkey flower exhibits a bright yellow petal that, together with orange spots, attracts insect pollinators near streambeds at elevations of 7,000 to 9,000 feet all summer. It is also found near thermal areas and Yellowstone Lake.

Shooting Star

Yellow Monkey Flower

FAIRYSLIPPER (also known as the **Calypso Orchid**)   Finding this beautiful orchid might require some serious detective work, but the payoff is worth the effort. It is one of 15 orchid species found in the parks and is considered by many to be the most beautiful and striking. Seen during May and June, it usually has one small, green leaf and a red-pink flower that resembles a small lady's slipper, hence the name. It is found in cool, deep-shaded areas and is becoming rare because its habitat is disappearing.

Fairyslipper (aka Calypso Orchid)

Bitterroot

BITTERROOT   The state flower of Montana, the bitterroot, with its fleshy rose and white petals, which extend to 1 inch in length, makes its first appearance in early June in dry, open, sometimes-stony soil and in grassy meadows. It was a source of food for Indians, who introduced it to Captain Meriwether Lewis of Lewis and Clark fame, hence its botanical name *(Lewisia rediviva)*.

Columbia Monkshood

COLUMBIA MONKSHOOD This is a purple, oddly shaped flower with a hood-shape structure that has two sepals at its side and two below (these make up the calyx, the leafy parts surrounding the flower). Its stem varies in height from 2 to 5 feet. You'll find these flowers in wet meadows and on stream banks from June to August, often near thermal areas, streambeds, and Yellowstone Lake.

4 Wildlife in the Parks

For many, the primary reason for a visit to these parks is the wildlife: bear, bighorn sheep, bison, elk, bald eagles, river otters, and moose all wandering free, often within roadside view of travelers. Yellowstone and Grand Teton are home to the largest concentration of free-roaming wildlife in the Lower 48. This includes one of the largest herds of elk in North America, the largest free-roaming herd of bison in the country, and the only significant population of grizzly bears south of Canada.

But it doesn't stop there. Also in the parks are eight species of ungulates (hoofed mammals), black bears, and three species of wildcats, as well as coyotes, wolverines, pine martens, about 60 smaller species of mammals, and 322 species of birds. Add to that the wolves reintroduced in 1995—they now number about 375 in the entire ecosystem—and you have a rich array of wildlife. Most of these creatures steer clear of humans. But humans, never shy, want to get ever closer to the animals, and that can cause problems. Unlike the critters that inhabit petting zoos, the animals in the Greater Yellowstone Ecosystem are wild and pose an unpredictable threat to the safety of visitors.

Death is a day-to-day affair in the parks. In the spring, you'll see carcasses of elk and bison that died during the long winter, attracting bears and other carnivores looking for a free lunch. That's part of the picture when you vow to interfere as little as possible with nature's way.

Tips **Photo Tip**

Photographers need a telephoto lens, preferably a zoom, to get good shots of wildlife. Even the biggest animals in the park present minimal risks to humans, unless you move in for a close-up. Invest in a 300-millimeter lens, or 100- to 300-millimeter zoom, and you should get some good shots without disturbing the wildlife or putting yourself at risk.

Park naturalists generally agree that every major vertebrate wildlife species that was present during the most recent ice age (over 10,000 years ago) is a resident of the parks today, as are several rare or endangered species, the most notable being the grizzly bear and the bald eagle.

MAMMALS

BEAR (BLACK & GRIZZLY)   In recent years, grizzly bears have enjoyed a comeback, in part because of the reintroduction of wolves—which create plenty of carcasses for bears to scavenge. But unless you have the patience to spend weeks outdoors in bear country, such as the Lamar and Hayden valleys, your chances of seeing a grizzly in Yellowstone or Grand Teton aren't all that good—you might have to go to the grizzly zoo in West Yellowstone. However, it's the bears that tourists are always asking to see; it's just not as easy an order to fill since park garbage dumps were closed in the early 1970s.

Estimates vary, but there are probably 400 to 600 grizzly bears in the Greater Yellowstone Ecosystem today, and an equal or greater number of black bears. Rangers say you're most likely to spot the black bears, especially during spring months after they emerge with new cubs from their winter dens. However, the black bears are probably

Black Bear or Grizzly?

Because a black bear can be black, brown, or cinnamon, here are some identifiers. The grizzly is the larger of the two, typically 3½ feet at the shoulder with a dish-face profile and a pronounced hump between the shoulders. The black's ears are rounder, just like those you see on stuffed animals. The grizzly's color is typically more yellowish-brown, but the coat is sometimes recognized by its cinnamon color, often highlighted by silver tips. In terms of tracks, the black bear's toes follow an arc around the foot pad while the grizzly's toes are arranged in a nearly straight line. The grizzly's claws are also considerably longer.

Caution: Park rangers attempt to keep track of grizzlies to avoid human/bear incidents. However, it is best to assume that they are always around; make noise when traveling in isolated spots.

more visible because they are more likely to venture near human development than are grizzlies, meaning that an encounter with a grizzly is most likely to occur in the backcountry. Neither type of bear sits along park roads, the way both once did, begging for food or wrestling over park-lodge garbage while tourists sat watching on bleachers. Bears that get a taste for human food, or get too comfortable around human campsites, are relocated to the depths of the wilderness. Black bears are most commonly sighted in the Canyon-Tower and Madison–Old Faithful areas, where they feed on green grass, herbs, berries, ants, and carrion.

Grizzly bears are most commonly seen in the northeast area of the park, in the meadows on the hillsides of the Lamar Valley, or wandering the Hayden Valley north of Yellowstone Lake. They also feed on trout spawning in Yellowstone Lake tributaries during the late spring (campgrounds by these streams are closed during spawning times). They are most active in spring, when they emerge from hibernation hungry, and in the fall, fattening up for winter.

Grizzly bears can do you the most damage, particularly when their cubs are around or when they think you're after their food.

Black Bear

Grizzly Bear

BIGHORN SHEEP   If there's a hint of a foothold, a bighorn sheep will find it. Its hooves are hard and durable on the outside but soft and clamplike underneath—perfect for steep, rocky terrain. You'll often hear them clattering before you spot their stocky, gray-brown bodies and white rumps. Six feet long, the males weigh up to 300 pounds. Their horns are coiled; the females' are straight. The Greater Yellowstone Ecosystem probably contains the largest concentration of bighorns in the United States. Look for them on Mount Washburn, along Specimen Ridge, and in the Gallatin Range in Yellowstone; they are also seen occasionally in the Heart Mountain area in southern Yellowstone. In Grand Teton, smaller herds are found in the Gros Ventre Valley, as well as the western slopes of the Tetons. In the winter, east of the Tetons, in the Wind

River Range, a large herd of bighorn sheep congregates south of the town of Dubois in Whiskey Basin.

BISON   Bison (or buffalo) appear indifferent to humans as they wander the roads and go about their grazing, but don't think for a minute that they're docile. Their prodigious size, cute calves (which look like cattle calves), and fearless nature ensure that bison are very visible symbols of Yellowstone. On ballerina-thin ankles, these burly brown animals carry as much as 2,000 pounds, concentrated in thick shoulders and massive chests. Those big heads help them clear snow for winter browsing, but during harsh winters they instinctively migrate to lower elevations (some biologists insist that both grizzlies and bison were driven up on the plateau from their natural home on the prairie). Bison are very easy to spot in the summer; you'll see them munching grass and wallowing in dust pits in Hayden Valley, Pelican Valley, the Madison River area, and the geyser areas near the Firehole River. In the winter, snowmobilers often have to make way for the shaggy beasts because bison take advantage of the snow-packed roads to travel around.

*Bighorn
Sheep*

Bison

COYOTE   The wily coyote is the predator most often spotted by park visitors. Looking something like a small, lanky shepherd dog with grizzled, gray-brown coat, the coyotes number around 450, living in about 60 packs that make their homes in burrows and caves. Numbers have dropped some since wolf reintroduction, but coyotes are very adaptable. Active hunters year-round, they feast on small animals, such as squirrels and rabbits, as well as the carcasses of animals that died naturally or were killed by larger carnivores, such as bears and wolves. They are seen near most park roads, in the meadows, and in the sagebrush. Coyote pups are considered a delicacy by great horned owls, eagles, cougars, and bears.

WOLF   In a controversial move, gray wolves were reintroduced to Yellowstone in 1995 for the first time since the 1920s, when they

Wolf or Coyote?

Wolves and coyotes both bear a striking resemblance to large dogs. Here are some ways to distinguish them.

- Coyotes are more delicate looking; wolves are sturdy, almost massive.
- Coyotes grow to a height of 20 inches; wolves often grow to 34 inches.
- Coyotes have long, pointed ears; wolf ears are rounded and relatively short.
- Coyotes have thin, delicate legs, similar to those of a fox; wolves' legs are thick and long.

were eliminated by hunters operating under a federal predator control program designed to protect cattle herds. The population of Canadian gray wolves is thriving in its new environment; in 2007, some 375 animals had spread from Montana down to Grand Teton, where they're now denning in Gros Ventre and the valley. They are high-profile occupants of the Lamar Valley, under constant observation by visitors with binoculars or spotting scopes who travel the area.

Coyote

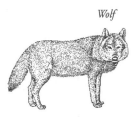

Wolf

ELK   It is estimated that the Yellowstone herd has about 10,000 elk (also called wapiti), down from its mid-1990s high of 19,000, and other herds spend time in the park as well. The most common large animal in both parks, elk are rather sociable and travel in small groups. Males are easily identifiable by a massive set of antlers. Although they shed them every spring, by early summer, bulls are beginning to display prodigious racks that, by year's end, are the envy of their cousins in the deer family. Their grayish-brown bodies, which typically weigh as much as 900 pounds, are accented by chestnut brown heads and necks, a shaggy mane, a short tail, and a distinctive tan patch on their rumps.

One herd can often be located in the vicinity of Mammoth Hot Springs, often on the lawn of the main square. Others are found throughout each park. During winter months, the northern Yellowstone herd heads to a winter grazing area near Gardiner, while their cousins in Grand Teton head for the National Elk Refuge, just north of Jackson, where the Forest Service supplements their diet with bales of alfalfa.

MOOSE Perhaps because of their size, their homely appearance, or the broad antler racks that can grow to 6 feet across, moose sightings provide park visitors with unequaled excitement. The largest member of the deer family, a typical adult male weighs 1,000 pounds and is most easily recognizable by a pendulous muzzle and fleshy dewlap that hangs beneath its neck like a bell.

Elk

Moose

Moose sightings are most frequent on the edges of ponds and in damp, lush valley bottoms, where they feed on willows and water plants, especially along the Moose-Wilson Road and near the Jackson Lake Lodge in Grand Teton.

The plodding, nibbling moose in a meadow is not to be approached—and is not likely to budge if you do. Although it appears ungainly, a moose is capable of traveling at 30 mph. Cows

---

Impressions

The most remarkable animal of these regions is the moose, and the most unearthly, hideous-looking monster that roams the mountains on four legs . . . the most uncomely animal in the West.

—Edwin Stanley, from Rambles in Wonderland (1878)

Antlers or Horns?

Most of the larger, four-legged animals roaming the parks have lavish headpieces that are either horns or antlers. But what's the difference? Antlers are shed every year; horns last a lifetime. Male deer, elk, and moose shed their *antlers* every spring, so they're as bald as cue balls when the parks open. By early June, though, new velvet-covered protuberances are making their appearance. In comparison, both sexes of bison and pronghorn grow only one set of horns during their lifetimes.

will charge any perceived threat to a calf, and bulls become particularly ornery in the fall; so give them a wide berth.

MULE DEER   Not to be outnumbered by their larger cousins, an estimated 2,500 live within the park borders. They are most often spotted near forest boundaries or in areas covered with grass and sagebrush. Their most distinguishing characteristics are their huge ears and a black tip on their tail that contrasts with their white rump. When they run, they bounce, with all four legs in the air. Fawns, often in pairs, are typically born in late spring.

PRONGHORN   The often-sighted pronghorn graze near the north entrance to Yellowstone and on the valley floors of Grand Teton, but they are shy and difficult to approach or photograph because of their excellent vision and speed. Often mistakenly referred to as antelope—they're actually unrelated to true African antelope—the pronghorn is identified by its short, black horns, tan-and-white bodies, and black accent stripes. They can run 45 mph, but they can't clear fences. In the past decade, Yellowstone's pronghorn population has dwindled from 600 to about 200, due to development, wolves, and harsh weather.

Mule Deer

 *Pronghorn*

5 Birds in the Parks

The skies above the parks are filled with predators on the wing, including eagles and 27 species of hawks, not to mention ospreys, falcons, and owls.

BALD EAGLE The bald eagle holds a position in the pecking order that parallels that of the grizzly. Of all the birds in the park, visitors are most interested in spotting this photogenic species, once almost wiped out by the pesticide DDT. The Yellowstone/Grand Teton area is now home to one of largest populations of eagles in the continental United States; more than 200 of these magnificent birds make their homes in the parks. Bald eagles are most recognizable by a striking white head, tail feathers, and wingspans up to 7 feet. They typically live within 2 miles of water, so the Yellowstone Plateau, Snake River, Yellowstone Lake, and headwaters of the Madison River are prime spotting areas for this spectacular bird.

GOLDEN EAGLE The bald eagle's cousin, the golden eagle, is similar in appearance, although it is smaller and does not have a white cowl. The golden eagle goes after small mammals, such as jack rabbits and prairie dogs. It works out in the open country; sometimes you'll find one feeding on roadkill.

Bald Eagle

Golden Eagle

OSPREY The osprey, which is nicknamed the "fish eagle" (on account of its diet), is a smaller version of the eagle, growing from 21 to 24 inches and with a white underbody and brown topsides. It is recognizable by a whistling sound it makes while hunting. Ospreys tend to create large nests made of twigs and branches that are found on the tops of trees and power poles. Look for this handsome, interesting bird in the Snake River area and the Grand Canyon of the Yellowstone River, a popular nesting area.

RAVEN Sporting a 50- to 60-inch wingspan, the raven is jet-black and markedly larger than the crow. The most intelligent bird

Tips **Birding Spot**

Take a picnic lunch, or plan a relaxing break, at the **Oxbow Bend** overlook in Grand Teton. Weather permitting, you can soak up some sunshine and observe the great blue herons, osprey, pelicans, cormorants, and, just maybe, a bald eagle. Although it's a popular spot, there's always room for one more vehicle.

in the parks, the raven plays an interesting role in the Greater Yellowstone Ecosystem: Biologists have observed ravens communicating with wolves, leading them to carcasses, and even playing with the pups. Ravens benefit from wolf kills because they are scavengers, so this relationship is symbiotic. They can be seen just about everywhere in both parks.

TRUMPETER SWAN   The trumpeter swan, one of the largest birds on the continent, has made the Greater Yellowstone Ecosystem a sanctuary. Easily recognizable by their long, curved necks, snowy white bodies, and black bills, they are found in marshes and on lakes and rivers, namely the Madison River in Yellowstone and Christian Pond, Swan Lake, and Cygnet Pond in Grand Teton.

Osprey

Trumpeter Swan

OTHER RAPTORS   American kestrels, prairie falcons, and **red-tailed hawks** are seen on Antelope Flats–Kelly Road in Grand Teton, where they search for small rodents.

OTHER AQUATIC BIRDS   The **great blue heron,** a skinny, long-legged wading bird, is found in wetlands and rocky outcrops, especially near the end of Jackson Lake. Yellowstone Lake is a prime viewing area for the best fishers in the park, the **American white pelicans** that capture fish in their long, yellow-pouched bill. The

American
Kestrel

Prairie
Falcon

Red-Tailed
Hawk

American dipper, the only aquatic songbird in North America, revels in cold, fast-flowing mountain streams. The slate-gray dipper is tiny, only 7 to 8 inches tall, and is recognized by its long bill and stubby tail.

Great Blue
Heron

American
White Pelican

American
Dipper

Index

See also Accommodations and Restaurant indexes below.

RESTAURANTS

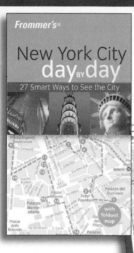

FROMMER'S® COMPLETE TRAVEL GUIDES

Alaska
Amalfi Coast
American Southwest
Amsterdam
Argentina
Arizona
Atlanta
Australia
Austria
Bahamas
Barcelona
Beijing
Belgium, Holland & Luxembourg
Belize
Bermuda
Boston
Brazil
British Columbia & the Canadian
  Rockies
Brussels & Bruges
Budapest & the Best of Hungary
Buenos Aires
Calgary
California
Canada
Cancún, Cozumel & the Yucatán
Cape Cod, Nantucket & Martha's
  Vineyard
Caribbean
Caribbean Ports of Call
Carolinas & Georgia
Chicago
Chile & Easter Island
China
Colorado
Costa Rica
Croatia
Cuba
Denmark
Denver, Boulder & Colorado Springs
Eastern Europe
Ecuador & the Galapagos Islands
Edinburgh & Glasgow
England
Europe
Europe by Rail

Florence, Tuscany & Umbria
Florida
France
Germany
Greece
Greek Islands
Guatemala
Hawaii
Hong Kong
Honolulu, Waikiki & Oahu
India
Ireland
Israel
Italy
Jamaica
Japan
Kauai
Las Vegas
London
Los Angeles
Los Cabos & Baja
Madrid
Maine Coast
Maryland & Delaware
Maui
Mexico
Montana & Wyoming
Montréal & Québec City
Morocco
Moscow & St. Petersburg
Munich & the Bavarian Alps
Nashville & Memphis
New England
Newfoundland & Labrador
New Mexico
New Orleans
New York City
New York State
New Zealand
Northern Italy
Norway
Nova Scotia, New Brunswick &
  Prince Edward Island
Oregon
Paris
Peru

Philadelphia & the Amish Country
Portugal
Prague & the Best of the Czech
  Republic
Provence & the Riviera
Puerto Rico
Rome
San Antonio & Austin
San Diego
San Francisco
Santa Fe, Taos & Albuquerque
Scandinavia
Scotland
Seattle
Seville, Granada & the Best of
  Andalusia
Shanghai
Sicily
Singapore & Malaysia
South Africa
South America
South Florida
South Korea
South Pacific
Southeast Asia
Spain
Sweden
Switzerland
Tahiti & French Polynesia
Texas
Thailand
Tokyo
Toronto
Turkey
USA
Utah
Vancouver & Victoria
Vermont, New Hampshire & Maine
Vienna & the Danube Valley
Vietnam
Virgin Islands
Virginia
Walt Disney World® & Orlando
Washington, D.C.
Washington State

FROMMER'S® DAY BY DAY GUIDES

Amsterdam
Barcelona
Beijing
Boston
Cancun & the Yucatan
Chicago
Florence & Tuscany

Hong Kong
Honolulu & Oahu
London
Maui
Montréal
Napa & Sonoma
New York City

Paris
Provence & the Riviera
Rome
San Francisco
Venice
Washington D.C.

PAULINE FROMMER'S GUIDES: SEE MORE. SPEND LESS.

Alaska
Hawaii
Italy

Las Vegas
London
New York City

Paris
Walt Disney World®
Washington D.C.